UNIFYING HUMANITY SPIRITUALLY
THROUGH THE CHRIST IMPULSE

UNIFYING HUMANITY SPIRITUALLY

THROUGH THE CHRIST IMPULSE

Thirteen lectures held in Berlin, Dornach, Basel and Bern between
19 December 1915 and 16 January 1916

TRANSLATED BY CHRISTIAN VON ARNIM

INTRODUCTION BY CHRISTIAN VON ARNIM

RUDOLF STEINER

RUDOLF STEINER PRESS

CW 165

The publishers gratefully acknowledge the generous funding of this publication by the estate of Dr Eva Frommer MD (1927–2004) and the Anthroposophical Society in Great Britain

Rudolf Steiner Press
Hillside House, The Square
Forest Row, RH18 5ES

www.rudolfsteinerpress.com

Published by Rudolf Steiner Press 2014

Originally published in German under the title *Die geistige Vereinigung der Menschheit durch den Christus-Impuls* (volume 165 in the *Rudolf Steiner Gesamtausgabe* or Collected Works) by Rudolf Steiner Verlag, Dornach. Based on shorthand transcripts not reviewed by the speaker, and edited by Ulla Trapp and Urs Dietler. This authorized translation is based on the latest available edition (2006)

Published by permission of the Rudolf Steiner Nachlassverwaltung, Dornach

© Rudolf Steiner Nachlassverwaltung, Dornach, Rudolf Steiner Verlag 2006

This translation © Rudolf Steiner Press 2014

A catalogue record for this book is available from the British Library

ISBN 978 1 85584 399 8

Cover by Mary Giddens
Typeset by DP Photosetting, Neath, West Glamorgan
Printed in Malta by Gutenberg Press Ltd.

CONTENTS

EDITOR'S PREFACE

The lectures of Rudolf Steiner collected in this volume were given in the second winter of the First World War. Rudolf Steiner had moved from Berlin to Dornach, Switzerland in 1914 where building work on the Goetheanum (called 'Johannesbau' at the time) had been in progress since the autumn of 1913. But several times a year he undertook lecture tours to various German cities. At the end of one such trip, he spoke in the Berlin branch at a pre-Christmas celebration on the fourth Sunday of Advent about the Provenance of the Cross—the first lecture in the present volume. The motif of the legend, according to which a seed from the tree of knowledge was laid in Adam's grave, continued to grow and propagate down the generations until its wood was used to make the cross on Golgotha, is inwardly connected with the Dornach lectures of 26, 27 and 28 December 1915 and with the Oberufer Christmas Plays which were performed for the first time in Dornach during these days.

This volume furthermore contains the lectures for members given in Dornach, Basel and Bern at the turn of 1915/1916. One motif that occurs as a linking element in these lectures is the question as to the quality of the knowledge about the mystery of the appearance of Christ on earth. Rudolf Steiner creates an arc from the pre-Christian mysteries through Gnosticism and the older patristics of the early Church Fathers to Scholasticism and neo-Scholasticism. After the old clairvoyance had faded, which was still able to perceive Christ as the coming one, the question arose as to how a transformation could be achieved of the qualitatively ever narrower range of knowledge which no longer reaches beyond our world of appearances. Only the transformation of thinking to produce a living inner conceptual life, which now however is also conscious, can obtain an understanding of the relationship between the earthly Jesus and the cosmic Christ which accords with reality—a question on which there continue to be differences. The single lecture in Bern, the title of which is also the title of this volume, furthermore indicates the power which lives in the Christ impulse as a source of unity; it is this which gives the continuing diversification and frag-mentation of humanity the opportunity for a conscious and newly acquired connection between human beings.

There is little evidence in these lectures of the increasingly critical attitude towards Rudolf Steiner and anthroposophy from certain quarters in Switzerland, which was on the rise from this time onwards. He did however respond to these criticisms in an important public lecture in Liestal on 11 January 1916—'The task of spiritual science and its building in Dornach'—which he had printed as a pamphlet in the same year (in GA 35).

In mid-January 1916, Rudolf Steiner took leave from the members in Dornach 'for a few weeks' to embark on another lecture tour to Berlin and other German cities. His absence was to last for more than six months.

Ulla Trapp
Urs Dietler

INTRODUCTION

The lectures in this volume cover a wide range of subjects. Held in a number of different places over the Christmas and New Year period 1915/1916, they range from thoughts connected with the Oberufer Christmas Plays—which Rudolf Steiner and his audience had just watched—and ancient streams of wisdom, to New Year's reflections on the earthly and cosmic year and the transformation of the nature of thinking and the human soul life from ancient Greece to our time; and there is much else (as outlined in the Editor's Preface).

The question thus arises whether there are certain themes which underlie this series of lectures and give them a certain unity despite the diversity of the subjects which Steiner discussed.

Perhaps the first thing to note is that these lectures were held against the background of the First World War and its terrible slaughter. This explicitly comes to expression in the first lecture but it is something that can be felt in the mood of many of the others as well. The apparent meaninglessness of things in time of war, the senselessness of the sacrifices it demands, will only grow worse unless human beings begin to have a deeper understanding at a spiritual level of the forces driving the development of the earth and humanity. The light of spiritual life has to enter human development out of the winter darkness.

The birth of Jesus at Christmas can lead us to the thought that even out of suffering something can arise which will help human beings to develop. The hate and enmity with which human beings oppose one another on earth are tied to the earth. Christmas—understood as the profound event in earth development that it is—can serve to remind us that even souls which fight one another to the death, become united through something higher than anything that will ever be able to divide human hearts on earth as soon as they cross the threshold of death and the hatreds of earth fall away: namely the thought of Jesus Christ. But that thought needs to grow and become infinitely more powerful in human minds before humanity will be able to achieve those things by different means that are now still the subject of bloody conflict.

While humanity is splintering through the influence of the adversary powers of Lucifer and Ahriman, an awareness of the unifying power of Christ can introduce something to the warring groups which transcends conflict.

Another theme which in one form or another runs through these lectures deals with some of the streams in human history which have been a source of knowledge about spiritual matters. In this context it is the spiritual science established by Rudolf Steiner which can provide a balance for the materialism of his (and indeed our) time. Speaking against the background of conflict, Steiner argues that the prevalent materialism must lead to despair because it ultimately has no answer to those events and leads to an outlook which can only perceive life as futile. A deeper understanding which can give meaning to events is provided by spiritual science.

However, Steiner has no illusions about the immediate public impact of spiritual science. It may not be possible to do much at present against the prevailing materialistic mood, he says, but a first step would be if at least some people recognize it for what it is and the constraints it imposes. In this context he criticises the disordered thinking of modern times; we must stop what he describes as 'flailing about' in our thinking in the attempt to make sense of things. Different forms of thinking are required to understand the finite material world and the infinite world of the spirit.

That does not mean rejecting materialistic science and knowledge as such—although Steiner can be very critical about some of its repre-sentatives. It is neutral, he says, and can be used both to bring progress to humanity and to create the instruments of terrible destruction. But it is a matter of understanding its limits, and those limits are reached when we move from the material world into the world of the spirit. And if we see materialism as the only form of knowledge there is, then we are cutting ourselves off from a real understanding of existence. Steiner warns against a blind belief in the claim to ultimate authority asserted by materialist thinkers and thinking. He warns of a future in which nothing but the officially approved orthodoxies will be allowed in our places of learning and public institutions to the exclusion of everything else.

Much must be left unsaid or cannot yet be formulated in a straightforward way in the present time, Steiner tells his listeners, because we do not yet have the language to express it in the right way. Furthermore, people do not let the words reach their souls where they can be understood properly before rushing to judgement. And something of that can be felt in these lectures, too. There is a sense that Steiner expresses himself quite circumspectly, hinting at things rather than always stating them explicitly—which sometimes makes their language quite difficult to penetrate.

Steiner uses these lectures to discuss a variety of themes in the sacred mood which is part of the time of year they were given. In this sense the lectures cover many aspects of human development. But what also underlies them is that everything is connected on the micro- and macrocosmic level. Discussing the nature of mineral and plant consciousness in lecture six, he draws parallels between the passage from one earth year to the next every twelve months and the passage from one cosmic year to the next every twelve millennia.

Who better than Steiner himself to sum up this interconnectedness of all things:

> And that is the secret of our existence. Everything is the same, both on the large scale and the small scale. And we will only understand the small scale, what happens in the course of the year, if we see it as a symbol of the great cosmic events, of what happens in the course of millennia. The year is the image of the aeons. And the aeons are the reality for those symbols which we encounter in the course of the year. If we understand the course of the year in the right way, then in this sacred night, when the new year starts its course, we will be imbued by the thought of the great cosmic secrets.

Christian von Arnim, May 2014

LECTURE 1

BERLIN, 19 DECEMBER 1915

LET us this day begin once again with particular strength of devotion in our hearts by thinking of those who are posted out in the fields where the events are happening and who today have to devote their life and soul to the great tasks of our time:

> Spirits of your souls, active guardians,
> May your wings bear
> The beseeching love of our souls
> To the human beings on earth committed to your keeping,
> That, united with your power,
> Our prayer may radiate in help
> To the souls it lovingly seeks.[1]

And for those who have already passed through the portal of death in this time of grave human duties as a result of the great demands of the present, let us say these words once more in the following form:

> Spirits of your souls, active guardians,
> May your wings bear
> The beseeching love of our souls
> To the human beings in the spheres committed to your keeping,
> That, united with your power,
> Our prayer may radiate in help
> To the souls it lovingly seeks.

And the spirit we seek through our spiritual striving, the spirit who went through the Mystery of Golgotha for the salvation of the earth, for the freedom and progress of humanity, the spirit whom we should particularly remember today—that spirit be with you and your grave duties!

Let our thoughts turn to the verse ringing forth out of the profound secrets of earth development:

> Revelation of the divine in the heights of existence
> And peace on earth to human beings
> Who are filled with good will.

And as Christmas approaches, there is something we must particularly reflect on this year. What sentiments unite us with this verse and its deep cosmic meaning? The deep cosmic meaning which many people feel in such a way that the word peace rings and sounds through it at a time in which peace avoids earth existence to the greatest extent. How can we reflect in this time on the Christmas verse?

But there is one thought which might touch us even more deeply at the present time than at other times in connection with this verse resounding through the world. One thought! Nations are facing one another in hostility. Our earth is soaked in blood, much blood. We have been forced to see, forced to feel many deaths around us. The atmosphere of sentiments and feelings weaves unending suffering around us. Hate and dislike flock through spiritual space and can easily show how far, far removed the people of our time still are from that love which the one whose birth is celebrated at Christmas wanted to proclaim. But there is one thought which particularly comes to the fore: we imagine how enemy can face enemy, opponent can face opponent, how people can bring death to one another and how they can pass through the same portal of death with the thought of the divine light-bearer, Jesus Christ. We reflect how across the earth, throughout which war and pain and disunity are spreading, those who are otherwise so disunited can be in unity because they bear in the deepest depths of their heart their connection with the one who entered the world on the day we celebrate at Christmas. We think how despite all hostility, all dislike, despite all the hate, a sentiment can penetrate human souls in these times, penetrate out of the midst of all the blood and hate: the thought of the intimate connection with the One, with Him who has united hearts with something that is higher than anything that can ever separate human beings on earth. And so this is a thought of infinite magnitude, a thought of infinite depth of feeling, the thought of Jesus Christ uniting human beings however much they may be disunited in all matters concerning the world.

If we grasp the thought in this way, then we will want to grasp it all the more deeply in our present time in particular. Because then we will have a notion of how much is connected with this thought in terms of the things that must become large and strong and powerful within human development so that much can be obtained in different ways by human hearts, by human souls which at present must still be obtained in such a blood-soaked way.

That He make us strong, that He vitalize us, that He teach us across the earth to feel in the truest sense of the word the consecrated words of Christmas despite all that separates us: that is what those who truly feel united with Jesus Christ must vow to themselves on Christmas Eve.

There is a tradition in the history of Christianity which keeps recurring in later times and which over centuries became a custom in certain regions. In ancient times already, believers in various regions had presented to them the mystery of Christmas, mostly by the Christian churches. In these most ancient times, in particular, this presentation of the Christmas mystery began with a reading, sometimes even a presentation of the creation story as it is set out at the beginning of the Bible. The first thing to be presented, particularly in the Christmas period, was how the cosmic Word sounded from the depths of the cosmos, how creation gradually came about out of the cosmic Word, how Lucifer approached the human being and how as a result human beings started earth existence in a different way from the existence that was intended for them before Lucifer approached them. The whole story of the temptation of Adam and Eve was performed and then it was shown how the human being was incorporated, as it were, into the whole of ancient pre-Testament history. Only then, in the further course of events, were the things added in plays in greater or lesser detail which then in the fifteenth, sixteenth, seventeenth and eighteenth centuries developed into the plays of which we saw a little one just now.[2]

Little remains of that which, in an infinitely great thought, linked the start of the Old Testament with the secret story of the Mystery of Golgotha in the Christmas festival, which combined those two stories in that thought. The only thing left today in that respect is that the feast day of Adam and Eve occurs in the calendar on the day before Christmas Day. That has its origin in the same thought. But in more ancient times a great, a comprehensively symbolic thought was presented to those who through their teachers and out of deeper thoughts, deeper feelings or a deeper knowledge were to grasp the secret of Christmas and the secret of Golgotha: the thought of the origin of the cross.[3] The god who is presented to human beings in the Old Testament instructs the human beings represented by Adam and Eve that they may eat of all the fruits in the garden except the fruit on the tree of knowledge of good and evil. They were driven out of the original setting of their existence because they ate of it.

But this tree—this was now represented in a great variety of ways—in some way came into the possession of the generations which were then also the original lineage from which the physical body of Jesus Christ emerged. And it happened—this is how it was presented at certain times—that when Adam was buried as a sinful human being this tree, which had been removed from paradise, grew out of his grave. Thus we see the thought suggested: Adam rests in his grave; he, the human being who passed through sin, he, the human being who was seduced by Lucifer, rests in his grave and has united himself with the body of the earth. But the tree grows out of his grave—the tree which can now grow out of the earth with which Adam's body has been united. The tree of this wood continues down the generations, including Abraham, including David. And the wood of this tree, which stood in paradise and which grew again out of Adam's grave, the wood of this tree was used to make the cross on which Jesus Christ hung.

This was the thought which was made clear by their teachers to those who were to understand out of deeper foundations the secrets of the Mystery of Golgotha. There is a deep meaning in the fact that in more ancient times—and we will shortly see in this meaning that it still holds good also in the present time—profound thoughts came to expression in such images.

We have acquainted ourselves with the thought about the Mystery of Golgotha which tells us: the Being who passed through the body of Jesus distributed across the earth what He can bring to it, distributed it into the earth's aura. What Christ brought into the earth has since then been combined with the complete corporeality of the earth. The earth has turned into something else since the Mystery of Golgotha. That which Christ brought down to earth from heavenly heights lives in the earth's aura. If together with that we cast our mind's eye on that ancient image of the tree, this image shows us the complete context from a higher vantage point: the luciferic principle entered human beings as they started their earth existence. Human beings as they now are in their association with the luciferic principle belong to the earth, are part of the earth. And when we place their bodies into the earth, then that body is not just the thing that anatomy sees, but this body is at the same time the external cast of what is also contained inside physical human beings. It can be clear to us through spiritual science that it is not only what goes through the portal of death into the spiritual world that belongs to the nature of the human being but that human beings are united with the earth through all that they do, through all their deeds on earth—that they are truly united with it in the same way that those events are united with the earth which geologists, mineralogists, zoologists and so on find connected with the earth. When human beings pass through the portal of death, the only thing that is closed off to the human individuality to begin with is what ties them to the earth. But we consign our outer form in some way to the earth; it enters the body of the earth. It carries within it the manifestation of what the earth has become because Lucifer entered earth development. What human beings do on earth bears the luciferic principle within it—human beings introduce this luciferic principle into the earth's aura. It is not just what was originally intended with the human being that arises or blossoms from human deeds, from human activity; human deeds give rise to what was mixed in with the luciferic element. That is contained in the earth's aura. And when on the grave of Adam, the human being seduced by Lucifer, we now see the tree which has become something different from what it was at the beginning because of Lucifer's seduction, the tree of knowledge of good and evil, then we see everything that human beings have provoked because they left their original position, because they turned into something else through Lucifer's seduction and therefore introduced something to earth evolution that was not previously intended for them.

We see the tree growing out of what the physical body is for the earth, what has been stamped into its earthly form, what makes human beings on earth appear in a lower sphere than what they would have become if they had not passed through the luciferic seduction. Something grows out of the human being's whole earthly existence which has entered into human development through the luciferic seduction, temptation. By seeking knowledge, we seek it in a different way to the one originally intended for us. But that means that what grows out of our deeds on earth is different from what it could be in accordance with the original decision of the gods. We shape an existence on earth that is not the same as the one determined for us by the original decision of the gods. We mix something else into it which we have to think of in a very specific way if we want to understand it properly. We have to tell ourselves: I have been placed in earth development. That which I contribute to earth development through my deeds bears fruit. It bears fruits of knowledge which I have obtained because I have been given knowledge of good and evil on earth. This knowledge lives in the development of the earth, this knowledge is there. But in looking at this knowledge it turns into something else for me from what it should originally have been. It turns into something else for me which I must change if the goal of the earth and the task of the earth is to be achieved. I see something grow out of my deeds on earth which must change. The tree grows which becomes the cross of earth existence, the tree which becomes the thing to which human beings must develop a new relationship—because it is the old relationship which makes the tree grow. The tree of the cross, that cross which grows out of luciferically tinged earth development, grows out of Adam's grave, out of the kind of human nature which Adam has become after the temptation. The tree of knowledge must become the trunk of the cross because human beings must unite with the properly perceived tree of knowledge, as it is now, in order to achieve the goal of the earth, the task of the earth.

Let us ask ourselves (and here we touch on an important secret of spiritual science): how is it with regard to the components which we have come to know as the elements of our human nature? Well, we know that our I is the initially highest component of human nature. We learn to say I to ourselves at a certain time during childhood. We enter into a relationship with this I from the time onwards to which we can remember back in later years. We know from various spiritual-scientific observations that up to that time the I itself acts in a formative and creative way in us, up to the moment that we acquire a conscious relationship with our I. This I is also present in the child but it is at work in us; it first forms the body in us. To begin with it works with supersensory forces from the spiritual world. Once we have passed through conception and birth, it continues to work for some time, which may be years, on our body until we have our body as a tool so that we can consciously grasp ourselves as an I. A profound secret is associated with this entry of the I into human physical nature. We ask a person when we met him: how old are you? He tells us his age as the years which have passed since he was born. As I said, we touch on a certain secret of spiritual science here which will become increasingly transparent to us in the coming time but which I only want to raise, to tell you about today. What a person tells us about his age at a certain time of his life only relates to his physical body. It tells us no more than that his physical body has developed for the period since his birth. The I is not involved in this development of the physical body; it remains stationary.

And this is the secret which is so difficult to understand, that the I remains stationary at the point to which we can remember back. It does not change with the body; it remains stationary. That, precisely, is the reason why we always have it before us, why it reflects our experiences back to us when we look into it. The I does not join us on our earthly journey. Only when we have passed through the portal of death do we have to take the return path we call kamaloka to our birth to meet our I again and take it with us on our further journey. The body takes precedence during these years—the I is left behind, the I remains stationary. This is difficult to understand because we cannot imagine that something remains stationary in time while time progresses. But that is how it is. The I remains stationary, and it remains stationary because it does not actually unite with what approaches human beings during their earth existence but remains united with those forces which we call ours in the spiritual world. The I remains, the I basically retains the form in which it was given to us, as we know, by the spirits of form. This I is kept in the spiritual world. It must be kept in the spiritual world because otherwise we would never as human beings during our earth development be able to achieve the original task and original goal of the earth. Everything that human beings go through because of the Adam part of their nature, of which they carry an imprint into the grave when they die as Adam, that adheres to the physical body, etheric body and astral body, emanates from them. The I waits, waits with everything it contains, for the whole time that the human being spends on earth, only looking towards the future development of the human being—until human beings pick it up again when they take the return path after they have passed through the portal of death. In other words, we remain—I mean that in a specific sense—with our I in the spiritual world, as it were. Humanity should develop an awareness of that. And it could only become aware of that because at a certain time Christ came down from the worlds to which human beings belong, the spiritual worlds, and, as we know, prepared in the body of Jesus in dual form[4] which was to serve Him as a body on earth.

If we understand ourselves in the right way, we will always look back to our childhood for the whole of our life on earth—because the spiritual part of us was left behind in childhood. We will always look back at that if we have understood the matter in the right way. And humanity should be educated to look at the thing to which the spirit from the heights can say, 'Let the little children come unto me',[5] not the human being who is linked with the earth but the little children. Humanity was to be educated in this respect by being given the festival of Christmas which was added to the Mystery of Golgotha. Otherwise the latter would only have been needed to be given to humanity in respect of the last three years of Christ's life when Christ occupied the body of Jesus of Nazareth. This festival shows how Christ prepared the human body in childhood. That is what should underlie what we feel about Christmas: knowing how human beings have actually always remained connected through what remains behind as they grow up, what remains in the heavenly heights, with what is now entering. The form of the child is there to remind human beings of the divine part of being human from which they have become separated by descending to earth but which in turn has come to them; this childlike element is what human beings were to be reminded of. It was not particularly easy, but precisely the way in which this cosmic festival of the child, the Christmas festival, came to appearance in the regions of central Europe illustrates its wonderfully supportive power.

What we saw today was only a small one of the many Christmas plays. Of the kind of Christmas plays from ancient times which I spoke about, a number of the so-called paradise plays have remained which are put on at Christmas and where the story of the creation is performed. The connection with the shepherds' play and the Three Kings play bringing their gifts has remained. Very many of these things were alive in many different plays. Most of them have now been lost.

The mid-eighteenth century is the period when they begin to disappear in rural areas. But it is wonderful to see how they were alive. Karl Julius Schröer,[6] whom I have told you about many times, collected such Christmas plays in the 1850s in the western regions of Hungary, in the area around Bratislava and from Bratislava down towards Hungary. Others collected such Christmas plays in other regions, but what Karl Julius Schröer discovered at the time about the traditions associated with the performance of these Christmas plays can touch our hearts particularly deeply. Handwritten versions of these Christmas plays were kept by certain families in the village and were considered to be something particularly sacred. They were put on in such a way that, as October approached, thought began to be given as to how to prepare for their performance in front of the farmers of the village at Christmas. Then the most courageous lads and lasses were selected and during this period, as they began to prepare themselves, they stopped drinking wine, drinking alcohol. They were not allowed to engage in fighting on a Sunday, which was otherwise permitted in these places, or engage in other excesses. They really had to live a 'chaste life' as they say. And so an awareness was created that a certain moral mood of soul was required in those who were engaged in the performance of such plays during Christmas. Such plays should not be performed with a normal worldly consciousness.

Then they were performed in all the naivety with which farmers can perform such things, but the whole performance was governed by a profoundly serious attitude, an infinitely serious attitude. The plays which Karl Julius Schröer in his time and, before him, Weinhold[7] and others collected in various regions all have this profoundly serious attitude with which the mystery of Christmas was approached. But it was not always like that. And we need go no further back than a few hundred years to find that things were different and to come across something very remarkable. Particularly the way in which the Christmas plays established themselves in central European regions, how they arose and gradually developed, can show us the overwhelming effect of the Christmas idea. They were not always received in the way I have just described: that they were approached with awe and reverence, with great seriousness, with an awareness of the significance of the events which lived in the feelings. Oh no! In many regions it started, for example, by a manger being set up in front of a side altar in some church—that still happened in the fourteenth and fifteenth centuries but it also goes back to earlier times. A manger was set up; that is, a stable with an ox and ass inside and the child and two puppets representing Joseph and Mary. So it was first done with a naive set of figures. Then greater life was to be introduced, but at first by the clergy. Priests dressed up as Joseph and Mary and they acted out a performance instead of the puppets. At the beginning they even performed it in Latin; this was considered very important in the ancient church because it appears that a very deep meaning was attached to those watching or listening understanding as little as possible of the matter but only observing the outward gestures. But they soon got fed up with that; they also wanted to understand something of what was being performed for them. So a start was made in putting some sections into the local language. Then, finally, a feeling awoke in people that they wanted to be involved and experience it themselves. But the whole thing was still quite alien to them. We have to remember that as late as the twelfth and thirteenth centuries there was no familiarity with the holy secrets—of Christmas for example—which we so much take for granted today. We have to remember that the people heard the mass year after year, at Christmas also the mass at midnight, but they did not hear the Bible—that was only available for the priests to read. They only knew individual bits of Holy Scripture. And it was really also to acquaint the people with what had happened long ago that it was performed as a drama by the priests to begin with. They only became familiar with it in this way.

Now I have to say something which I have to request very much that it should not be misunderstood. But it can be said because it corresponds to pure historical truth. The involvement in these Christmas plays did not immediately result from some kind of mystery mood or something like that—that's not what it was like. It was the desire to take part in what was being presented to them, to be involved, to act which brought the people to the plays. And in the end they had to be permitted to be involved. The plays had to be made more comprehensible to the people. Making them more comprehensible was a gradual process. For example, the people did not understand to begin with that the baby lay in the manger. They had never seen that, a baby in a manger. Previously, when they were not allowed to understand anything, they had accepted it. But now, when they were to be involved, the whole thing had to be comprehensible for them. So only a cradle was put there for them. And the people became involved as they walked past the cradle; everyone stood next to it and rocked the baby for a while and so this kind of involvement developed. There were even regions in which things started seriously but once the child was there everyone became very boisterous and shouted and indicated with dancing and shouting the joy which they felt now that the child was born. It was received in a mood that arose from the desire to be in motion, the desire to experience a story. But the story contains such great, such mighty things that a very profane mood—it was a profane mood at the beginning—gradually developed into the sacred mood which I have just spoken about. The subject itself spread its sanctity over a reception which could not at the beginning be described as holy. It was particularly in the Middle Ages that the holy Christmas story first had to take hold of the people. And it took hold of them to the extent that they wanted to prepare themselves morally in a very intensive way as they were performing their plays.

What was it that captured human feelings, the human soul? The sight of the child, the sight of those things which remain holy in human beings while their other three bodies unite with earth development. Even if in certain regions and at certain times the story of Bethlehem took on grotesque forms, it lay in human nature to develop this holy view of the child's nature, a view which is connected with the aspect which entered Christian development right from the beginning: an awareness of how that which remains at rest in human beings when they start on their earth development has to enter into a new connection with that which has combined with the earthly human being. So that human beings give to the earth the wood from which the cross must be made with which they must enter into a new connection.

In the more ancient periods of central European Christian development it was actually only the idea of Easter which was widespread among the populace. And the idea of Christmas supplemented that gradually in the way I have described. Because what is written in the *Heliand*[8] and similar works is the work of individual people but it was certainly not widespread.

The popular aspect of Christmas arose in the way I have just described; it shows in a truly magnificent way how the idea of the connection with the childlike aspect, the pure, true childlike aspect which appeared in a new form in Child Jesus, took hold of people. If we combine the power of this idea with the thought that this idea in the souls is the only one which to begin with can live in our earth existence, then it is the right Christ idea. And thus the Christ idea grows in us, thus the Christ idea turns into what must gradually grow strong in us if the further development of the earth is to happen in the right way. Just consider how far human beings are still removed in our present existence on earth from what is concealed in the depths of the Christ idea.

A book by Ernst Haeckel[9]—you might have read about it—is being published in these days: *Ewigkeit. Weltkriegsgedanken über Leben und Tod, Religion und Entwicklungslehre* (Eternity. Thoughts in a Time of World War about Life and Death, Religion and Evolutionary Theory). A book by Ernst Haeckel is undoubtedly a book that is the result of a serious love of truth, is undoubtedly a book that most earnestly seeks the truth. The book is said to be roughly about the following. It aims to describe what is currently happening on earth, how the nations are living in war, how they are living in hate with one another, how there are innumerable deaths each day. All these thoughts which impose themselves on human beings in such a painful way are also mentioned by Ernst Haeckel, always against the background of a view of the world as it is seen by him from his perspective—we have often spoken about it, because we can recognize Haeckel as a great scientist even if we are scientists of the spirit. That is, from the perspective which, as we know, can also lead to other things but which leads to what we can observe in the more recent phases of Haeckel's development. Now Haeckel is reflecting on the World War. He too thinks of the blood that is flowing, of the many deaths that surround us. And he poses the question: can religious thought persist in the face of these things? Is it possible to believe in any way—Haeckel asks—that some wise providence, a benevolent God governs the world when we see that the lives of so many people are cut short, that they are dying daily by pure chance—as he puts it—through no cause which could in any way be shown to be connected with any wise cosmic governance but through the chance—as he says—that one might be hit by a bullet or have an accident? Do all these thoughts of wisdom, of providence have any meaning in the face of these things? Is it not precisely events such as these which prove that human beings simply have to accept that they are nothing more than what externally, materialistically conceived evolutionary history shows us, and that basically it is not wise providence but chance which governs all earth existence? Is it possible to have any other religious thought—Haeckel thinks—than to resign oneself, to tell oneself that we simply give up our lives and are absorbed into the great universe? But if this universe—we can ask further, Haeckel does not go on to do so—is nothing more than the interplay of atoms, does this life of human beings really give meaning to earth existence? As I said, Haeckel does not go on to ask this question but he gives the answer in his Christmas book: it is precisely events of the kind which touch us so painfully now, it is precisely such events which show that we have no right to believe that benevolent providence or wise cosmic governance or anything of the kind is interwoven with and living in the world. So, resignation and acceptance that this is simply how things are!

Also a Christmas book! A Christmas book which has very honest and sincere intentions. But this book will be based on a significant preconception. It will be based on the preconception that we must not seek meaning in the world by spiritual means, that humanity is prohibited from searching for meaning by spiritual means. If we only look at the external course of events, we will not see any meaning. Then it is as Haeckel thinks. And we would have to accept that life has no meaning—Haeckel thinks. We should not look for meaning!

In contrast, could not another person come and say: 'If we only keep looking at current events in such an external way, if we only ever keep pointing out the countless bullets that strike people at this time, if we only look at these things and they seem to be senseless, that precisely shows us that we have to seek their meaning at a deeper level. They show us that we cannot simply seek their meaning in what is happening on earth right now and believe that these human souls will pass away with their bodies, but that we have to search for what they embark on once they have passed through the portal of death.' In short, someone else may come who says: 'It is precisely because no meaning can be found in external events that such meaning must be sought elsewhere, must be sought in the supersensory sphere.'

Is this any different from the same situation in quite another field? Haeckel's science can lead anyone who thinks as Haeckel does today to deny that our existence on earth has any meaning at all. It can lead people to want to prove on the basis of what is happening to such great sorrow today that our life on earth has no meaning as such. But if we interpret it in our way—we have, after all, done that quite often—then that same science becomes the starting point for showing the profound, immense meaning in world events which can be deciphered by us. But the spiritual must be at work in the world for that to happen. We must be able to unite with the spiritual. Because people do not yet understand in the fields of scholarship how they can allow the power to act on them which has so wonderfully conquered hearts and souls that a holy perception could arise out of a downright profane one when we look at the Christmas mystery, because scholars have not been able to grasp that, because they cannot yet combine the Christ impulse with what they see in the outside world, it is impossible for them to find any meaning, any real meaning, with regard to the earth.

And so we have to say: science itself, with all the great progress it has achieved of which people today are rightly so proud, is not of itself in a position to lead to a view which can satisfy human beings. In following its paths, it can be interpreted either way: as leading to a lack of meaning or as giving meaning to the earth, just as happens in quite a different field. Let us take external science, which has developed so proudly in the last few centuries and particularly the nineteenth century to the present day, with all its wonderful laws. Let us take everything that surrounds us today: it is the product of this science. We no longer burn a night light in the way that Goethe still did; we light and illuminate our rooms in quite a different way. And let us take everything that lives in our souls today through science: it has been created through the great progress in science of which humanity is rightly proud. But this same science—how does it work? It works beneficially when human beings develop beneficial things. But today, precisely because it is such a perfect science, it produces the invincible instruments of murder. Its progress serves destruction in the same measure that it serves development. Just as the science to which Haeckel has pledged himself can lead to sense or nonsense, so the science which has achieved such great things can either serve development or it can serve destruction. And if this science were left to its own devices, it would produce more and more terrible works of destruction from the same sources from which it brings development. It does not directly contain within itself an impulse which takes humanity forwards. Oh, if only people would recognize that, then they would be able to judge this science in the right way. Only then would people know that something has to exist in human development in addition to what human beings can achieve through science! This science—what is it? It is, in reality, nothing other than the tree that grows out of Adam's grave and the time will come ever closer in which people will recognize that this science is the tree that grows out of Adam's grave. And the time will come when people will recognize that this tree has to turn into the wood that is the cross of humanity, that it can only turn into a blessing when that is crucified on it which unites in the right way with what lies beyond death but already lives in human beings here: that to which we look in the Holy Nights of Christmas when we experience the mystery of these Holy Nights of Christmas in the right way; that which can be represented in a childlike way but which bears within it the highest mysteries. Is it not wonderful that the populace can be told in the simplest way that something has entered which acts on earth through human life, something that must not actually go beyond childhood? It is related to the aspect of which human beings are a part as something transcendental. Is it not wonderful that this pre-eminently transcendental invisible part could come so close to human souls in such a simple image—to the simplest human souls?

Those with learning will also still have to tread the path trodden by these simple human souls. There was a time in which the child was not depicted as sleeping in a cradle, in a manger but in which the child was represented as sleeping on a cross.[10] The child sleeping on the cross! A wonderfully profound image, completely expressive of the thought to which I wanted to give arise in your souls today.

And can this thought basically not be expressed in quite simple terms? That it can! Let us, then, search for the origin of the impulses which face each other in the world today in such a terrible way. Where do these impulses originate? Where do all the things which make life so difficult for humanity today originate? Where do they have their origins? They have their origins in all the things which we only become in the world from the time onwards to which we can remember back. If we go further back than this time, we go back to the time when we are called as little children who can enter the kingdom of heaven. In this time nothing originates, nothing lies in human souls of that which is conflict and discord today. The thought can be expressed as simply as that. But today we have to see spiritually that there is something so archetypal in human souls that it goes beyond all human conflict, all human disharmony.

We have often spoken about the ancient mysteries which aimed to awaken in human nature those things which allow human beings to look up to the supersensory sphere; and we said that the Mystery of Golgotha placed this supersensory mystery in the arena of history so that all human beings could perceive it. Fundamentally, that which unites us with the true idea of Christ is present in us, truly present, because there can be moments in our life—in a real sense now, not in a metaphorical sense—in which we can bring to life what we have received as children despite of everything that we are in the external world; and we can do so by going back, feeling our way back to our childhood perspective, by looking at human beings as they develop between birth and death, by being able to feel that within us.

I lectured publicly about Johann Gottlieb Fichte[11] last Thursday. I could have added something—which would not have been fully understood then—which explains much about what lived particularly in this, in his own way, pious figure. I could have talked about why he became as special as he did and I would have had to say: because he retained more of his childlike nature than other people, despite his old age. Such people have more of the childlike nature within them than others. They become less old, such people. Truly, such people retain more of what is present in childhood than other people. And that indeed is the secret of many great people, that they can remain children in a certain sense right into old age—that even when they die, they die as children, expressed relatively of course as we have to keep with life.

The mystery of Christmas, sight of the divine child who was chosen to become the vehicle of Christ, addresses that which lives as childlike nature in us; we look to him as the child over whom Christ is already poised who in truth went through the Mystery of Golgotha for the salvation of the earth.

Let us bear in mind: when we commit the imprint of our higher human being, our physical body, to the earth, that is more than just a physical process. Something spiritual happens as well. But this spiritual event only happens in the right way because the Christ being who passed through the Mystery of Golgotha has flowed into the earth's aura. We do not see the whole earth in its entirety if we do not see Christ united with the earth since the time of the Mystery of Golgotha, Christ whom we pass by like we pass by all supersensory things if we only feel equipped in a materialistic sense—but whom we cannot pass by if the earth is to have a real, a true meaning for us. That is why everything is dependent on us being able to awaken in us that which opens our view into the spiritual world.

Let us turn Christmas into the celebration which it should be especially for us: a celebration which serves not just the past but which should also serve the future—the future which gradually must bring the birth of spiritual life to the whole of humanity. Let us unite with the prophetic feeling, the prophetic prescience that such a birth of the spiritual life must be made accessible to humanity, that such a great Christmas must influence the future of humanity, must influence the birth of something that gives meaning to the earth in the thoughts of human beings. The earth has objectively received this meaning because the Christ being has united with the earth's aura through the Mystery of Golgotha. Let us reflect at Christmas how light has to enter human development out of profound darkness, the light of spiritual life. The embers of the old light of spiritual life that existed before the Mystery of Golgotha must die out and it must be resurrected, reborn after the Mystery of Golgotha through the awareness in human souls—that these human souls are connected with what Christ has become for the earth through the Mystery of Golgotha.

As the number of people grows who know to grasp Christmas in such a spiritual-scientific sense, Christmas will develop a power in human hearts and human souls that will retain its meaning at all times: at times when human beings can give themselves over to feelings of happiness, but also in those times in which human beings must give themselves over to that feeling of sorrow which cannot but fill us today when we think of the great suffering in our time.

The way in which looking up to what is spiritual can give meaning to the earth has been expressed by a person in beautiful words[12] which I wish to quote to you today:

> What gave my eye the strength
> To see deformity dissolve away,
> The nights turn to bright suns,
> Disorder turn to order and decay to life?
>
> What through the confusion of time and space
> Guides me safely to the eternal spring
> Of truth, beauty, goodness and delight
> And therein immerses all my striving for destruction?
>
> It is: since in Urania's eye the deep,
> Clear-in-itself, blue, calm, pure
> Flame of light myself I saw;

Since then this eye rests deep within me
And *is* within my being—the eternal One,
Lives in my life, *sees* in my seeing.

And in a second small poem:

There is nothing but God and God is nothing but life,
You know it, I know it as you do;
But how can knowledge be,
Were it not knowledge of God's life!

How much, alas, I wanted to devote myself thereto
But where to find it? If it flows in some way
Into knowledge, transformed it is into appearance,
Mixed up with it, surrounded by its cloak.

The cloak clearly rises up before you,
It is your I, let everything destructible die off,
And henceforth only God lives in your striving.
See through to what your striving lives beyond,
Then you will see the cloak as what it is
And you will see divine life as it is unveiled.

It is, however, the case that people no longer know how to respond to those who point them to a vision of the spiritual that gives meaning to the earth. It is not only the materialists who do not know how to respond. The others, who think they are not materialists because they always have 'God' or 'Lord' on their lips, they often do not know either what to make of these guides who point us towards the spiritual. Because what could have been achieved with a person who says: 'There is nothing but God! Everything is God! God is everywhere, everywhere!' The person who said these words

See through to what your striving lives beyond,
Then you will see the cloak as what it is
And you will see divine life as it is unveiled.

sought God everywhere. He, who wants to see divine life everywhere, he could be accused of not admitting to the world, of denying the world—

people could call him a denier of the world! His contemporaries accused him of denying God and therefore forced his dismissal from university. Because the words I read to you come from Johann Gottlieb Fichte. He, in particular, is an example of how—what in the Mystery of Golgotha and, following on from the Mystery of Golgotha, in the Christmas mystery can resound as an impulse in tones of the soul if it continues to live in the human soul throughout earth existence—this can open a path on which we can find the consciousness in which our own I coalesces with the earth's I; because the earth's I is Christ through which we develop something in the human being which has to keep growing if the earth is to head towards the development to which it was destined from the beginning.

So, in the sense set out once again today, let us allow the idea of Christmas to become an impulse in us particularly in the spirit of our spiritual knowledge. Let us attempt by looking up to this idea of Christmas not to see the senselessness of earth development on the basis of what is happening around us but let us also see something in suffering and pain, in conflict and hate which ultimately will help human beings to progress, which really does take humanity a step forwards.

Rather than looking for the causes, which can in any case easily be covered up in the dispute between the parties, rather than looking for the causes of what is happening today, it is more important to cast our eye on possible effects, those possible effects which we have to think of as healing, as bringing healing to humanity.

The nation, the people will do the right thing which is capable of turning what can grow out of the blood-soaked soil into something healing for the future of humanity. But something healing for humanity will only arise if humanity can find the way to the spiritual worlds, if people do not forget that there must not just be a Christmas on a specific date but a lasting Christmas—a lasting birth of the divine spiritual in physical human beings on earth.

Let us enclose the sanctity of this thought in our souls particularly today, let us hold it over the Christmas period which can also be a symbol for us in its outward course of the developing light. In these days, this season there will be darkness, darkness on earth to the maximum extent that can happen here on earth. But while earth is living in such profound outer darkness, we know the earth's soul is experiencing the light of Christmas, is beginning to keep watch to the greatest extent.

The Christmas period is associated with the time of spiritual watch-keeping, and this time of spiritual watch-keeping should be linked with a commemoration of the spiritual awakening of earth development through Jesus Christ. That is why the consecrated Christmas festival is set specifically at this time.

Let us unite the idea of Christmas with our souls in this cosmic and at the same time earthly and moral sense. And then, strengthened and invigorated, let us to the extent that we can look at all these things with this idea of Christmas in mind, desiring that events proceed in the right way, but also desiring what is right for the course of those things which are developing out of the actions of the present time.

And in starting immediately to make active in our souls what we can absorb from this Christmas festival as strength, we look once again to the spirits protecting those who have to bear the brunt of the great events of our time in hard places:

> Spirits of your souls, active guardians,
> May your wings bear
> The beseeching love of our souls
> To the human beings on earth committed to your keeping,
> That, united with your power,
> Our prayer may radiate in help
> To the souls it lovingly seeks.

And for those who have already passed through the portal of death in this time of grave human tasks as a result of the great demands of the present, let us say these words once more in the following form:

> Spirits of your souls, active guardians,
> May your wings bear
> The beseeching love of our souls
> To the human beings in the spheres committed to your keeping,
> That, united with your power,
> Our prayer may radiate in help
> To the souls it lovingly seeks.

And the Spirit who went through the Mystery of Golgotha, the Spirit who announced His coming for the salvation of the earth and for progress in what human beings will increasingly also learn to understand the Christmas mystery to be, may He be with you and your grave duties!

LECTURE 2

DORNACH, 26 DECEMBER 1915 [13]

Two Christmas plays have passed before our souls. We may perhaps raise the thought: do both Christmas plays deal in the same way with the great affairs of humanity which are so alive in our souls during these days? The two plays are fundamentally different, quite different from one another. We can hardly imagine anything more different devoted to the same subject as these two plays. When we look at the first play, it breathes a wonderful simplicity in all its parts, childlike simplicity. It contains a profound depth of soul but infused, alive with childlike simplicity. The second play moves at the highest levels of external physical existence. The immediate thought is that Jesus Christ enters the world as a king. He is contrasted with that other king, namely Herod. Then we are shown that two worlds open up before us: the one which promotes the development of humanity in a good way, the world which is served by Jesus Christ, and the other world, which is served by Ahriman and Lucifer and which is represented by the diabolical element—a cosmic, a cosmically spiritual image in the highest meaning of the word. The link between human development and the stellar script is clearly evident: not the simple, primitive clairvoyance of the shepherds which finds its 'heavenly reflection', which can be found in the simplest of circumstances, but the deciphering of the stellar script which requires all the wisdom of past centuries and which reveals what is to come, which shines into our world what comes from other worlds. The things which are to happen are guided and directed in dream and sleep states; in short, occultism and magic infuse the whole play.

The two plays are fundamentally different. The first one approaches us in what we might truly describe as childlike simplicity and naivety. Yet it is infinitely admonitory, infinitely empathetic. But let us, to begin with, consider the main thought. The human being who is to become the vehicle of Christ enters the world. His entry into the world is shown, we are to be shown what Jesus represents to human beings into whose surroundings he enters. Well, my dear friends, this idea did not automatically capture the attention of the circles in which such plays as this one were subsequently watched with ardour and devotion. The person whom I have often mentioned to you, Karl Julius Schröer, was one of the first who in the nineteenth century collected Christmas plays. He collected the plays in western Hungary, the Oberufer plays, heading eastwards from Bratislava, and he was able to study the way in which these plays lived among the people there. And it is very, very indicative to see the way they were handed down in handwritten form from generation to generation and how those who were found suitable in the village prepared themselves to present the plays not just before Christmas but when Christmas was still a long way off. Then we can see the intimate connection between the content of the plays and the life of the people throughout the cycle of the year in whose villages such plays were performed. The time at which Schröer for example collected these plays in the mid-nineteenth century was already the time in which they started to die out in the way they had been cultivated until then. Many weeks in advance of Christmas, the boys and girls in the village who were suitable for presenting such plays were selected. And they had to prepare themselves. But such preparation did not just consist of learning by heart and rehearsing the content of the play to perform it, but the preparation consisted of these boys and girls having to change their whole way of life, their outer way of life. From the time that the preparations began, they were no longer allowed to drink wine or imbibe alcohol. They were no longer allowed to wrestle with each other as was otherwise customary in the village on a Sunday. They had to be very well behaved, they had to become gentle and mild, were no longer allowed to bloody each other and not allowed to do a number of other things which were quite common in villages in those times. Thus they also prepared themselves morally through their inner mood of soul. And then it really was as if they carried something holy around the village when they performed the plays.

But that came about only slowly and gradually. It is certainly true that a mood existed in many villages of central Europe in the nineteenth century that something holy was received with these plays at Christmas. But we only need to go back perhaps to the eighteenth century or a bit further and this mood becomes increasingly less holy—less holy. This mood was not there from the beginning when these plays came to the village, not at all from the beginning, but it only developed and appeared over time. There was a time, we do not even need to go back that far, when other things could be found. It could be found how villages in central Europe gathered together and a cradle was brought in with the child lying in it, with a small child lying in it, a cradle with the child lying in it and with it there was the most beautiful girl in the village—Mary had to be beautiful—but an ugly Joseph, a very ugly-looking Joseph. Then a similar scene was performed as you can still see today. But above all, when it was proclaimed that Christ is coming, the whole community stepped forward and everyone put their foot on the cradle. Above all things, everyone wanted to have put their foot on the cradle and rocked the Christ child a little, that was important for everyone; and they made an incredible racket which was meant to express that Christ had come into the world. And in some of those older plays Joseph was terribly mocked who in these times was always presented as a doddery old man whom everyone laughed at.

How did plays of this kind actually get among the people? Well, we have to remember of course that the first form of the greatest, mightiest earthly idea, the appearance of Jesus Christ on earth, was the idea of the Saviour who had passed through death, who through His death had given meaning to the earth. It was the suffering of Christ which first came into the world in early Christianity. And the offerings in the various events which were held in the course of the year were made to the suffering Christ. The child only conquered the world very slowly and gradually. The dying Saviour first conquered the world; the child did so only slowly and gradually. We must not forget that the liturgy was in Latin, that the people did not understand anything. Beginning with the mass, which was held at Christmas, a start was gradually made to show the people not just the mass—which was held three times at Christmas—but also something else. Perhaps not altogether without justification, the idea of revealing the mystery of Jesus to the faithful at Christmas is attributed to St Francis of Assisi[14]—if not him then his followers—who indeed maintained his whole teaching and his whole being out of a certain opposition to the old church forms and the old spirit in the church. And so we can see gradually, slowly how something was to be offered to the community of the faithful at Christmas which was connected with the great mystery of humanity, the descent of Jesus Christ to earth. At first a manger was simply set up and a few figures were made: the baby and Joseph and Mary—as sculpted figures. Gradually they were replaced by priests who dressed up and who presented it in the simplest way. And it was not until the thirteenth and fourteenth centuries that the mood arose outside in the community which could be described as people saying to themselves: we also want to understand something of what we see here, we want to delve deeper into the matter. And then people began to be allowed to take part in individual sections of what had previously only been acted out by the priesthood. Now we have to know something about life in the high Middle Ages, of course, in order to understand how what was connected with the most sacred was at the same time taken in the way I have indicated. That was quite possible at the time through a responsiveness in the mood of the community so that it could say, 'I also rocked the cradle in which Christ was born a little bit with my foot'—there was such a responsiveness. It could be expressed in this and in many other things—in the singing which sometimes escalated into yodelling, in everything that happened. But that which lived in the matter had the strength within itself, we might almost say, to transform itself into what is most holy out of something that was profane, from a profanation of the idea of Christmas. And the idea of the child appearing in the world conquered for itself what is most holy in the hearts of the simplest people.

That is the wonderful thing particularly in these plays, such as the first one, that they were not simply there in the form they appear to us now but that they became like that: only developing a mood of devotion out of impiety out of the power of what they represent. The child first had to conquer hearts, first had to find entry to hearts. Through what was holy in himself he made hearts holy which he first encountered in roughness and exuberance. That is the wonderful thing in the history of the development of these plays, how the mystery of Christ had to conquer hearts and souls a bit at a time—a bit at a time. And tomorrow we will place before our souls a few more things about this gradual conquest. Today I just want to add: not for nothing I pointed out the admonitory way in which even the simplest things are presented in the first play—the admonitory way.

As I said, slowly and gradually the things which came into the world with the mystery of Christ entered the hearts and souls of people. And the situation is really like this: the further back we go in the tradition of the various mysteries of Christ, the more we can see that the form of expression becomes elevated, spiritually elevated. I would almost say we enter into an 'expressiveness at a cosmic level' the further back we go. We have already included some of that in our reflections and in last year's lecture[15] here I also showed how Gnostic ideas were used to understand the profound Christ mystery. But even if we still see some of those things in the later periods of the Middle Ages, we find that in the high Middle Ages something was present in the Christmas poetry of the time which later fell away: a highlight of the early Christian thought that Christ comes down from cosmic expanses, from spiritual heights. We find it in the eleventh or twelfth centuries when, for example, we place a Christmas song such as the following before our souls:[16]

> The honour of the Son of God turned human[17]
> Is proclaimed joyously by heavenly hosts in exultation
> And out of the shepherds' mouths there loudly resound
> The glad tidings.
>
> 'Praise be on high! And peace to all people!'
> Thus it sounds in solemn song;
> People watch in amazement today
> What has never happened before.
>
> The heavens shine brightly with a new star;
> Under its guidance, from afar come

The wise men and welcome with delight
The one they behold.

With him truth has now been reborn.
Replaced has been what was lost through sin;
More wonderfully there blossom in the light of grace
The fruits of blessedness.

The apprehension of the past has now been revealed
Since this fruit has sprouted from the earth
Which grants us life and refreshment,
Nourishing us eternally.

There has come, dressed in our flesh,
The good shepherd who leads all peoples to pasture;
He has lived, like us, in pilgrims' huts,
Suffering for us.

Salvation now for earth which has seen his light!
Blessed through him for all time and eternity,
Let everyone vow gratitude and love to him, the Saviour,
With the purest desire.

Help, Christ, yourself so that we can fulfil your law,
Let good deeds succeed through you,
That someday at your side the crown of eternal life
Reward us too!

That was the tone which came from those who still understood something of the full cosmic meaning of the Christ mystery.

Or there was another Christmas poem on the Christmas festival from the high Middle Ages, a little after the Carolingian period:[18]

The Son of God, engendered by eternity, who is invisible and
   without end,
Through whom the fabric of heaven and earth, and everything
   that lives thereon, has been created,
Through whom the days and hours pass away and then return;
Whom angels always praise in heaven's castle in full harmonious
   song,

Has clothed himself, free of original sin, in a weak body
Which out of Mary, the Virgin, He took, the sin of the first father
    Adam,
As well as the lustfulness of mother Eve to destroy.
The exalted splendour of the glorious day today bears witness that
    now the son,
The true sun, scatters the old darkness of the world through the
    light's rays.
Now night is illuminated through the light of that new star
Which once amazed the Magi's gaze knowledgeable in heavenly
    things,
And lo, the light shines on the shepherds who were blinded
By the sublime light of heaven's occupants.
O Mother of God, be happy, you who at the birth by an angelic
    host,
Singing the praise of God, are served.
O Christ, you, the Father's only Son, who for our sake
Assumed human nature, give sustenance to those who are yours in
    supplication here.
O Jesus, hear in mildness the entreaties of those
Whom you have dignified with your attention,
In order, O Son of God, to let them partake in your divinity.

That is the tone which, I might say, sounds down to the people from the heights of more theologically tinged scholarship.

    Now let us hear a little of the tone which at Christmas sounded from the people themselves when a soul was found which reflected the feelings of the people:[19]

Er ist gewaltic unde starc,
der ze winnaht geborn wart:
Daz ist der heilige Krist.
Jâ lobt in allez daz dir ist
Niewan der tiefel eine
dur sînen grôzen ubermuot
Sô wart ime diu helle ze teile.

In der helle ist Michel unrât
swer dâ heimuote hât,
Din sunne schînet nie sô licht,
der mane hilfet in niht,
Noh der liechte sterne,
jâ müet in allez daz er siht,
jâ waer er dâ ze himel also gerne.

In himelrich ein hûs stat,
ein guldîn wec dar în gâtm
Die siule die sint mermelin
die zieret unser trehtîn
Mit edelem gesteine:
dâ enkumt nieman în,
er ensî vor allen sünden also reine.

Swer gerne zuo der kilchen gât
und âne nît dâ stat,
Der mac wol vrôlichen leben,
den wirt ze jungest gegeben
Der Engel gemeine,
wol im daz er je wart:
ze himel ist daz Leben also reine.

Ich hân gedienet lange
leider einem Manne
Der in der helle umbe gât
der brüevet mine missetât,
Sin lôn der ist boese.
Hilf mich heiliger geist,
daz ich mich von sîner vancnisse loese.

That is the prayer which the simple people said and understood. We read
the sound coming down from on high, now we have the sound rising up.

I will try to give a rendering of this Christmas song from the twelfth
century so that we can see how the simple person also grasped the full
magnitude of Christ and brought it into connection with the whole of
cosmic life:

He is mighty and strong, who was born at Christmas. That is the Holy Spirit. He is praised by everything that there is, only not by the devil alone, who was such through his great pride that hell was his lot. In hell there is great filth. Anyone who has his home there, in other words, who lives in hell, must see: the sun never shines there, the moon does not help, illuminate anyone, nor the bright stars. Because of what they see there, everyone must think how nice it would be to go to heaven. They would like to be in heaven. In heaven there is a house. A golden path leads up to it. The pillars are of marble, decorated with precious stones. But no one can enter it who is not purified of sin. Those who go to church and stand there without jealousy, they will have higher life because youth is given to them, that is, once their life is ended. If you recall, I once introduced the term 'younging'[20] with regard to the etheric body. Here you even have it in the vernacular! So when they are given 'young' to the angelic community they can happily wait for that because in heaven life is pure. And then the person who prays this Christmas song says: Sadly, having been captured, I served a man who goes about in hell, who devised my certain deed. Help me, holy Christ, that I am released from his prison, that is, that I am released from the prison of evil.

So that is the language of the common people:

He is mighty and strong,
Who was born at Christmas . . .

LECTURE 3

I drew your attention yesterday to the way in which the fact of the birth of Jesus gradually conquered the hearts and souls of people: how the Christmas play, in the way we were able to let it act on us, basically only gradually developed into this noble and beautiful form together with the whole Christmas mood with which it arose at the time in which it blossomed; how it was basically possible to say about the first forms of this Christmas play that people did indeed try, out of a quite profane mood, to participate in what they had seen for centuries in a way which they could not understand. The Christ child only gradually conquered human hearts. And this conquest of human hearts actually took quite a long time. When we see in the eighth, ninth, tenth, eleventh centuries the things which the priests at first began to play being transformed into participation by the people, then such participation as I described to you yesterday has not yet taken the noble form which these Christmas plays later assumed—of which we have just become acquainted with two examples.

I tried to make you aware that these two plays[21] are quite different in origin and that this can be clearly seen. The first play has something simple and popular so that it is easy to see that the main thing is to present how the child in which the great cosmic spirit was later to be incarnated and active on earth, how this child entered the world, how he was received on the one hand by the innkeepers, the two innkeepers, and on the other hand by the shepherds. And basically this Christmas play, this first one which we watched yesterday, reveals specifically the difference of the reception by the innkeepers and the shepherds. That is what we particularly remember from it.

The other Christmas play is quite different. It is immediately made clear to us that wise men—which for the peoples to which this applied at the time also meant wise kings, the Magi—read in the stars the significant destiny which was in store for humanity. So we see ancient occult wisdom contained in the action of the play. And then we see in the further course of events how the being which now enters earth events as foreseen by this occult wisdom, this knowledge obtained from the stars, is opposed by a figure at whose side we can clearly see evil, the principle which has fallen behind, the diabolic, the ahrimanic and luciferic principle—Herod. We see how the Christ principle and the luciferic and ahrimanic principle are set in opposition. But we also see how in the course of events that asserts itself which is revealed out of spiritual spheres. The angels appear as if announcing their guidance from spiritual spheres and guide and control events so that what Herod wants does not happen and something else occurs. The will of human beings is filled with impulses which come from the spiritual worlds. So we have a play which, in terms of the forces within, points beyond purely earth events.

If we consider how these two plays relate to one another, the one perfused with a primitive popular view, the other perfused with a wisdom which truly refers us back to the original wisdom of earth development, we will be led to reflect on what has happened in the course of time and what is connected with the full meaning of the Mystery of Golgotha with regard to earth development. Let us consider that at the time—at the time in a wider sense—when the Mystery of Golgotha took place, a profound wisdom about spiritual matters existed in certain circles. We refer to what existed as such profound wisdom as gnosis. In the outer world, in the progression of the intellectual culture of Europe, it would be true to say that this gnosis, which existed as a profound spiritual knowledge of the secrets of the spiritual world, had disappeared within the culture of Europe as far as the external world was concerned; in the third, fourth, fifth, sixth centuries there was precious little idea in intellectual life of what was contained in this system of knowledge. Those who knew something—I am referring to those who knew what could be known if one was a Christian priest or Christian scholar—they really knew about gnosis because there were opponents of gnosis in the first centuries of Christianity and these opponents fought against gnosis. Imagine if it were to happen today that all the books which we count among our literature and all the lecture cycles were to be weeded out, were to be burnt so that nothing remained of them and only the things remained which the opponents had written. And a few centuries later someone would lay their hands on these books of the opponents and on that basis would have to form an idea of what was written in our books. That is what it was like with gnosis!

One of the most important church authors to have written about gnosis is Irenaeus,[22] the pupil of Bishop Polycarp[23] of Asia Minor who himself was a pupil of the apostles. But Irenaeus wrote as an opponent of gnosis. The things which were taught by the Gnostics could only be learned over the centuries by looking at what Irenaeus had written, what he had recorded in his book to refute them. So everything had to be taken into consideration which resulted from this ancient wisdom only being reported by an opponent. You can see from this that actually the whole development of the West was designed such that something which came from ancient times was rooted out, thoroughly rooted out. Outwardly this fact alone shows how new the start was for western culture that was given with the Mystery of Golgotha, how basically something new started everywhere. Truly, just like what might be described as a lost city buried in the earth, the ancient writings were thoroughly buried under what was now newly developed on the basis of the ancient Church Fathers by St Ambrose, St Augustine, Scotus Eriugena[24] and so on. A new start! And just like a new city rises on apparently new ground, so something new arose—a new city, but on ground in which was buried the ancient city without anyone knowing what it looked like. That is how European culture developed. But from that it can also be seen that, in our time, if there is to be a renewed spiritual deepening it is necessary for this deepening to be achieved out of the strength of human beings themselves; human beings themselves must find once again what was not passed down to them outwardly, at least within the course of the European development of ideas. And—I cannot speak about this today because it would take us too far off the subject—there is no point in referring to the eastern records as a sub-stitute for the external records which have disappeared in western thought for the simple reason that the eastern records indeed provide something much, much more primitive than that which developed in the world spreading across Asia Minor, North Africa, southern Europe and even partly across central Europe. What spiritual knowledge had developed into had been thoroughly rooted out in the first centuries of Christian development; that really was only passed down to posterity through the writings of its opponents.

Now these writings which were rooted out not only contained the knowledge, the spiritual knowledge, which related to the spiritual worlds in addition to Christ, but the application of all the compre-hensive ancient spiritual wisdom to the mystery of Jesus Christ was also lost with these writings. The Gnostics tried to understand in their way—if we wish to call them Gnostics—the course of earth develop-ment, the nature of the being of Christ. The time had not yet come at that time to understand the matter in the way we understand it now by fetching truths from the spiritual worlds themselves which do not need to be written down because they exist directly in the spiritual world in a living way. It was not possible for them to acquire knowledge about the being of Jesus Christ in this way. That has only become possible in our time. But in this more ancient way certain things were known about Christ in knowledge which truly had been lost. It is only recently that a few, scarce remains have been found:[25] the *Pistis Sophia* text and then the text about the 'Secret of Jeu'. They are now available as if through them the attention of people was also to be drawn outwardly to the fact that the knowledge of Christ we are now striving for in our way is not as stupid as the opponents of our movement would like to make out. The Books of Jeu—little remains of it in Coptic script, but what does remain is like a pointer. See what exists in the Gospels; that is not the only thing which filled the thinking of people in the first centuries of Christian development. The Books of Jeu contains information about how Christ after the resurrection, after he had gone through the Mystery of Gol-gotha, spoke to those who could understand him at the time, who had become his disciples. The curious thing is that this Books of Jeu—I mean the small fragment we have of it—speaks clearly about Christ and what he is in quite a different way from even the Gospel of John. The curious thing is that a word keeps recurring in this book which clearly tells us that attention is to be drawn to something. And I would like to describe the thing to which attention is to be drawn by paraphrasing it as follows. If we assume that someone at that time had wanted to explain why Jesus Christ had entered earth development, he would have said, he would have told those who could understand it: 'See, a time will come when human beings will approach the development of the consciousness soul. A time will come when human beings will have to understand the world through their external, physical organs, through the organs which are essentially anchored in their physical body. The time is past when human beings had archetypal revelations through original primitive clairvoyance. The time is past when human beings knew something not just by applying their physical body with its tools but by being able to use their etheric body independently of their physical body for obtaining knowledge. Human beings will now have to use only their physical body as a tool. But in future human beings will also be able to know something of the things which hitherto were known only through the etheric body. In the external world there will only be one sort of knowledge which is tied to the physical body subject to death. But knowledge about the spiritual world cannot be obtained through the tools which are tied to the physical body. To that end, a helper must come who ignites in human beings those things which only the etheric body can know. Someone must come who does not ignite what is dead in the physical body but who ignites what is alive in the human being, what is alive in the etheric, who is with the living, who is with those things which are not physical in human beings on earth. Someone has to be there who rips out of this sluggish, dead physical body the reason which can understand the spiritual world, the reason which is in human beings and which is united with heaven—the reason which cannot be crucified by the world because it belongs to heaven, which itself crucifies the world, that is, overcomes the world.'

We have to understand that human beings in earlier times, when they could not yet see Christ in his true being as he passed through the Mystery of Golgotha, felt themselves united with the spiritual world with their etheric bodies in primitive clairvoyance. How the physical body grew increasingly hardened and thereby turned into an instrument, how someone had to come (that is, Christ) to extract the living element out of the sluggish instrument of the physical body—that is what we have to understand.

And now let us look at the Books of Jeu:[26] how Christ, having passed through the Mystery of Golgotha, speaks to those who have learnt to follow Him, to follow the wisdom contained in His words: 'I have loved you and wished to give you life.' We can discern it in his phrase: 'and wished to give you life'. He wished to take the sluggish physical body out of its sluggishness and to give what only the etheric body can give.

'Jesus the living one is knowledge of truth.' The living one—that is, the one who has passed through the Mystery of Golgotha—speaks while depicting himself as the representative of life.

Then the text continues, 'This is the book of knowledge of the invisible God by means of the concealed mysteries,' that is, the mysteries which are concealed in human beings, 'which show the way to the chosen essence of the human being, leading in the silence to the life of the cosmic Father, in the coming of the Saviour, the deliverer of the souls who will receive in themselves the Word of life, which is higher than all life, in the knowledge of Jesu, the living one, who through the Father came forth from the aeon of light in the allness of the pleroma,' that is, other aeons, all the spiritual beings, 'in the teaching apart from which there is no other, which Jesus, the living one, taught his apostles in saying: this is the teaching in which rests all knowledge.'

This is how we have to imagine that the risen one, who went through the Mystery of Golgotha, spoke to the disciples who had learnt to belong to him.

'Jesus, the living one, commenced and spoke to his apostles: "Blessed is the one who has crucified the world and the world has not crucified him,"' who can thus grasp that part of the human being which is not overcome by matter, by external physical matter.

'The apostles answered as one in saying: "Lord, teach us how to crucify the world so that it not crucify us and we might perish and lose our lives."

'Jesus, the living one, answered and said: "He who has crucified the world is the one who has found my Word and has fulfilled it in accordance with the will of the one who sent me."

'And the apostles answered: "Speak to us Lord so that we hear you. We have followed you with all our hearts, have left father and mother, have left vineyards and fields, have left goods, have left the magnificence of the external king and followed you so that you teach us the life of your Father who sent you."'

And in response to this request from the apostles, Jesus Christ, the living one, now says what He has to tell them: 'Christ, the living one, answered and said: "The life of my Father is this, that out of the essence of the human being you receive that understanding of your soul which is not earthly."'

So that is what the living one wants, that those who are his disciples learn to understand that there is a knowledge of spiritual things in the human being which can tear itself away from the physical body, which is not earthly. If they can activate that within themselves they will understand his word.

'"This essence of all souls, which becomes comprehensible through what I say to you in the course of my Word. So that you fulfil it and are saved from the archon,"' from the being of the aeon, this epoch, '"and his persecution,"' the luciferic-ahrimanic being, '"and his persecution, which is never-ending, so that you are saved therefrom. But you, my disciples, make haste to receive my Word carefully so that you recognize it, so that the archon of this aeon,"' that is Ahriman-Lucifer, '"does not quarrel with you because he can find none of his commands in me,"' who thus finds his commands outside the one who went through the Mystery of Golgotha, '"so that you yourself, O my apostles, fulfil my Word in relation to me and I myself make you free, and you become holy through the freedom which is immaculate. Just as the spirit of the Holy Spirit is holy so you too will become holy through the freedom of the spirit of the Holy Spirit."

'All the apostles answered with one voice, Matthew and John, Philip and Bartholomew and James, and they said: "O Jesus, you living one whose benevolence extends across those who have found his wisdom and his form through enlightenment, O light, which in the light that has illuminated our hearts has received the light of life as we have, O true

Logos, so that through gnosis we learned true knowledge, taught out of what is alive."

'Jesus, the living one answered, and said: "Blessed is the person who has recognized this and has brought heaven down," ' that is, who has become aware that there is something in him which is not connected with the physical body but which is connected with the beings of the heavens and who introduces into events on earth what is connected with heaven in him, what is above.

' "Blessed is the person who has understood this and has brought down heaven and supported the earth and sent it to heaven," ' has united what is earthly in him with what is heavenly in him so that, when he passes through the portal of death with the fruits of what is earthly, he can guide the earth back to heaven through what is heavenly.

'The apostles answered and said: "Jesus, you living one, explain to us the way in which one brings down heaven. Because we followed you so that you teach us the true light."

'And Jesus, the living one, answered and said: "The Word which exists in heaven," ' by which he meant that which one can have as wisdom, as knowledge independently of the physical being of human beings. ' "The Word which exists in heaven before earth was created, the earth which is called the world. But you, if you recognize my Word, will bring heaven down and the Word will live in you. Heaven is the invisible Word of the Father. But if you recognise this, you will bring heaven down. I will show you how to send the earth to heaven, how it is, so that you know it; sending earth to heaven is: the hearer of the Word of knowledge who has stopped being no more than the reason of earthly human beings, but has become a heavenly human being," ' who has thus torn the understanding within himself away from the outer physical body, who has stopped being an earthly human being and become a heavenly human being. His reason has stopped being earthly, it has become heavenly.

' "That is why you will be saved from the archon of this aeon," ' from the ahrimanic-luciferic being.

Here you have a fragment which has survived, which was found again and which could make people aware of the infinitely profound knowledge which was linked in the first Christian centuries with the secret of the Mystery of Golgotha. As a rule, the theologians in our time tend to blow their top about anyone who wishes to draw attention to this or other writings in some way. They admit that they exist, that is true. They work on them externally, historically, and publish editions of them. But they are convinced, these normal theologians of our time, that these writings have to a certain extent been rightly forgotten because they only contain all kinds of incredible fantasies which any reasonable person of today should no longer bother with, that they are not appropriate for an enlightened spirit. But in a certain sense they are an indication that through these things which we retrieve out of the wellspring of the spiritual worlds we do connect with something which has already been in earth development, with something which only had to keep flowing subterraneously for a time like certain waters in the Alps run subterraneously after they have flowed on the surface for a while. Then they disappear into the depths and appear again later. In the same way, spiritual knowledge has continued to flow as in subterranean worlds through the centuries and now it must emerge again. In order that those who cannot believe at all that the spiritual sources flowing into earth existence could have come from such springs should also receive an outward indication, history has preserved a few fragments, some scraps of a rich ancient literature which was widespread, which was great and powerful, and which is really only known about through the writings of its opponents—for example the writings of Irenaeus[27] and similar people who only wanted to rebut it.

Thus we have to say: the Mystery of Golgotha has found its way into western culture under extraordinarily difficult circumstances. And it started with the result of the mighty saying of Paul which flowed out of him as he had the vision on the road to Damascus: the secret of death, of the passage through the Mystery of Golgotha. That in turn led into the wide-ranging discussion about the way that Christ was connected with Jesus, how his divine and human nature were connected, how the three forms of manifestation of the divine are related which entered western cultural development as three figures, and similar things. We can say: that which was human wisdom receded. The power of knowledge also receded. The power of wisdom in those people was incredibly strong, allowing them to produce the kind of thing which I just read out to you—a strong power of wisdom. It receded completely. And people much preferred to listen to those who were able to say: Jesus, Christ, was here on earth in person; we know that he was here because I knew Polycarp and Polycarp knew the disciples of Jesus! That was a directly personal account. In a certain sense belief starts in just those things which physically existed, in physical progression. As the spiritual wisdom gradually ebbed away, the belief grew in what was only physical. We can ask: what kind of a mind was Irenaeus? He was a mind who said: 'Here we have the Gnostics. They claim to know something through a reason which can act independently of the physical body. That is all wrong, that is all—as people said at the time—heretical. People must not believe that.' And he refuted it. Such opponents kept growing in number. And what of course remained was the Mystery of Golgotha, the power of that fact, the power of that tradition. Christianity now progressed through what was handed down by tradition, what now took on the role of fact. What progressed as science actually ebbed away. And the successor of Irenaeus in our time is once again fighting against everything which is based on a real knowledge of the spiritual world. Who is the predecessor and who the successor? Irenaeus, the Bishop of Lyon who fought the Gnostics; and the Irenaeus of our time, the bishop of matter from Jena, is Ernst Haeckel. In terms of the way of thinking, there is a direct line from Irenaeus, the Bishop of Lyon, to Ernst Haeckel. These things have to be seen with historical objectivity, not with some feeling of critical sympathy or antipathy but with complete historical objectivity.

If we imagine the course of this spiritual development, we can obtain a feeling for something which has already been touched on here from a different perspective, namely that what people were capable of understanding could not accommodate this Christian development. Such understanding, such a spiritual grasp is something that is meant to come only now, because people had lost the power to understand something that could only be understood spiritually, such as was the Mystery of Golgotha. The way in which the Mystery of Golgotha conquered humanity was not through reason but through fact. And this fact actually also acted in a very peculiar way.

Only a very weak echo now remains of this matter. But in the first centuries, when the story of how Christ appeared on earth at Christmas was told, the first chapter of the creation story was read out to begin with. A direct connection was made between the creation story, the start of the Bible, and the Christmas mystery. Now only one such connection remains: if you look at the calendar, you have Christmas on 25 December and the feast of Adam and Eve on 24 December. This direct connection in the calendar is the last remnant of what existed in people's consciousness: that once the Christmas festival had been set in a specific season, the creation story was thought of in association with the Christmas mystery. But it was not just that outwardly the creation story was first presented and then the Christmas mystery; people were regularly made aware of one of the most profound legends by those who wanted to show the connection between the world, the beginning of the earth, and the Mystery of Golgotha. People were made aware how, when Adam was driven from paradise, the tree through which he had sinned, the tree of knowledge of good and evil, was also removed from paradise; how fruits, seeds from this tree were planted on the grave of Adam and how the tree grew out of it. And then the wood of this tree, the tree of paradise, was passed down the generations until the time when Christ appeared on earth. And this wood, this wood which had grown out of the grave which was the grave of Adam, this wood was used to make the cross on which the Saviour was suspended.

This legend about the connection between the beginning of the world and the Mystery of Golgotha was continuously repeated in early centuries to the people who were able to understand such things. They were told: the tree of paradise, through which human beings have sinned, was thrown out of paradise and its seeds fell on the earth which covered Adam's grave. And the tree through which human beings had sinned in paradise grew again from these seeds. And the wood from this tree was passed from generation to generation until it came by all kinds of circuitous routes into the era of the Mystery of Golgotha, and the cross on which Christ was suspended was made from this wood.

This legend thus also includes the connection between the beginning of the earth and the Mystery of Golgotha. But these things are so closely connected, so intimately connected, that there are certain plays which are not just plays about Christ performed at Christmas but paradise plays—paradise plays in which the mystery of Adam and Eve and the Fall was directly presented to the people when Christmas, or rather Epiphany, Three Kings' Day, on 6 January approached.

Consider, my dear friends, the profound spiritual facts of which we are made aware in this way. We think of the luciferic-ahrimanic temptation of the human being, of what became of human beings through luciferic-ahrimanic temptation; we think of it as represented by the figure of Adam who had succumbed to temptation. If we fully understand this luciferic-ahrimanic temptation, we cannot but think that earth development would have turned out quite differently if there had been no luciferic-ahrimanic temptation of the human being; things would have turned out quite differently. But this luciferic-ahrimanic temptation only has meaning in relation to life on earth in a physical body. It can thus only acquire meaning from the moment at which we enter life on earth out of the spiritual world through birth or, let us say, through conception. The luciferic-ahrimanic temptation cannot have any meaning for the life between death and a new birth because it has its meaning here in life on earth.

When we therefore see the child enter life on earth, we experience it in the right way if we say: 'You appear, soul that you are, here in the flesh; you appear out of a cosmic sphere which is still untouched by luciferic-ahrimanic nature. You only enter luciferic-ahrimanic nature as you increasingly grow into the flesh.'

And that is how we can look at the child, that is how we can look at the child in sensing a spiritual cosmic mystery. As they enter earth development, human beings are already predetermined through their earlier incarnations to grow as one with the flesh. But people should also experience on one occasion what it means to enter the earth without being predestined for earthly life. For this thought to awaken in human beings—the thought about what actually lives in humans as a being through which they are connected with something heavenly, sunlike— that this should awaken in humans is why the Christ child conquered the spiritual development of humanity. And this Christ child conquered the spiritual development of humanity in the way that he was able.

There were basically two streams in the whole of Christian development. We are well able to understand these two streams. To begin with, Christ entered the world through two bodies: through the Jesus from the line of Nathan and the Jesus from the line of Solomon. He entered through the Jesus from the line of Nathan as what I might call the earth child.[*] You need only look at how I have explained it in the lecture cycles and also in *The Spiritual Guidance of the Individual and Humanity*. Through the Jesus from the line of Nathan, Christ entered earth such that this Jesus from the line of Nathan was like a being who had been preserved from earth development up to that time, like the substance from the beginning of the earth. But the Jesus from the line of Solomon: this was progressive development which had gone through many, many earth incarnations. Two paths, then, which were subsequently to converge in the way I have set out.

But now imagine all of this happening in a time in which spiritual wisdom is dying out, in which there is no way of understanding these things. The infinite profundity occurs that there are two Jesus children through which Christ is to enter the world. The infinite profundity occurs which the people who understand nothing about the whole thing—although they are called upon to do so by their office—today slander and brand as heretical. The event occurs which could only have been understood with that wisdom which has been rooted out. It is hardly surprising that this fact has happened in a way of which an understanding can only gradually be achieved once again through our science. That is why the following was endeavoured. When more of the old wisdom was still trickling through, trickling through drop by drop, people wanted to place even greater value on the appearance of Jesus Christ on earth, on his entry into the great events of the world, and so 'Three Kings' Day' was set as the day when the Lord appeared, which is

---

[*]Editors' note: Some readers have suggested that this sentence should be amended to read correctly: 'He entered through the Jesus from the line of Solomon as what I might call the earth child.'

The editors did not feel that they could go along with such an amendment. The original shorthand note clearly says 'Nathan'; and that Rudolf Steiner might have made a slip of the tongue can be excluded in the context of the other content. This lecture highlights in particular the childlike nature of the Jesus from the line of Nathan—whereas the Jesus from the line of Solomon is described as the bringer of heavenly wisdom, as can also be seen from the following pages.

6 January. But that is connected to a greater extent with the Jesus from the line of Solomon, with the Jesus who appeared as a king, who entered from the royal line. He was indeed understood to a greater extent through what was royal occult knowledge. In contrast, the other one, the Jesus from the line of Nathan, who really carried nothing of what had happened on earth in his substance, was set in deepest winter which is now the Christmas festival. People did not understand that these things belong together and even set the birth dates apart. Because in centuries further in the past, 6 January was indeed felt to be the birth date of Jesus. But the feeling that there were two birth dates can easily be explained by anyone with a knowledge of the two Jesus children. There are even two versions of the way Jesus was thought about. The one relates more to the Jesus who entered without previously having been connected with what through nations and the estates and races created differentiation on earth: the Jesus who enters and can be understood with the simplest popular feeling—the Luke Jesus, the Jesus from the line of Nathan. The other Jesus, the Jesus from the line of Solomon, is better understood with what is heavenly wisdom, the wisdom through which those things trickled through that still remain as droplets of ancient occult wisdom.

It would not be at all incorrect to say: we saw the first play about Jesus, the simple play about Jesus to which the ancient remains of occult wisdom cannot be applied in any way, that is, the Jesus child from the line of Nathan. In the other one the wisdom is at work which still remained: the Jesus who entered the world from royal stock—the second play which acted on us. People were not aware of it, but the two Jesus children continued to have an effect in that people created such fundamentally different plays about these things.

Thus I wanted to give some indication to begin with about the way in which the paradise play and the Christmas play coalesced so that everything together has a meaning. We will speak more about it tomorrow. But today I want to commend to you once more the words I said in conclusion yesterday and also in the course of our considerations, that these Christmas plays—in a certain sense even the simplest one—are also an admonition. And they were also an admonition for all those who heard them.

We should endeavour once again to return to a kind of cosmic Christmas in a spiritual sense. Christ should once again be born in a spiritual way at least for human understanding. All the work in spiritual science is actually a kind of Christmas festival, a birth of Christ in human wisdom. The question is whether the numbers of people can be found who understand that. Indeed, sometimes the farmers could be heard saying things to one another as they sat there when such a Christmas play, like the first one yesterday, was performed in earlier centuries. The whole community came and the farmers sat there. Then this might happen. One of the farmers might say to another: 'Tell me, are you a shepherd or an innkeeper?' Then he might reflect on whether he was a shepherd or an innkeeper. I think in respect of the way Christ is seen in more modern science we might also ask people: 'Are you an innkeeper or a shepherd?' Because we can hear the innkeepers fulminating and saying: 'How dare you come to my door? Clear off, go and find somewhere else to stay, not here!' The others are the shepherds. There are also sceptics among them—there is Mops who does not want to understand the bright light but who nevertheless out of a certain sense of truth allows himself to be led by Koridan.[28] I think the question and answer in their soul with which the farmers in the sixteenth, seventeenth and eighteenth centuries left the Christmas play they had just watched might well give us pause for thought: 'Well tell me, are you an innkeeper or a shepherd?' Let us hope, my dear friends, that gradually a good many shepherds arise in our way so that the innkeepers who can, after all, be heard in great numbers, are gradually silenced.

LECTURE 4

DORNACH, 28 DECEMBER 1915

I attempted yesterday to draw attention to an important fact in the context of the Christ problem, a fact which undoubtedly has a surprising aspect: the fact that a whole swathe of wisdom has actually disappeared and is only known about today in a few fragments, in a few remains. Something from one of the remains was presented here yesterday, namely the start of the Books of Jeu. Now we have to ask ourselves: can wisdom which existed simply disappear like that? Can there just be external reasons for such a disappearance? I made a comparison: I said that it was conceivable that everything of ours that is printed and in existence could be burned, that all that remained were the writings of our opponents from which people could at a later time reconstruct what we said. Now, such a case could certainly occur. However, it is not actually a hypothesis which we can just put like that. Because just imagine for a minute that all the books were suddenly to disappear; there would still be many of us—at least we may assume that to be the case—who know what is written in the books and who could continue to speak about it without needing the writings of our opponents. In this way our wisdom would be able to be handed on.

In order for the matter completely to disappear, it would be necessary that in a certain way the ability to understand the matter also gradually disappeared, the ability to retain a memory of the matter in order to implant it in each new generation. But that is what must have happened at the time. It must have happened in a certain way at the time that people lost the ability to understand something like the gnosis of

Valentinus,[29] like the content of the *Pistis Sophia* writings, like the content of the Books of Jeu and so on. And that is what really did happen. We do have to imagine that on the broad basis of the ancient heritage which came to expression in more ancient times as primitive clairvoyance and then gradually withered and dimmed, that on this basis a higher knowledge also developed, a spiritual knowledge which was, however, only maintained by a few who were trained in the mysteries but which did exist in a wider setting. And we further have to imagine that through the gradual paralysis of these abilities to understand these things the whole matter not only began to be forgotten but to disappear. People simply no longer had the ability within western culture to understand these things. That was the only way in which that wisdom could be lost. So that we can truly say: when we look at the time which directly preceded and followed the Mystery of Golgotha, we look at a time in which to the greatest extent ancient abilities disappear and people work out of something fresh, something new. We can indeed say: as human development progressed towards the Mystery of Golgotha, there was a dimming, disappearance of a very particular perspective, a way of thinking of a spiritual kind through which it would have been possible to understand the entry of Christ into the world as a spiritual being.

So just at the time at which Christ unites with earth development, the knowledge disappears through which the nature and essence of Christ could have been understood in a real, deeper sense. That is an important fact. I have also already at various times in our reflections referred to something that is very important. I said: the annunciation of Christ as such is not something which was completely new with the event of Golgotha. No, Christ was referred to as the coming one already in the mysteries. There were teachings in the mysteries that Christ would come. This Christ Being was understood in the sense of the spiritual wisdom which has disappeared. But these mysteries had gradually fallen into ruin so that just at the time when Christ came the time approached in which human beings were least able to speak about this Christ. We can see this not just in everything I have indicated just now, we can also see it in everything that has remained from people who wanted to conceive of the Christ mystery out of what was fresh, what was new.

Right in the first centuries of Christian development we have such great minds as, for example, Clement of Alexandria and Origen,[30] two eminent minds. If we wish to characterize them from a particular perspective—Clement of Alexandria who followed after the Gnostics when gnosis had already dimmed, equally Origen—then we have to say that they strove to understand the true nature of the Mystery of Golgotha. On the one hand we are dealing with Christ—that they still knew. This Christ can only be understood as a spiritual being who is connected with spiritual, with supersensory impulses. This Christ descends from cosmic regions of the spirit. They no longer knew properly how the ancient gnosis had been able to understand Christ, but they knew that He has to be understood as a spiritual being with spiritual abilities. That is what they knew about Christ. On the other hand Jesus was a historical figure for them. The appearance of Jesus was a historical fact for them. A given number of years ago a personality was born in a certain part of Asia Minor, Jesus, who was the bearer of Christ, a person in whom God was present. That became a riddle for them. In historical developments we are dealing with a historical figure, they said to themselves; in our understanding of the spirit we are dealing with Christ. How should the unity of both be thought? And we see a struggle in such eminent, such great minds as are Clement of Alexandria and Origen, a struggle to understand how Christ is in Jesus, is in him.

If we look first at Clement of Alexandria, who was head of the Catechetical School of Alexandria where the Christian teachers were trained, if we look at this important figure, we find the following among what this figure taught. Clement of Alexandria told himself: 'Christ belongs to those forces which were already at work in the creation of the earth. Naturally, He is part of the spiritual world. He entered earth development through the body of Jesus of Nazareth.' So Clement of Alexandria first looked at Christ as a spiritual being, sought to understand Him in spiritual regions. Now Clement of Alexandria also knew the following, which we have often previously emphasized. He knew that Christ was actually always there for human beings but not in earth regions; only those could reach Him who developed forces in themselves through the mysteries by means of which they could leave the body. When they, those people, left their body through the mystery forces and entered the spiritual regions, they recognized Christ and experienced him as the one who would come. Clement of Alexandria knew that. He knew that Christ was spoken of in the ancient mysteries as the coming one who is not yet united with earth development. He expressed it like this: people were undoubtedly inspired to anticipate the coming of Christ. And he went as far as to say: what could be prepared for the descent of Christ in particular was cultivated in two centres of the spiritual development of humanity. Clement of Alexandria said: it was cultivated on the one hand by Moses and the prophets. What entered the world through Moses and the prophets, he said, was such preparation. Human beings were first to learn what came through Moses and the prophets so that they could then with the help of their own sentiments develop a feeling: we have Christ. That is what they were to imagine. However, he knew nothing of the ancient Gnostic wisdom, or at least he did not use it. But he said about what entered human abilities through Moses and the prophets that it was 'preparation'. And then—this is very important—the second thing which Clement of Alexandria said was to act as preparation alongside Moses and the prophets was the Greek philosophers: Plato and Aristotle— Greek philosophy. He said, in so many words: Moses and the prophets and the Greek philosophers existed to prepare humanity for the event, for the fact of the Mystery of Golgotha.

And Origen, in turn, said to himself: we are dealing with Christ, with the Christ who can be understood using spiritual forces as a spiritual being; we are dealing with the historical Jesus, with that figure who once existed as a real figure in the sensory world. How can the two be combined—the God and the human being? How is God-man created? And Origen worked out his own theory. He told himself: the God cannot just live like that in the physical human being but there must first be a special soul in Jesus so that this soul can mediate between the God and the human being, that is, between the God as a pure spiritual being and the physical human being. He inserted the soul. And so he distinguished in Jesus Christ between the God, the pure pneuma being, the pure spiritual being; then between the psyche, the soul; and finally between the physical body of Jesus of Nazareth. So he tried to gain an understanding of how Christ could be in Jesus of Nazareth. He no longer had the ancient gnosis to be able to understand Christ dwelling on earth and Christ uniting Himself with earth evolution. People had to work with what was fresh, what was new. They made great efforts to do that. So just at the time that Christ had united himself with earth development as a real being human beings had the greatest difficulty in understanding this fact at all. The ability to do so existed to the least possible extent.

And Clement of Alexandria had at least a trace of an understanding why that was so. He told himself: 'What was it that inspired these ancient mystery people? The ancient mystery people were inspired, Clement of Alexandria told himself, because Christ also had an effect on them, but transcendentally, when they had come out of themselves. That happened,' as Clement of Alexandria says quite clearly, 'because he sent them the angels.' So Clement of Alexandria more or less said it: when there is reference in the Old Testament to the appearance of an angel, it means that Christ has sent this angel. Indeed, Clement of Alexandria expressly lets it shine through: when Yahweh appears to Moses in the burning bush,[31] it is actually also Christ who appears there, who appears through the physical-soul-spiritual phenomenon. So that Clement of Alexandria expresses it clearly: in antiquity, before the Mystery of Golgotha, Christ appeared to human beings through angels. If they could develop the ability to hear the message of the angels, they were actually facing Christ himself in higher worlds, having left their bodies, as initiates who had left their bodies.

That far Clement of Alexandria was still able to go. And then he said (that also was still preserved in him): 'As time progressed, Christ made the transition from being of angelic nature to being in the nature of the son. He became the son. Previously he was able to manifest, reveal himself through the angels or as an angel, as a multitude of angels, as many angels. When he wanted to appear to one person as one angel and another person as another angel, he appeared in many forms. Then he appeared in the one form: as the son.'

A very important element occurs here. Take good note, this is exceptionally important! Clement of Alexandria takes the view that Christ was already present before the Mystery of Golgotha in spiritual regions. He was so far that he could announce his presence through angels, through messengers. But then he went further, he went as far as being able to manifest himself as the son. That is exceptionally important.

What actually enters human understanding in this way? If we go through the whole of ancient gnosis, there is something peculiar. If I wanted to draw a diagram of this gnosis[32] for example, I could say the following: this gnosis imagined a person in evolution which started from the Father, the primal Father, from the so-called silence or σιγή, from the primal spirit. The ancient Gnostics set out 30 different such stages. They called them aeons. I could set out 30 here. Then a second stream, in a sense; whereas the first stream is a spiritual one, they indicated a second stream which belongs to the soul. Within this stream they knew two main primal aeons in Christ and in Sophia. Then there were a number of further aeons. And they set out a third stream: the demiurge with matter. And these came together and formed the human being.

We can draw such diagrams from the way of thinking which the Gnostics had. These ideas are not completely unreal because humans are complicated beings. Once when I spoke about the number of sevenfold parts in the human being—it is contained in one of the Norwegian cycles, I think it is called *Man in the Light of Occultism, Theosophy and Philosophy*[33]—our dear friends were quite disconcerted at the number of differences which actually have to be sought in the human being. These differences remind us of what the Gnostics already knew from their perspective. But if we look closely at gnosis, there is always one thing: the concept of time plays little part. Gnosticism can be expressed through spatial diagrams. The concept of time does not play any particular role, at least there is no meaningful understanding of it. And in that respect it is a step forward from gnosis to Clement of Alexandria. Even if the whole comprehensive fullness of spiritual wisdom was lost, it was nevertheless a step forward to Clement of Alexandria in that he introduced the concept of time into the development of Christ and said: Christ announced His presence, was able to announce His presence in earlier times through angels, then as the son because He Himself progressed. Development was introduced, that is the important thing. It cannot be stressed often enough that the purpose of western cultural development was to introduce the concept of time into our understanding of the world in the right way, to understand the idea of development in the right way. It is of such great importance, it is of overriding importance to look at development and to see how Christ originally could only announce His presence through the angels and then, after He passed through the Mystery of Golgotha, He appeared as the son. Through the angels He is the messenger of something that is external to the world, which does indeed penetrate the world but which, if it is to be recognized, must be recognized outside the world: a herald. Later, when He appears as the son, He penetrates everything. Just as a son is of the same blood, is one with his father in the physical world, so the spiritual son must be imagined as of one being with the Father in the spiritual world. Being a son is something different from just being an angel. So if this being reveals Himself as the son, it is progress with regard to the earlier revelation where He was able to reveal Himself only as an angel, as a herald.

So in Christianity there was a kind of further-reaching understanding than the understanding within ancient gnosis. But what I might call the after-effects of gnosis were required to express even just that which Clement of Alexandria said. When gnosis gradually disappeared altogether, it was no longer even possible to say what Clement and Origen had said. People increasingly found their way into those impulses which were the impulses of a later time, the purely materialistic impulses. And so it came about that the teaching of Origen was condemned. It was declared to be heretical. The element which caused it to be declared heretical was, namely, that people no longer wanted an understanding of these things which originated in human beings themselves and their powers. People felt: that must no longer exist. But how do we see these things now? How must it appear to us? After all, we can see that an ancient spiritual wisdom had spread on the basis of ancient clairvoyance. It was there and gradually disappeared. Even if it related to a transcendental being, such spiritual wisdom contained knowledge about Christ. Just when Christ had descended to earth, this knowledge disappeared. The real Christ was united with the earth. The knowledge about Christ disappeared at this time. You have another situation on a large scale which I ask you simply to observe properly. We can look across the earth of the time, across the earth before the Mystery of

Golgotha. The further we go back, the more knowledge about Christ we find, even if it is the Christ who must be thought of in supersensory regions. But He is a being who can only be communicated through angels. That is evolution. This knowledge, these ideas about Christ spread across many people. Christ lives as the inspirer of many people: evolution.

This knowledge gradually recedes, disappears, is dimmed and everything that was previously distributed is concentrated in the one being, in Jesus of Nazareth. Think of evolution as one drop of Christ's inwardness in one mystery priest, in a second, a third and a fourth one, and so on within evolution. In each of the mystery initiates we would find that they had something of Christ within them when they left their body with their spirit. Christ is multiplied in them. Then everything disappears. And in one place, in the body of Jesus of Nazareth, everything is drawn together which was distributed: involution.

All the things specifically which had been withdrawn from all the others appeared in the one body. And so we see that what was distributed, what lived in evolution had to disappear from the earth in that it was concentrated in the one point, in the body of Jesus of Nazareth. That is the important fact. Evolution stops within the most significant involution. So now the time begins in which Christ lives with the earth but the knowledge about Christ does not live in the earth, in which the knowledge of Christ first has to develop again.

Now great difficulties arise—we have already indicated them. On the one hand we have Jesus, on the other we have Christ. And consider that the ancient wisdom of the connection was lost in humans. The whole period knew nothing of what the human being is actually like. Only now do we start to differentiate the human being again into physical body, etheric body, sentient soul and so on. We are only just starting with that again. We distinguish once again in the individual human being the physical earthly element which continues in the line of heredity and the higher spiritual element which comes down from spiritual worlds. Origen did not know that, Clement of Alexandria did not know that. They did not know about the soul and spiritual entity and the physical part of each human being walking on earth. That is why they found it difficult to understand the individual component elements of the Christ being. Knowledge of the human being had been lost—hence this difficulty in understanding the God-man. And thus the knowledge about Jesus and the knowledge about Christ diverged ever more. And it is incredibly important for an understanding of our time to realize how this in turn has an effect on our time to the extent that the content of our spiritual science has to appear in it. It is incredibly important to look particularly at this divergence of Jesus and Christ. That is an incredibly serious, and incredibly important matter. And we encounter it in so many different ways.

We have seen the Christmas plays pass before us. In the one Christmas play we still felt something of Christ, in the second one; the pure figure of Jesus in the first one, in the simple and primitive one. We can say: the Jesus child, that is the starting point of Jesus, has conquered people's minds. It is only from the high Middle Ages onwards that people begin to look to the child. Previously Christians attended mass, heard about the mystery that Christ went through death, the Pauline teaching and so on. But the Bible was not popular, the Bible was only in the hands of the priests. The faithful had to attend mass which, furthermore, was provided for them in Latin. But there was no participation in the processes of the holy service. And the things which are contained in the Gospels only gradually conquered minds and souls. And thus such plays, such presentations of the appearance of Jesus and so on could only be offered to people really properly from the high Middle Ages onwards. Today we tend to think: the Mystery of Golgotha happened and from that moment onwards people knew something about the Mystery of Golgotha. Well, what they knew was that Christ had died on the cross. The people primarily experienced the Easter happenings. But the Christmas happenings were quite unknown. They only very slowly and gradually crept into the minds, the hearts of people. That was the outer side, how people began to learn through images what happened in Palestine. It was only gradually through the dramatic performances that people began to have an idea of what happened in Palestine. That was the aspect of the Jesus mystery. At the same time—just consider—at the same time on the other side the mystics Tauler and Meister Eckhart[34] and the others sought Christ again through mysticism. So we have on the one hand the initial rise of

the Christmas plays. Jesus is sought as outwardly as possible, namely in
direct outer presentation: Jesus is sought. And the mystics seek Christ,
they seek to develop their soul to such an extent that they see Christ rise
in themselves; they seek to experience the wholly unformed, wholly
distanced from the world, purely spiritual Christ in their soul. Mysticism
on the one side, the Christmas plays on the other side—Jesus and Christ
sought at the same time by two different, greatly divergent paths!
What in Origen was a theoretical difficulty, not being able to combine
Christ with Jesus, that we can see out there in the villages. Jesus is
shown to the people as a child. The profound mystics seek Christ in that
they want to guide their own soul as far as inwardly sensing, almost as
far as inwardly touching Christ. But where is the connection? Where is
it, the connection? Things are happening in parallel. Think how far
what the simple person, the simple eye sees in the Christmas plays is
removed from the profound mysticism of a Meister Eckhart or a
Johannes Tauler. But the beginnings of the Christmas plays fall into this
period. And mysticism also continues.

And in our time today—just think what the whole Mystery of
Golgotha has become for many theologians. Take those who are the
most progressive theologians, what are they actually looking at? They
see that at one time at the start of our calendar in Nazareth or Bethlehem or somewhere a select human being was born, so select as to be
able gradually to fulfil the connection between human beings and the
spiritual world within himself, a noble human being—the most noble
human being there is, a human being so noble that we might say he was
almost—and furthermore—you see, this is where a problem arises!
People do not know quite what to do, what else there is to say in respect
of the fact that he was perceived wholly as a god in the course of
Christianity. They squirm and twist and come out with all the various
Eukenisms and Harnackisms[35] which are so—well, it is beyond belief
but people want to be clever in some way and still have the possibility of
understanding Jesus as one thing and Christ as some form of Christ. So
people take the Gospels. They are of course embarrassed as modern
people to believe in miracles. So they cut what can be cut and thus
construct something highly naturalistic, something for which there is a
reasonable explanation. And then they come to the event of Jerusalem

and the death on the cross. This is still all right when we get to the death. But it is no longer all right when we come to the resurrection. People then go as far as Harnack does, for example, who says: well, this resurrection, this tomb from which Christ is said to have arisen—the Easter mystery—yes, well, the Easter mystery, we have to bring ourselves to accept the knowledge that this Easter mystery originated in the garden by Calvary, the Easter mystery arose there, the thought of the resurrection came from there and that is what we have to keep in mind and in all other respects not look too closely at what actually happened there; that is where the view of the resurrection had its origin.

Isn't that something? Read Harnack's *Das Wesen des Christentums* (The nature of Christianity), that is where you will find these extraordinary thoughts about the resurrection! I once spoke about it at a meeting of the Giordano Bruno League[36] in a certain town and said: it is a strange thought, is it not, that people want to deal with the idea of the resurrection in such a way that they say, we do not want to go near what actually happened there but want to point out that the belief in the resurrection, the belief in the Easter mystery climbed out of that grave. In response, someone said to me: 'Harnack can't have written that. That is little short of Catholic, that is little short of Catholic superstition. That is the same as if one still were to believe that the holy robe of Trier had some meaning! That is superstition, Harnack cannot have written that.' Well, Harnack did write it and there was little I could do—I did not have the book to hand—other than to write the gentleman a card the next day telling him that it was written on page so and so. These are things which become difficult. People cannot do it when they are asked to find the way from Jesus to Christ. Someone[37] once told me: 'We are no longer able to make anything of Christology, we modern theologians, we really only have need for a Jesuology.' It was he who said it, not I: a pity that the term Jesuit is already in use because actually the confessors of modern theology should be called 'Jesuits'. Please note, I did not say it but a person who confessed to be a modern theologian!

Well then, that is the one side of the story. The other side is this, that a number of modern theologians in turn adhere more to Christ. They study the Gospels. They take certain statements in the Gospels not in the way that those whom I have just told you about take what reasonable people believe about another person, even if he is a divine person. But here people are unclear when they refer to a 'divine person' how far they should go with the application of divine: a noble person, but greater than Socrates—a slight problem here. Well, those are the one lot, the Jesuologists, because theologians is a word that cannot really be applied to them—theology as meaning wisdom about the divine. But the 'divine' part is precisely what is to be got rid of here. Then there are the others; they take these claims a bit more seriously. They find with regard to certain statements that it is not acceptable that the one who made them is seen merely as an ordinary person. After all, there are statements in the Gospels which cannot simply be attributed in all honesty to a person, a mere person. And they furthermore take the story of the resurrection seriously and so on. They make themselves Christologists in contrast to the Jesuologists.

But now they reach a different conclusion. Read the book *Ecce Deus*[38] and other books and you will see that they say: 'If we read the Gospels honestly, we cannot say that the Gospels refer to a human being. They refer to a god, a real, proper god.' These people in turn lose Jesus. And they lose him seriously because they now say: 'The Gospels refer everywhere to a god; but that god cannot have existed, so we have to retain Christ'. Those people speak about Christ, but not as someone who lived on earth. Christology without Jesuology, that is the other direction. But the two directions cannot come together. And so it really is the case today that those who refer to Christ have lost Jesus and those who refer to Jesus have lost Christ. Christ has become an unreal god and Jesus an unreal human being. They will inevitably continue along these tracks unless something else is added.

That which is added must be spiritual science which in turn can understand how Christ lived in Jesus. And that is basically one of the most important points in the teachings of spiritual science, that it can lead to an understanding of how Christ by way of the two Jesuses really could become the being who placed Himself at the centre of the earth development of humanity—because spiritual science has a concept of what the human being is, how spiritual, soul and physical aspects intermesh in the human being. So, building on this, we can in turn understand how Christ comes together with Jesus. That is of course complicated and not easy to understand, but it can be understood. And so you can see how out of the origins those things must in turn be restored through spiritual science which were lost to humanity, including in relation to an understanding of the Mystery of Golgotha. When Christ appeared in the world, it was not possible to understand him. Such understanding must gradually be re-acquired. His work is based in reality. But the starting points are everywhere. And such starting points can be found even in the simplest Christmas play.

What is it that is presented? What is presented with particular clarity as far as the paradise plays are concerned is how a human being enters the world about whom it only becomes clear through peripheral events that he is Jesus. The human being enters the world as a child. I said that the paradise play is connected with that—the start of earth development, the Mystery of Golgotha. How so? Here we have to take into consideration how at the start of earth development human beings were subject to the luciferic temptation. In that way they became a different being from what they would have become if they had progressed ordinarily. So if, speaking symbolically, we have Adam before us outside paradise, he is a different being to the being he was destined to be before the luciferic temptation. How is that revealed? Imagine that Lucifer had not approached human beings, they would be living without the luciferic impulse and would live quite differently in their etheric body. When human beings pass through the portal of death and still have their etheric body and then shed it, the etheric body remains behind but all the things are imprinted in it which human beings do and think as a result of the luciferic temptation. You see, human beings die and pass through the portal of death. The physical body is given over to the elements. A few days later the etheric body detaches itself from the being of the person. The human being then proceeds on his or her various ways. But the etheric body contains what it has become as a result of the way that human beings think, feel and act as they must do after the luciferic temptation.

So now imagine the earth. The human physical body is put in the earth and is given over to the elements of the earth. But its etheric body remains linked with the earth. So we have the etheric bodies of human beings which are present in the earth's atmosphere. They are different to how they would be if they had not been subject to the luciferic temp-tation. Everything I have said elsewhere about the etheric body of course relates to them. But what I say today also relates to them so that we can say: a human being is embedded in the earth. But that which human beings leave behind on earth, what has become their etheric body during life, is more arid, woody than it would be if the luciferic temptation had not happened. More woody, arid—this difference really does exist. Imagine that the luciferic temptation had never happened, then people would leave a much more 'youngified' etheric body behind on death, a much greener etheric body, as it were. They leave a much more arid, dried out etheric body behind through the luciferic temp-tation than would have been the case without the luciferic temptation. That already comes to expression in the legend that the wooded tree of paradise grows out of Adam's grave. But what lives in the earth there lived before the Mystery of Golgotha in the luciferically infected etheric body. That was precisely the element into which the phantom of the body of Jesus of Nazareth went to redeem it, as I once indicated in the Karlsruhe lectures.[39] So now imagine Adam's grave: Adam given over as a physical body to the elements of the earth, coming out of Adam's grave the wooded etheric body as the representative of that which is luciferically infected in the human being and remains after death. That is also the wood on which the human being can be crucified. And this crucifixion comes about in that the phantom of Jesus of Nazareth remains behind after the Mystery of Golgotha, combining with the earth with his help. That is expressed in the legend when it is told that the wood was passed from generation to generation and in turn formed the wood of the cross at Golgotha. This image is an image which corresponds to a real fact, namely that through the crucifixion the phantom of Jesus of Nazareth combined with what lives etherically in the earth in terms of all the luciferically infected etheric bodies which were, of course, spread out and had become diluted and dissolved, but which were still there in their forces. It is a very important, profoundly deep fact which we are considering here, which casts a light on mysteries of the earth.

But how is the relationship between human beings and this luci-ferically infected etheric body established? Because they enter into this world in which they start as children. It has not yet, of course, happened when they are children. That is why we can truly see the non-luciferic human being when we look at children with the right feelings as they enter the world. And if we are able to look at children with the right feelings as they enter the world, we can see human beings as they are related to Christ. That is the feeling which was to be created in those to whom Jesus was given in the Christmas play: to feel what I indicated right at the beginning in the first pages of the small text about the progress of the human being and humanity,[40] where I spoke about the first three years, about this arrival. Because if that which imbues human beings at that point could infuse them in the middle of their lives—that is what I indicated—then we would have an idea of the way in which Christ lived in Jesus. Being able to look in this way at what is not yet luciferically infected in the child, that is precisely what can happen in the Christmas play.

And think what all of this ultimately represents. It actually represents something colossal, when we look at the child in this way. I drew attention in this small text to the way we are more clever in youth, albeit unconsciously more clever, because we only have to build our body gradually, something we can no longer do later on. We are much cleverer, we are much wiser than we are later on as we pervade the human being, the essence of the human being, but there is nothing luciferic yet. By working inwardly in this way when we are children, up to the point to which we can subsequently remember back, we are working on the delicate refinement of the body. We work there in accordance with infinitely wise laws of which we subsequently have not the least idea in our luciferically and ahrimanically infiltrated thinking. When we are at work within this being we are still free from everything which enters later on when we experience the world in our body. We are free of all differences, even the great differences between male and female. We do not yet as children live within the male and female aspect. We are not yet within differences of status and race, are not yet within national differences. We are human, purely human. The reality in which we are as children is the one in which once lived even those who now oppose one another in war through something which they first experience outwardly, through hate. That we face one another in the world in hate as belonging to different nations only comes about through the forces into which we enter in life together with the physical body. Before they have lived their way fully into the physical body, children still live in those things which are beyond differences of nation and status. They live in those things in which souls can truly live wherever they are born on earth. Just think, people can fight one another in terrible ways, face one another in battle, shoot and kill one another—and those who shoot and kill one another can pass through the portal of death together in the community of Christ, in that of which they are a part when they are not yet marked with the differences between human beings. The things which face off in hate are only acquired by human beings in the physical body; they have nothing to do with what is outside the physical body. There is a great deal that our present time can learn, particularly our present time, by finding its way back to the veneration of Jesus in the time in which he is represented as a child, when he has not yet entered into what differentiates people and brings them to quarrel and strife. War and disputes only arise through what people experience when they become something different from what the child is about whom we speak at Christmas. The things which are acted out in the Christmas plays represent the human being truly connected with the cosmic powers, but in such a way that outwardly on the physical plane something is revealed in unique form which does not get into a quarrel, which those who fight one another outwardly to the death can in the same way carry in their hearts.

There is something immensely profound in this aspect being placed before humanity in the Jesus child from the line of Nathan; so that human beings are touched by the aspect through which they enter the world without the shadow of differentiation, before they have entered into nations, into other differences, differences which they do not enter into until they coexist with the body. The Jesus idea on the one hand, which can only come to full expression in the Jesus child, touches the Christ idea. The latter comes to expression if in purity we can grasp in Jesus between the age of 30 and 33 what now is also spiritual, the Christ being. In a dual way, through the Jesus from the line of Nathan and from the line of Solomon a body has been prepared which can now stand aside from everything that causes differences between human beings. And Christ can only be revealed in such a body.

Thus we can see the Jesus idea in our spiritual-scientific sense, as I have indicated in the booklet about the progress of the human being and humanity, can see the Christ idea and how they grow together. That is the greatest, the most significant requirement of our time. Hitherto people only had one Christmas and one Easter but they did not belong together—because Easter is a Christ festival, Christmas a Jesus festival. Easter and Christmas only come together if we can understand how Christ and Jesus belong together. The bridge between Christmas and Easter is built by spiritual science. And a bridge is built from the simple shepherds' play to the most subtle understanding which may be acquired if we study spiritual science so far that we can find Christ through it. But we have to have the ability to go with the attitude of the shepherds, not with the attitude of the innkeepers. The contrast between materialism and spiritualism is set out in a wonderful way in the 'innkeepers' and 'shepherds'. And that is basically the major question of our time, whether people want to be innkeepers or shepherds. A large part of the events in our time have come about because people are innkeepers. Being an innkeeper is widespread throughout the world. We must try to be shepherds again, to become shepherds. But even among the shepherds there will still be some doubters. And when one person says: I believe I can see a light over there, meaning I perceive something spiritual, someone else will nevertheless come along and say: that is all just fantasy. That may be, but if people can develop now in themselves the aspects which are not based on what can be acquired on earth but can find the connection with the things which human beings have brought in their inner being from the spiritual, the heavenly worlds, then they will be able to be shepherds. People today stand too firmly in the house in which they have what the innkeeper has, the things that have been introduced from what is of the earth. That can only be measured with earthly values. But those who still have a certain connection with the things that flow and pulse through the spiritual world, who have retained the shepherd nature within themselves, they shall find the paths—be able to find the paths where basically with outer knowledge we only find outer appearances. We will gradually begin to understand Christmas when we learn to distinguish the inn-keeper nature from the shepherd nature and when we know how much there is of an innkeeper nature in our time. But there is a small matter which we will have to try and deal with. We do of course have to distinguish between the innkeeper and shepherd natures, we are after all surrounded by a whole lot of innkeepers; wherever we go we are surrounded by a whole lot of innkeepers and feel quite the shepherd. Naturally we always feel ourselves to be shepherds! But we do have to get over it and should at least search a little bit for the innkeeper element we bear within ourselves and not see ourselves purely as shepherds. Sometimes we will have to ask ourselves: can I already see the light which is to come? We will have to cultivate everything that can bring the feeling to life in us of being able to celebrate Christmas in our hearts on the basis of this new spiritual direction: seeking the light in the darkness, and seeking, really wanting to seek, in the light; and in seeking truly having the sentiment that just once is not enough, that we have to keep coming like the shepherds did who also promise that they will return; that they do not want to let it be just once.

Yes, there is a lot to learn still from this simple Christmas play in particular. And that is why I think it is good that we have started to cultivate among us a little also of this simplest form of the Christmas mystery, an experience in the simplest form of the Christmas mystery. Because spiritual-scientific striving in particular will have to face many serious battles in the coming time. And only those will find the way who have truly learnt to become shepherds through a spiritual under-standing of the Christmas mystery with all the humility of the shep-herds, but also with all the wise seeking of the shepherds who are connected with the world in loyalty. Let us inscribe this in our hearts, in our souls at this Christmas time so that we become seeking shepherds to an ever greater extent and learn in time to seek what is holy in the innermost soul mood of human beings, just as it was found out of the profane mood I characterized for you when the most solemn form of the Christmas play gradually arose out of carnival rather than holy entertainment.

Let us try to seek the spiritual by building on precisely what the Christmas plays have shown us. Then we will find it in the right way as shepherds, not as innkeepers who have already lost—that is the symbolic message of the Christmas play—the connection with the Christmas child. That is something which is very necessary, very much necessary in our time, our time in which materialism has taken hold of such large, large swathes of the external world, of inner human feeling, and in which a spiritual view of the world has such difficulty even just to find the rights words, to say what the right words are in the face of the abused words which are spoken.

LECTURE 5

You have just heard about the way that the Christmas festival is intimately entwined with spiritual nature.[41] It is true that this thought can penetrate our spiritual-scientific branch of work in a particularly profound and warm fashion when we see the tree festooned with lights in the dark middle of winter, in the night of winter. Of all the symbols that have entered spiritual life out of a certain elementary, not superficial consciousness, the Christmas tree is actually one of the most recent. If we go back about two hundred years in the time that European spiritual life has developed, we find that the Christmas tree occurs at most very occasionally here or there. It is not yet old as a Christmas symbol. We combine with this thought of the Christmas tree as one of the most recent Christian symbols—which arouses joy, the impulse of gratitude in the childlike heart—a slightly different thought that we have become very fond of this Christmas tree in many of our branches and that we do not want to do without it when we celebrate the Christmas festival in our branches.

Although it has only turned into a Christian symbol of Christmas in recent times—even if out of unconscious depths of the human heart— the Christmas tree is truly connected with a deep sense of and feeling for the nature and meaning of Christmas. In the Middle Ages it became common practice to perform Christmas plays around the time of Christmas, New Year and Epiphany. Farmers who had prepared for it for a long time went from one village to the next and presented the birth of Christ. They presented the Three Kings, the three Magi, coming to the newly born Christ. But in the so-called paradise play they also presented what is described in Genesis as the creation of our earthly world[42]—the scene which we have to visualize so often, revealing to us as it does the secrets of our own soul in such a mighty, illuminating way, the beginning scene of the earth into which the meaningful words resound, 'Of every tree of the garden thou mayest freely eat: But of the tree of the knowledge of good and evil, thou shalt not eat of it.' Now the only thing that remains of the inner connections between the beginning of the creation of the earth and the Christmas festival is that our calendar shows 'Feast of Adam and Eve' on 24 December and the festival of the birth of Christ on 25 December.

And yet we cannot but feel—not, as I said, out of reflection but out of a feeling—did the impulse perhaps not arise out of the darkest substrates of the Christian human heart to put up that ancient cosmic tree, the tree from the centre of paradise, the fruit of which should not actually have been eaten, on the day that Christ is born? The paradise play was performed. What remained of the memory of paradise was the tree of paradise and the tree of paradise was able to be combined with the feeling we can have about the birth of Jesus Christ.

I do not want to develop theories here. That is not what this feast day is about. There is certainly more that could be said about the reasons why the Christmas tree became popular. But in looking at the Christmas tree, we want to speak out of the feeling which might arise in us as we stand next to it, as we let just those feelings illuminate our soul which unite us at this festival with the most childlike human feelings, because we see in it something like the renewal of the tree of paradise. The Christmas tree does not really present itself as a heathen symbol, not even as a Nordic heathen symbol. When our earth was covered in snow, when the icicles hung from the eaves of the houses and from the trees and people fled inside from the regions of their world where for months greenery and colourful flowers delighted the eye and fruits offered themselves which people needed to live, when people had to escape inside from all the things which they felt were there for them outside and with which they had to concern themselves throughout spring and summer, when they had to escape inside into their houses with the snow and icicles looking in and warm them from inside, then the heathen might have sensed something of what might become of this world if it was left to its own devices. The great winter at the end of earth existence was experienced by heathens when they were abandoned in this way by the spirits of nature, by everything which they sensed as gnomes, undines and sylphs, when they had to escape inside to the warmth of the stove, escape from what left them feeling abandoned by their beloved nature and only saw through a slit what they could not be part of. When they experienced that abandonment, they felt the end of earth existence, the great cosmic winter in a wintertime expanded to infinity, submerging everything, drowning out everything.

Christ would have answered them, once again perhaps not through a theoretical understanding but through a feeling understanding: you may be right, that is what would have happened to the world if the effect of the tree had spread, the tree from which human beings enjoyed the fruit of knowledge of good and evil without permission as a result of luciferic temptation. And if we think in this way of earth development and the goal which everything would have had to face after the abandonment and loneliness of winter, after the coldness and frost, also with regard to the soul element, and if we connect this with the consequences of the luciferic temptation, with the enjoyment of the tree of knowledge of good and evil, then on the other hand we can feel very well what the real meaning of the Christ idea is.

Before the Christ idea, human beings who were part of Christian development were aware of the Easter idea, the idea which the Easter symbols relate in such a significant way and through which human beings have been liberated from everything that is in the luciferic temptation. The magnificence of experiencing the Easter idea can send tremors, a breeze through the soul in spring with awakening nature. But the Christmas idea is something different, this other side of the Christ idea. In order to understand the Easter idea, some knowledge is indeed necessary which we must have obtained beforehand. The Christmas idea can be understood through the feelings by, I might say, the smallest child. And what really is this Christmas feeling idea if we investigate it in the children who are summoned once the Christmas tree has been decorated, the candles have been lit, the presents laid out underneath? What is this Christmas feeling idea when the children are led to the Christmas tree, when they receive their gifts, when they are told that they were brought by Christ the holy one—what is the essential thing?

The children might not know it, but they feel it subconsciously in those depths which are located so deeply in the human soul that they cannot always be called to consciousness. What is this essential thing, if we investigate it properly, which lives in the children when they are called to the Christmas tree and hear that the presents were brought by a transcendental being? These are not the kind of presents which they can go and pick outside by the stream in summer or spring; no, they have received them from something transcendental. What is it that then lives in the children? I mean, we can say, particularly when we look deep into the hearts of children with the eyes we call clairvoyant which we acquire gradually: the most important, the most intensive feeling which lives unconsciously in the children's hearts is an infinite, deep-seated gratitude. And then, if we feel our way into that, we feel something like the thought which triggers these feelings of gratitude: why does such gratitude spread like this in the hearts, in the souls of the children? Why? Because actually these hearts tell themselves in their deepest unconscious: we human beings must be grateful that we have not been abandoned, that a being has turned towards us from spiritual heights which has wanted to take up residence within human earthly existence, that on the earth—which would have had to remain dark as a result of the temptation in paradise, which would have had to grow cold and frozen with the onset of the great winter—a being entered into this impending petrified existence, and enters anew each year, in a time which symbolically already indicates the end of the earth in the frost of winter, the darkness and the obscurity of winter. We have to be grateful to the cosmic spirit which has descended, has united with the earth development of human beings so that we do not need to fear the coming of the great winter. But we may hope that when, through the outer natural development of the earth, the great winter with its earthly-cosmic frost follows, the being will be present who comes to us each year in the form of a child and rejuvenates the earth so that it is not carried out in its frozen form into its subsequent existence in the cosmos. Hence the infinite warmth which emanates particularly from the Christmas festival. And hence what I might call the peculiar affirmative character of the Christmas festival. The Christmas festival has something about it which affirms Christ.

We can feel in respect of the Christmas festival that what it aims to represent is true because as soon as the mere thought of the Christmas festival arises in the childlike human soul it immediately takes hold of the child's heart, the childlike soul of the human being in its full meaning, and that it really encompasses everything in the human being, irrespective of whether this childlike element comes to expression in childhood or in later years. Particularly the people who, on the one hand, have a proper feeling for outer nature with all its spring and summer beauty, who can also feel the peculiar abandonment of winter time, who can feel the holy mood of Christmas time, they can also feel this affirmative aspect of the Christmas festival.

A writer who throughout his life studied nature in minutest detail also wrote wonderfully beautiful words about the Christmas festival in one of his writings; this is the writer who said:[43] 'People say a thunderstorm is magnificent, a storm is magnificent, an earthquake or volcano could be magnificent. I think: a ladybird is magnificent as it runs across a leaf if we can only experience it in its true nature.' This is roughly what the writer Adalbert Stifter said.[44] And out of such acquaintance with the greatness in the minutiae of nature, with what pervades all of nature as spirit, he also produced a beautiful Christmas story in whose basic tenor there lives and is entwined the affirmative element of the Christmas festival.

The writer leads us into a secluded Alpine valley which has a neighbouring valley. There are villages in both valleys. As happens in the Alps—at least in earlier times—the inhabitants of the one valley have little contact with the inhabitants of the other valley. But then it happens that an inhabitant of the one valley—he is a cobbler—marries an inhabitant from the other valley. The latter, who was only born a short distance away on the other side of the mountain, is treated like a stranger. Then children came along. The grandparents are over in the other Alpine valley. The grandfather has little good to say about his son-in-law so he has little time for the children but the grandmother had often visited in the past. But as the children grew a little older, although they were still small, the grandmother was already old and could no longer come across to visit so often. So the children visited her. On one occasion, it was on so-called Christmas Eve, they were sent across to the village in the other valley in weather which seemed to contain no threat. They walked along. As they were still very young, the children had probably only stood a few times with any awareness in front of the Christmas tree in the silence of the Alpine hut at night and heard words about the mystery of Christ, only heard little. Now, still being relatively small children, they were let go. They were to go and visit their grandmother. The weather could be expected to stay good. They went to their grandmother in the neighbouring village. Grandmother gave them their presents and urged them to take care on their way home. But then the snow began to fall. They had to cross the mountains to the other valley. They lost their way and could not find it again. They were lost. The boy, who was a little older, was concerned to look after the little girl. They even had to cross glaciers. They were only able to keep going because their grandmother had given them some coffee which they took out. The boy had once heard that one could prevent freezing to death with coffee. But they could not find the way home. The night grew darker and darker and they were high up amid the snow and ice so that when at midnight the church bells everywhere began to ring they could not hear them. So that is how they spent the night of Christmas while of course in the village not just the parents but the whole village was gripped with fear and worry. The villagers had gone out to look for the children. But the children were high up lost and alone. They had to wait and keep warm with all the knowledge they had already learnt at their young age, had to wait until morning gradually arrived. As the description says, snow and ice were below them and the stars above. Then, as they looked towards the mountains, a wonderful brightness rose above them towards morning. Well, the children were found half frozen and taken home and put to bed. The mother—I won't go into all the scenes which the writer now describes in a deeply affecting way—sits down at the bed of the little girl and listens to the terrible ordeal the children suffered. Then the little girl who, as I said, has not yet heard many words about the whole meaning of the festival of Christ, says: 'Mother, when we were up there and it was so cold and we did not see anything except the snow and the stars, I looked at the stars and, you know, mother, what I saw as I looked up into the sky? I saw holy Christ!'

I said that a work like this has something affirmative because it affirms the intimate way in which the Christ idea is interwoven with the human heart even if a person has not yet heard much about the Christ idea. He is understood at every age, in youngest childhood. The writer Adalbert Stifter told the truth. He is understood in such a way that even as very small children we are already able to read the script in the stars of what holy Christ says. This is truly connected with the gratitude towards the cosmic fact that a God has wanted to descend to earth so that human beings are not abandoned with earth development. The divine helper has wrested us from loneliness. The child feels that. And this feeling of gratitude towards the cosmic powers, which can be so deep-seated, is the same infinitely warm feeling which glows in the hearts of human beings in the holy nights of Christmas; in a spiritual way it makes life in the holy nights of Christmas so warm in the coldness of winter, it makes life in the holy nights of Christmas so light in the darkness of winter when the sun is at its lowest.

And we, who seek knowledge, must seek it in a different way from the way it is when it comes from the tempter. And we do seek knowledge. Indeed, we seek spiritual knowledge. We must value the tree of knowledge. If we feel it in the right way it is also the tree of knowledge for us. But we must not let it be presented to us by luciferic powers. We receive it from Christ who descended to earth. Because that is how it may be received by human hearts, human minds, the human striving for knowledge, this tree of knowledge; that is how it may be received when Christ presents it to us. That which Lucifer should not present to human beings is presented to human beings by Christ. And that is how the tree of paradise is renewed: it becomes the Christmas tree. What Lucifer presented to human beings as temptation is in turn presented by Christ to human beings in reconciliation. And thus even the maturest thought in our striving for knowledge is linked to the childlike idea of the Christmas tree. Just as children receive the things which on other occasions they have seen from where they come, gifts of nature, gifts from society, just as they accept those things as a holy gift on Christmas Eve, we should have the same thoughts when we receive what is holy and valuable to us, the gift from the tree of knowledge, from Christ who has wanted to unite his impulses with the impulses of earth.

Particularly from the perspective of our view of the world, we will understand how we can bring to life that warm gratitude towards the Christ being who wanted to come to earth to liberate human beings from their loneliness symbolized by the darkness and coldness of winter. Symbolized on the other hand is the spiritual warmth of which human beings can partake together with the spiritual powers, the true warmth from that consciousness which we can allow to penetrate our hearts from our spirit if we understand the symbol of the Christmas tree in the right way, the renewed tree of knowledge, the tree of knowledge which is presented by Jesus Christ, if we allow this Christmas symbol which warms the cosmic chill to speak to our soul, to our heart.

LECTURE 6

SOME of the things we want to talk about with regard to the secrets of the spiritual world have to be indicated in pictorial form to begin with, or we might say indicated half-pictorially, which does not, however, mean that such images are not meant to be taken as reality. Indicating what I want to tell you today in pictorial form, so that you can meditate further on it in your own mind, is necessary because if we were to speak not in images but in concepts there would have to be long explanations. But everyone can themselves get to the deeper aspects if they let what I will say today be present in their mind and meditate on it, as it were.

Every year at this time of the year we pass from one period to the next. We can certainly see that to begin with as a convenient division of chronological order. But it is no such thing because the people who had to make the chronological divisions followed certain major laws of the division of time out of a profound instinct. We celebrate this festival of transition from one year to the next—and I refer of course to our part of the world—in the depth of winter, in the period in which the plants have stopped growing, blossoming and bearing fruit. Only certain evergreens, as people call them, continue to keep their leaves through the winter whiteness. The sun is at its weakest.

We know that spiritual events are interwoven with all the events which take place in front of our senses. We know that when we walk through the forest we not only have the trees of the forest with their green needles or their leaves around us but that spiritual and soul beings are also at work in the mysterious depths of existence. We have already found our way to experiencing as indicative of true reality those things which are viewed as childish superstition by the very clever people of our time.

And so it is clear to us that spiritual workings and development underlie everything of a sensory nature, be it fixed things or be it events that can be observed with the senses. And so we begin by looking at the non-living, the inorganic earth as it is called, at everything that is mineral realm on our earth—by looking at everything that is lifeless. Lifeless is all that it is to the outer materialist. For us, everything lifeless has a soul and spiritual element so that we can also speak of a soul and spiritual part of our whole, so-called lifeless and inorganic, purely mineral earth. Nevertheless, when we speak about such earth consciousness, we do not to begin with even see in the geological and mineral part anything that could be compared with the muscles and blood in human beings but only the skeleton, namely the firm part of the earth. So that when we speak about this earth consciousness we have to think of it as being connected with the whole earth, which comprises not only the skeleton but also water, air and so on, corresponding to muscles and blood. The whole earth has consciousness, a consciousness which belongs to its mineral realm. We need not concern ourselves with the change of this consciousness in a particular region throughout the year but we want to bring the idea to mind that the whole earth has its consciousness. And now we turn our gaze away from the whole mineral earth to that which grows out of the earth as the plant world.

When we look at it within the meaning of spiritual science, we have to begin by looking at this plant world as an independent being in comparison to the earth. And that the totality of plant existence is an independent being in comparison to the earth only emerges properly if we look at the consciousness of these two beings. We can speak of the consciousness of the whole mineral earth. But we can also talk of a consciousness of the whole plant world as it develops on earth. The laws of this consciousness are, however, different from the laws of human consciousness. If we speak of plant consciousness, we can only ever speak of a specific region because that consciousness changes depending on the region of the earth.

We do not take into account as human beings that there is actually a certain parallelism between our consciousness and the consciousness of, for example, the plant world of the whole earth because we take our daytime consciousness up into our full consciousness but not our night-time consciousness. We can simply say to avoid making our reflections too complicated: when we are awake during the day, the I and our astral body are in our physical body. But I have already pointed out that this actually relates only to our blood and nervous system, not to the other systems. Because when the I and astral body are outside our head, as it were, they are all the more strongly in the rest of our organism.

It is very parallel with this that when, for example, it is winter on one side of the earth, it is summer on the other side. That, too, is just a change of consciousness. That is the same as with us. We only do not take account of it because in us human beings the two consciousnesses do not have the same brightness. In us they are of different intensity. The night-time consciousness is subdued for us so that there is no consciousness to all intents and purposes and the daytime consciousness is a full consciousness of our other side. Our lower nature is awake at night when our higher nature is asleep, just as is the case with the earth when it is winter on one side and summer on the other. When there is a waking state on the one side there is a sleeping state on the other and vice versa.

The way I have explained the matter now and how we have already explained it many times actually only applies with regard to the plant world. The plant world sleeps for us during the height of summer, precisely while it is in abundant growth. It is asleep while it unfolds its physical side to the greatest extent. And it is awake with full consciousness when it undergoes no outward physical development but its physical development diminishes. Thus we speak of all plants on earth as a whole, and this totality of the plant world has a consciousness.

When we speak about this consciousness, which is therefore a second consciousness pervading the mineral consciousness of the earth, when we speak about this plant consciousness we can say in a true sense: this plant consciousness is asleep in our region during the height of summer and awake in the dark winter period.

But then something else also happens about this time. You see, the two consciousnesses, that is, this whole earth consciousness that belongs to the mineral earth and the whole plant consciousness are separate. They are two beings throughout the whole year. However, they are not only two beings but they pervade one another so that the one is pervaded by the other at the present time. At the point where the one year develops over into the next one, at that point our mineral things and processes on earth and the whole of the plant world have one consciousness; that is, their two consciousnesses pervade one another.

What, then, is the nature of the mineral consciousness of the earth which today, as I said, we do not intend to look at in its differentiation as we did plant consciousness, which we conceive of as waking in winter time and sleeping in summer time? What, then, is the particular nature of mineral consciousness, the consciousness of the great earth being? People who are only restricted to their physical senses, and restricted to a reason which they see as belonging to the physical senses, cannot to begin with know anything about this great earth consciousness. But spiritual science can teach us what this earth consciousness is actually thinking, thinks in the same way that we conceive of minerals, plants, animals, air, rivers, mountains and so on. The earth thinks in the same way that we think with our ordinary day consciousness about what surrounds us. But what does it think with its consciousness? Let us ask today: what does the earth think with its consciousness?

To begin with, the earth thinks with its consciousness about the heavenly spaces belonging to earth. In the same way that we look out with our eyes at trees or at stones, so the earth looks with its consciousness out at the heavenly spaces and thinks about everything that is happening in the stars. The earth is a being that thinks about the processes of the stars.

So basically the mineral consciousness contains the secret of the whole cosmos as a thought. While we human beings walk superficially across the earth and only think about the stones against which we stub our toe or about whatever else surrounds our senses, the earth thinks about the cosmos out there with the consciousness through which we walk as we walk through our spaces. It truly has more comprehensive, greater thoughts than we do. And it is basically incredibly uplifting when we know: you are not just walking through the air, you are walking through the earth's thoughts.

And now let us look back at the other thing, at plant consciousness. Plants cannot think as much as the earth. The consciousness, the thinking consciousness of the plant world, of all the plant world (not the individual plants) is much more restricted. It comprises smaller surroundings of the earth for the whole of the year, just not in these days. At this time plant consciousness becomes one with the whole of the consciousness of the earth. And because plant consciousness pervades the consciousness of the earth, our earth's plant world knows during the New Year period, that is now, of the secrets of the stars, takes up the secrets of the stars and uses them so that the plants in turn can develop in the spring in accordance with the secrets of the cosmos and can bear flowers and fruit. Because the whole secret of the cosmos is contained in the way that the plants can bear leaves and flowers and fruit. But while they are bearing leaves and flowers, the plants cannot think about it. They can only think about it in the current time, at the time when the consciousness of the plant world is united with the consciousness of the mineral world.

That is why we say in spiritual science: at this time, approximately on New Year's Eve, two cycles interpenetrate. And that is the secret of all existence as such, that two cycles interpenetrate and then continue their further development separately, then interpenetrate again. Just think how wonderful this secret of becoming is: plant consciousness, mineral consciousness—two developmental streams. They go their separate ways throughout the year and then unite in the time in which the one year passes over into the next. Then they go their separate ways again for the rest of the year and unite again in the New Year period. That is the cyclical progress of this story.

And now let us look from this process, which can fill us with a profound, holy awe regarding the secrets of the transition from one cycle of the year to the next cycle of the year—now let us look from this secret which, as I might say, we walk through directly, to another even greater secret. We know that we now live in the cycle of consciousness soul development, that this cycle was preceded by the cycle of intellectual or mind soul development, which was preceded by the development of the sentient soul; and then we come to the development of the sentient body. That takes us back as far as the fifth millennium before the Christian era if we go back as far as the time in which all human thinking developed within the cycle of the sentient body, the so-called astral body.

Right now we have to pass through the consciousness soul; human beings will develop through Spirit Self and further. The consciousness soul develops in our current time mainly in that human beings use their physical body alone as a tool. That is why we now have, as you have already heard in various lectures here, the deluge of materialism because people are primarily using their physical body. But a time will come in which they will not just use their physical body—I have described how human beings continue to progress—in which they will learn to use their etheric body again, will learn to use their astral body in the way they used it a long time ago in the developmental cycle in which the astral body provided the foundation of consciousness.

So we can say: we were once on earth in such a way that our soul was in contact with its consciousness, with the consciousness of the astral body. In the same way that at New Year plant consciousness passes through mineral consciousness, so our soul millennia ago passed through our astral body, through the consciousness which is central to our astral body. At that time our souls were one in their consciousness with our astral body. We go back millennia for that, into the sixth millennium before the Christian era. When this consciousness began, humanity on earth celebrated a New Year—a great New Year! Just as we now have New Year approaching us as the passage of plant and mineral consciousness, so New Year occurred on our earth six millennia before the Christian era, but as a great cosmic New Year of our earth. The consciousness of our soul united with, went through the astral consciousness of our body.

And what happened at that time? At that time, six millennia before the Christian era, when our inner soul consciousness passed through the astral consciousness of our body, our restricted human consciousness as we have it now expanded as much as plant consciousness expands at New Year. Just as the plant looks out into the heavens because its consciousness has united with mineral consciousness, so human beings saw and heard a wide field of wisdom at that time six millennia before the Christian era when their souls united with the astral body at cosmic New Year.

And that is the period in which the knowledge originates which has been lost—we spoke about it some days ago—as Gnostic knowledge. We have to look for the origin of this knowledge in the earthly-cosmic New Year about six thousand years before the Christian era; it is the knowledge on which Zarathustra drew, the knowledge whose last great rays shone on the Gnostics and of which only a few fragments are left, as I explained, and of which I gave an example. That goes back to earth winter, earth New Year.

And now add about another four thousand years to the years that have passed since the start of Christianity and our soul consciousness will once again pass through astral consciousness in the way I indicated just now, except at a higher level. Human beings will once again enter such a cosmic consciousness of the stars. And that is what we want to prepare for through our spiritual science so that there are people who are ready for it.

We want to prepare for the cosmic New Year! And if we prepare the Christmas festival in the way I have indicated here in a previous reflection, we will prepare in the right way. We will prepare for the new cosmic New Year, which will occur twelve millennia after the old cosmic New Year, by turning the birth of spiritual knowledge in us into the hallowed mood of Christmas.

Twelve months of the year pass from one union to the next of plant consciousness on earth with mineral consciousness. Twelve millennia pass from one cosmic New Year of earth to the next cosmic New Year of earth, from one passage of the human soul through the astral world to the next passage of the human soul through the astral world.

So in this hallowed hour we look from New Year on a small scale to the New Year on a grand scale, from the annual New Year to the New Year for which we prepare by trying to see now in wintertime the light which in a natural, elementary way only flows towards human beings as inhabitants of the earth in the cosmic New Year of earth.

Truly, we only see the world in the right light if we grasp what surrounds us not just as it presents itself through the senses, as it is understood by the materialistic spirit, but if we view what surrounds us in the external world of the senses as a symbol for the great secrets of the cosmos.

And so it can appear to us as New Year approaches, as if a messenger from the spiritual world came to us and revealed to us the secret of New Year's Eve each year by telling us: see how in the dark, cold midwinter plant consciousness unites with mineral earth consciousness. But let that be a sign to you that the earth also has a year, the great cosmic year, of which Zarathustra once spoke and which he meant as a reality extending from one New Year's Eve to the next New Year's Eve, from one cosmic New Year to the next cosmic New Year, which must be understood if the progression of human development is to be comprehended.

Zarathustra spoke about twelve millennia. He was referring to the twelve millennia of which I have spoken to you today. He set out one earth year in four periods of time as the developmental progression of humanity on earth. This is based on profound spiritual secrets.

And so let a hallowed mood take hold of our souls, our hearts, out of a deeper understanding of our spiritual science. Let us develop that inner warmth in our hearts which can come to us if we hear on a frosty winter's night the tidings of the descent of the Sun Spirit to us on earth and then of the secret of the course of the year.

The 13 days are the days in which plant consciousness combines with mineral consciousness. And if human beings can put themselves in plant consciousness, then they can dream, then they can see the manifold secrets which pass through their hearts in many different ways, as we let them pass through our souls here last year in the dream of Olaf Åsteson.[45]

But if we make such a hallowed mood our own, then we will find the right feeling out of that mood for what we want to achieve with our endeavours regarding spiritual knowledge: we want to use such heart warmth to prepare the new cosmic year, anticipate in solemnity the new cosmic New Year's Eve which must bring a new cosmic year. So when our souls live through the great cosmic New Year's Eve in following incarnations under quite different circumstances on earth, they will live through it in the way they live through it when the little New Year's

Eve, the day which occurs not after twelve thousand years but after twelve months, becomes the symbol for the great New Year's Eve.

And that is the secret of our existence. Everything is the same, both on the large scale and the small scale. And we will only understand the small scale, what happens in the course of the year, if we see it as a symbol of the great cosmic events, of what happens in the course of millennia.

The year is the image of the aeons. And the aeons are the reality for those symbols which we encounter in the course of the year. If we understand the course of the year in the right way, then in this sacred night, when the new year starts its course, we will be imbued by the thought of the great cosmic secrets. Let us try to put our soul in such a mood that it can look towards the New Year in the awareness: it wishes to carry within itself the course of the year as a symbol for the great course of the cosmos; the cosmos comprising all the secrets which the divine beings who stream through and weave in the world pursue with our souls from one aeon to the next, just as the more minor gods pursue the secret becoming of the plant and mineral realm in the course of the individual year.

LECTURE 7

IF yesterday at New Year's Eve it was good to immerse ourselves in some of the secrets of existence, in such things that are connected with great transcendental secrets such as the annual transition from one year to the next, and the great cosmic New Year's Eve and cosmic New Year—if it was good yesterday, as I said, to immerse ourselves in these secrets which address the depths of our soul far removed from the external world, it might be of particular importance, specifically at the start of the year, to let at least some of our great, important obligations pass before our soul. These obligations are, however, connected with what we can know about the development of humanity through spiritual science. They are connected with the knowledge about the path which humanity must follow as it strides towards its future. We cannot recognize the obligations about which we are talking if we do not try to take a candid look at our time in various fields. That is also what we have repeatedly done in the course of our reflections. But it might be appropriate to put some of the things—which we may already know about—before our soul today already, at the start of a new year.

Of course, my dear friends, all the things which pass before our soul in view of our materialistic time with all its consequences—so that we know that spiritual science must provide the foundations to advocate in a higher way the proper progress of mankind—of course all the things which we deem it necessary to do are so enormous, so incisive, so important, there is, in simple words, so much to do in the present time that it is inconceivable that we would be able with our weak forces to do a lot of the things that need to be done. It is nevertheless important that we show an interest in what has to be done, that our interest grows in what is necessary for humanity specifically in our time. Because that is where the start has to be made, that a group, however small, becomes interested in what humanity needs, that it obtains, and be it ever such a small group, a clear insight into what in the development of our time are forces of decline, harmful forces. Particularly at the start of the year it might be good to direct our interest a little towards the objective great interests of humanity away from our own personal affairs.

To this end, as I said, clear insights are required into what moves on a downward trajectory in the development of humanity. We only need to transfer thoughts that passed before our soul in the last few days to the current situation and we will find a lot, or at least we will find some of the things that humanity particularly needs in the present time. We saw how far-reaching wisdom disappeared from humanity at a particular developmental moment, how Gnostic wisdom was lost, and how now we have to work towards a situation in which a knowledge of spiritual things arises once again—in accordance, however, with our more advanced time. We also drew attention throughout last autumn[46] to the profound reasons why the wave of materialism rose particularly high just in the nineteenth century. And I had to keep emphasizing that the spiritual-scientific insights into the rise of this wave of materialism should in no way lead to a failure to recognize or a misunderstanding of the great progress of outer materialistic science. It should indeed be recognized and I keep emphasizing that such materialistic progress of natural science has to be recognized by us. But we are particularly obliged to understand that in the course of the nineteenth century up to our day the great progress in the outer material field was associated with a regression in the power of thinking, in clear, sound thinking. Clear, sound thinking has receded particularly in science. Specifically where science is being pursued, clear and secure, content-filled thinking has receded. And since the belief in authority has never been stronger than in our time, although people refuse to believe it, this desolate situation with regard to sound thinking has spread to the widest circles, to the whole of popular thought. We live in an age of disordered thinking and at the same time in the age of the most blind belief in authority. How much do people today suffer from the impression that they have to believe, they have to accept the authorities who are sanctioned by the external powers.

People want to be told whether they are entitled to do this or that. People have mostly stopped thinking about the fact that this might be a concern of the individual, that people themselves might think about it! No, people go to those in whom 'all laws and rights are passed down like an eternal disease from one generation to the next',[47] and allow themselves to be instructed without making any claim to thinking themselves about the things of which they are being informed. Because it is considered the right thing to do to follow authority blindly. People become ill, they completely refuse to make the effort to know anything about the simplest things. Why should they? After all, we have state-certified medics and it is their business to concern themselves with the body. This body is actually no concern of ours at all. If people want a decision about some other question they go to those who are supposed to know about it: the theologians, the philosophers, to this person or another. Anyone who continues this train of thought themselves will find innumerable other things within them which are based in the blindest belief in authority. And if they cannot find anything, my dear friends, then please don't be angry with me when I say that they have an all the greater dose of such a belief in authority the less they find in themselves!

But I would like to begin by showing how insufficient, inadequate thinking has crept particularly into the most subtle areas of intellectual life all over the world, without distinction of nation, race, colour—how a certain element of inadequate thinking exists particularly in the most subtle areas of our intellectual cultural life. Take the way some philosophy has developed. Who would not be convinced today on the basis of a belief in authority going through many channels that the human being simply cannot get to the 'thing in itself' but only has access to the outer appearance, the impressions on the senses, the impression on the soul of things. We can only have access to the 'effect' of things, we cannot have access to the 'thing in itself'. That is something which has become the basic outlook of nineteenth-century thinking. I described this whole miserable situation in the chapter in my *Riddles of Philosophy* called 'The World as Illusion'. Anyone who studies this chapter will be able to find my overview of this whole miserable situation. Human beings can only have access to effects, they cannot get to the thing in itself; the thing in itself remains unknown. The finest thinkers of the nineteenth century in particular—if finest is the right word here—have been infected by this thing in itself which has to remain unknown.

If we now look at the trains of thought which underlie what I have just said, we find the following. People demonstrate, rigorously demonstrate, that the eye can only reflect what it can produce out of itself by means of its nerve and other processes. If therefore an outer impression comes it responds in its specific way. We can only get as far as the impression, not the thing which makes the impression on the eye. Through the ear we can only get as far as the auditory impression, not to what makes that impression and so on. And in this way it is only the impressions from the outer world which act on the senses of the soul. Since Lange,[48] who believed he had determined these things for certain fields, for colour and sound and suchlike, it has now entered the whole of people's thinking that human beings can only obtain impressions of the world, can only obtain effects. Is that incorrect? It is certainly not incorrect because as I have often emphasized, it is not a matter of whether something is correct or incorrect, but quite different things come into play. Is it right that only images, only impressions on our senses can be called forth by things? Certainly that is right. There can be no doubt about it. But something quite different is actually the case.

Let me clarify that with a comparison. When we stand in front of a mirror and a second person also stands in front of that mirror, then it can in no way be denied that what one sees in it is an image of oneself and an image of the other person. It is images which we see in the mirror, no doubt about it. And to that extent all our sensory impression are also all images because the object first has to make an impression on us and it is that impression, our reaction as we would say, which comes to consciousness. We can therefore compare that quite correctly with the images that we have in the mirror, because those are also images. This way of thinking of Lange and Kant is quite right to claim that human beings are faced with images. But we are then faced with the conclusion that human beings cannot get to the 'thing in itself' with anything that is real because they are dealing with images. What is this based on? It is based merely on the failure to pursue the thought further from that prerequisite, that a halt is made at the prerequisite which is correct. Such thinking is not incorrect but it is truly frozen. Because these are proper images that we have in the mirror. But say the person who is standing next to me, with whom I am looking into the mirror, gives me a slap in the mirror. Will I say then, although they are just images: the one mirror image has given the other mirror image a slap? Here what happens in the images points to something very real. If our thinking is not frozen but is alive, and is actually connected with things, with realities, then we know that Lange's and Kant's prerequisites are correct that we are dealing with images everywhere. But if these images relate to living circumstances, then these living circumstances really express those things which are needed to enter the tangible thing in itself. So it is not the case that the gentlemen concerned, who have led thinking astray, start from the wrong prerequisites, but everything is based on the fact that we are dealing with frozen thinking, with thinking where people just say: correct, correct, correct—and stop there. Flexibility, vitality is missing from such disordered nineteenth-century thinking. Nineteenth-century thinking is frozen, truly frozen.

Let us take another example. I have often told you things in the past year about an honest thinker, Mauthner,[49] the great language critic. With Kant it was a 'critique of ideas'. Mauthner goes further, what comes later always has to go further—he developed a 'critique of language'. I gave you a few small samples[50] from this 'critique of language' in the course of the autumn, indeed, in the course of the year, you will recall. Today such a man has many followers. He was a journalist before he joined the philosophers. According to an old proverb, 'dog don't eat dog'. Not only do they not eat each other, but hungry dogs are even pointed towards a meal by other dogs if those other dogs happen to be journalists. As I said, I certainly do not want in any way to call into question the honesty, indeed the thoroughness and depth—'depth' as understood in our time—of such thinkers because I have to keep emphasizing that it is incorrect to say that we are criticizing natural science or any other endeavour here; I only wish to characterize it. Hence let me say expressly, Mauthner is an honourable man—'so are they all, all honourable men'[51]—but let us look at a line of thought which reflects the critique of language. He says, for example, that human knowledge is restricted—that is what Mauthner says. Restricted—why restricted in his sense? Well, because what human beings learn about the world enters their soul through the senses. Certainly, not very profound but nevertheless undoubtedly true. Everything from the external world, the world of the senses enters through the senses. But now Mauthner conceives of the idea that these senses are random senses,[52] in other words, that instead of the eyes and ears and other senses which humans have they might well not have had them and could have had other senses. Then the world out there would look quite different—a very popular thought indeed among some philosophers of our time. And thus it is actually a coincidence that we have the particular senses we have and so is the world. If we had different senses, we would have a different world. Random senses! One person[53] who parroted Fritz Mauthner said roughly the following, for example. The world is immeasurable, but how can human beings know anything about this immeasurable world? They only have impressions through their random senses. Some things drop into the soul through these random senses, the gateways of these random senses, and there they are ordered while outside the immeasurable world continues and human beings cannot know anything of the laws according to which this immeasurable world proceeds. How can human beings believe that what they learn about the world through their random senses can have anything to do with the great secrets of the world out there? That is what one imitator of Fritz Mauthner said, who does, however, not consider himself to be an imitator but one of the cleverest men of the present time. We can translate this line of thought into another one. I will stay complete within the character of this way of thinking but only translate the thought into another one.

We can never actually have an idea of what such a genius as Goethe gave to humanity because such a genius as Goethe cannot do anything other than to express what he has to give to humanity by grouping it into the 22 or 23 random letters we have which are grouped on the paper by their own laws. How can we ever know anything about the content produced by the genius Goethe through what is grouped on the paper by the 23 random letters? As clever as the person would be who believes that we cannot obtain anything of Goethe and his results because the genius had to express all his brilliance through the 23 letters A, B and so on—as clever the person would be who says that the world out there is immeasurable and we cannot know it because we have nothing in us other than what enters through our random senses.

It is however the case that such disordered thinking exists not just in the fields I have spoken about now. It only occurs there in a particularly crass form but it exists everywhere. It is at work in all our human interaction. It is at work in the deeply sad events of the present because they would not be as they are if not all the thinking of people were imbued with the kind of thinking which is only expressed particularly crassly in such a field as I have indicated. We will never be able to take a proper interest in this field—I mean the field of human activity of true progress as properly pursued in the spirit of spiritual science—if we lack the will to look at these things properly, if we do not want to see what humanity needs. We repeatedly hear the objections with regard to the results of spiritual science that they are only accessible to those who can look clairvoyantly into the spiritual world. And people will never believe that this is not true but that we can truly come to an understanding with the thinking of what the clairvoyant fetches out of the spiritual world. But we should not be surprised that people today cannot understand with their thinking what the clairvoyant has fetched out of the spiritual world if such thinking takes the form as has been described. Such thinking trumps everything else. Such thinking has flowed into all fields. And this is so not because it would be impossible to understand the results of spiritual science with the thinking, but because people allow themselves to be infected by the weak-minded, the disordered thinking of the present. The important thing is that spiritual science should encourage us to engage in intensive, strong-minded thinking! And spiritual science is very suitable for that, my dear friends. Naturally, for as long as we only receive spiritual science by merely allowing ourselves to be told what things are about we will not get very far with the kind of thinking which we should, let me say, donate to the future of humanity. But if we endeavour really to understand, really to grasp things, then we will make progress.

But something of this disordered thinking of the present has affected the understanding of spiritual science. I have demonstrated to you how such disordered thinking actually works. I said that effects only come from the outside world so we cannot get to the thing in itself. Then the thought immediately freezes. People do not want to go further. They no longer see that what the images are in a living context leads beyond their being merely pictorial in character. This is now transferred to an understanding of spiritual science. Because people are completely infected by such a thinking, they say to themselves: 'What the spiritual scientist says on page a, b or c is spiritual scientific fact. That is inaccessible unless one has the gift of clairvoyance.' And then they stop thinking whether they might not be able to access these things by relating the things the spiritual scientists say to one another; they make the same mistake that the world makes today. The terrible thing is that there is so little understanding of and insight into this fundamental error of contemporary thinking. And there really is very little such understanding. It reaches into our most mundane thoughts, asserts itself there as much as in the most advanced guard of philosophical or scientific thought. And people rarely realize the immense obligation which actually arises from such an insight into this fact, how important it is to have an interest in these matters, how irresponsible it is to blunt an interest in these matters.

Now it is a fact that in the course of recent centuries purely external sensory observation has become dominant in science, that people place the main value on those things alone which they can observe in the laboratory, the hospital or zoo—I have often emphasized the value which should be accorded to that. Certainly, immense progress has been made through this scientific method but such progress in particular has led to a total neglect of the thinking. And that gives rise to the duty not to allow those to come to power in the world who strive for power on the basis of a purely materialistic experimental knowledge—and power is what these people want. We are already at the stage today that as a result of the most brutal claim to power of materialistic scholarship everything else is to be removed from the world that is not materialistic scholarship. And those who today appeal also to the outer powers in the harshest way to ensure that their outer materialism is given a privileged and patented position include the people in particular who stand on the ground of materialist science alone. It is a matter of understanding how the balance of power in the world works. It is not enough for us to be interested purely in our own personal circumstances but we must develop an interest in the great affairs of humanity. It is true that we will not be able to do a great deal today as individuals or indeed as a small society, but the matter has to take its start from such small beginnings. What use is it if there are many today who say they have no confidence in official medicine and seek what they do have trust in by all manner of other paths. That is not what things are about to begin with. All of that is only personal endeavour in our own affairs. What matters is to have an interest that alongside today's materialistic medicine the thing that one trusts also has rights. Otherwise it means making the matter worse from day to day. It is not just a matter of someone who has little confidence in today's so-called scientific medicine going to see someone else. In that way they put the other person into a difficult position if they are not interested in creating a situation in which the other person is also entitled under law to be interested in the general human progress of the affairs of humanity. It may well be the case that today or tomorrow we are not yet able to do more than have an interest in the matter. But we have to carry such an interest in the great affairs of humanity in our souls if we want to understand the spiritual-scientific movement in the truest sense of the word. We still often believe that we understand the great interests of humanity because we often interpret our personal interests as if they were the great interests of humanity.

We have to search deeply, deeply in the depths of our soul if we want to discover within ourselves the extent to which we are actually dependent on the blind belief in authority of the present time, how thoroughly we are dependent on it. Strolling along in complacency is what prevents us from being at least inwardly ignited and inflamed to begin with for the great interests of humanity. But it is this which we can inscribe into our soul as the best New Year's greeting: becoming ignited by, becoming enthusiastic about the great interests of human progress, of true human freedom. For as long as we adopt a position which means that somewhere we still have something which makes us believe that the person who is proclaimed a great man by the world must have some correct thoughts about something—for as long as we have not torn this belief, which is connected with the disordered thinking organism of our time and is raised by the latter, thoroughly out of our soul—for that amount of time we have not yet acquired such an interest in the general great affairs of humanity.

The words I say are not directed in some way against individual great men. I know there are many who say, particularly when such things are referred to in public lectures, that current natural science is being attacked by spiritual science, figures of authority are being attacked. I choose precisely such figures of authority of which, on the other hand, I can say that they are important figures of authority in the present time, great men—in order to show precisely how in the great personalities of the present those things assert themselves which must be removed root and branch by spiritual science. And even if we are not great men we can develop something of an eye for seeing the disordered thinking in great men which is reared particularly through the progress, through the brilliant side of current experimental science.

One example, which can truly stand for many: let me take a book which comes from one of the most important men of the present time—it has also been translated into German—so, as I said, let no one say that in some way I do not wish to recognize someone's greatness. I say expressly: the book comes from one of the most important men of the present time in the field of experimental science. I open the book at a random page, the introduction to the second volume, which, after specific questions of current cosmology have been discussed by the great man, deals with the way belief systems have evolved, with the history of the development of belief systems. And he says, roughly, that people at the time of the ancient Egyptians, at the time of the ancient Greeks, the Romans, attempted to understand the world in one way or another. But then contemporary natural science came along in the last four centuries; it swept away everything that came before it, it finally won the big prize and found the real truth which now only needs to be consolidated.[54]

I have already emphasized many times that it is not so much what these people say in detail; it is rather that they are then immediately gripped by a demonic luciferic or ahrimanic disposition, they immediately become luciferic or ahrimanic. And so we then read at the end of this introduction the following, very peculiar words. Pay close attention to what is revealed in an undoubtedly great and important man of the present time who says after he has praised scientific knowledge: 'The period of sad decline lasted until the reawakening of humanity at the start of the modern age. The latter put the art of printing at the service of scholarship and the contempt for experimental work disappeared from the views of educated people. But it was slow progress given the resistance from old preconceived ideas and the lack of collaboration among researchers. The impediments have meanwhile disappeared and at the same time the number of people and their resources working in the service of science has rapidly increased. Hence the magnificent progress of recent times.'

And now the final sentences of this introduction: 'Occasionally we hear it said that we live in the "best of all possible worlds"; it is difficult to say anything well founded about that, but we—at least the scientific researchers—can claim with complete certainty that we live in the best of all possible times. In the firm hope that the future will only get better still ...' And now we come to the bit where—please excuse the harsh words!—we either fall off our chair laughing when we read it or we hit the roof! Now in our age the person concerned of course wants to allow the words which have been spoken in the past about nature and the world in the research of great men to pass before his mind's eye in review. So he says: 'In the firm hope that the future will only get better still, we can say in the words of the great authority on nature and judge of human character, Goethe:

> ... it is a great delight,
> On the spirit of the ages to set our sight,
> To see how wise men have thought before us,
> And we've finally made such magnificent progress.'

In all seriousness, my dear friends, a great man here refers in his reflections to a quotation from the 'great authority on nature and judge of human character Goethe', that is, to the words of Wagner whom Goethe, as we know, has say in *Faust*:

> Excuse me, but it is a great delight,
> On the spirit of the ages to set our sight,
> To see how wise men have thought before us,
> And we've finally made such magnificent progress.[55]

It is Wagner who says these words! But Faust replies to him—and perhaps he may say what Faust says in the spirit of the 'great authority on nature and judge of human character' Goethe:

> O yes indeed! To furthest stars!

It is particularly suitable for the man who has also made it 'to furthest stars'! Namely:

> O yes indeed! To furthest stars!
> My friend, those ages past
> Are like a book with seven seals;
> What you as spirit of the ages name
> Is just the spirit of the gentlemen
> In whom the times they are reflected.
> So often, then, there's disarray!
> People turn tail and run away.
> A rubbish pit and lumber room,
> At most a song and dance dramatic,
> With maxims fitting and pragmatic,
> Best suited to the mouths of puppets![56]

and so on. 'Let him not be a tinkling fool'[57] it says a little bit earlier. Thus writes one of the 'greatest men of the present time' in 1907, who has made it 'to furthest stars', and who has also managed, in looking back at all the others who were active before him, to use the words expressed by the 'great authority on nature and judge of human character' Goethe:

> It is a great delight,
> On the spirit of the ages to set our sight,

You laugh. But it would be nice if this laughter were also always to sound where such disordered thinking is applied within those situations in which power is exercised today. Because this is an example which really proves how those who in particular stand firmly, stand securely on the ground of today's scientific world view, who are even associated with great progress in this field, who have made great progress themselves, how they can produce disordered thinking. And it proves that what we call materialistic science today need not exclude at all the most superficial thinking there is. One can think in the most disordered way today and be a great man in the field of external science. But one has to know that and one must be able to behave in that way. That is a signature of our time. But if it continues in this way, that someone is marked out as a great man, is deemed to be a great authority and what he has to say in one field or another is quoted untested as something which probably is true, then we will never overcome the great plight of our time. I am convinced that innumerable people today will read across the section I have just read out to you and not laugh about it, even though this section is one which in a preeminent sense indicates where the profound problems in our time lie—problems which lead to the decline of humanity in the present and where a start has to be made with regard to the things which humanity needs. Despite the immeasurably great progress made by external science, it must be recognized that it has become possible for precisely the greatest scientists of the nineteenth century up to and including our day to have become the worst dilettantes with regard to all philosophical questions. It is to the great detriment of our time that people now do not see through that—do not see that the greatest scientists of the nineteenth century have to be just the worst dilettantes with regard to philosophical questions if they wholly give themselves over to the spirit which rules in materialistic sciences—and that people chase after these great personalities even when these great personalities do not hold forth just about their laboratory experiments and clinical studies but when they talk about the mysteries of the cosmos.

That is why we have in parallel with the popularization of science, which is beneficial in the best sense, useful in the best sense, a simultaneous decline in all philosophical questions, disordered thinking which is spreading like an epidemic because it is eating away at everything and because ultimately it goes back to the terrible dilettantism particularly of those who are great men.

This is where the tasks lie with which we at least have to unite our interest, my dear friends, even if to begin with we cannot do anything. We at least have to see through the situation and have to clearly understand that above all it would lead to much, much more sorrowful times than they are at present if the things which have been indicated here are not seen through by people, if such disordered thinking were not to be replaced once again by clear and sound thinking in humanity. It all goes back to this disordered thinking. That which we encounter as an external, often very sad phenomenon would not exist if it were not for this disordered thinking.

It seemed to me that these things which are connected with the character of the conviction connected with our task as a whole should be spoken about particularly at the start of the new year. Because if we get into the habit of looking in an unbiased way at the way in which people think today and how this thinking exercises a powerful influence in absolutely all situations, only then will we obtain a picture of what needs to be done and what humanity particularly needs. But for that we have to overcome quite some longing for disorganization, quite some longing for laziness and lethargy, must to begin with at least be able to imagine that the task of a spiritual-scientific movement is more than merely listening to or reading lectures—it is to familiarize ourselves with the appropriate ideas, as I have to keep emphasizing! Of course there is not much we can do, to begin with, as individuals and a small society. But our own thinking has to move in the right direction, it must know what things are about, must not be open to the danger of, if I may use the trite expression, falling for the philosophical dilettantism specifically of those who are the greatest men of our age in external science. Great men—who are however dilettantes with regard to philosophical questions—establish all kinds of philosophical societies, monistic ones and God knows what else, without the inherent contradiction becoming clear which would arise if people at least understood that when people like that found philosophical societies it is no different to saying: 'I will have a suit made by that person because he has shown himself to be an outstanding cobbler!' It is a nonsense, but it is just as much a nonsense if a great chemist or a great psychologist is accepted as an authority on questions of world conception. They cannot be blamed for doing it themselves, because they cannot, of course, know how inadequate they are. But that they are accepted is connected with the great problems of our time.

It seems to me, my dear friends, that our feelings about matters of eternity might be the subject of a New Year's Eve reflection, and that the things that must immediately be done with regard to the affairs of the day, what it is necessary for us to do with regard to our immediate obligations, might be connected with a New Year's reflection. So it does appear to me that the tone of a New Year's reflection and the tone of a New Year's Eve reflection are related to one another in the same way as the words which I have spoken today are related to the words which I spoke yesterday.

LECTURE 8

DORNACH, 2 JANUARY 1916

LET us imagine the human etheric body in connection with the physical body of the human being and let us capture it in a diagram. Purely diagrammatically, let this be the etheric body [R.S. draws] and let us draw the physical body—which of course completely fills the whole human etheric body with the exception of its outermost parts—like this surrounded in a kind of outer layer by the etheric body. You know, of course, the real relationship. So let this be the physical body

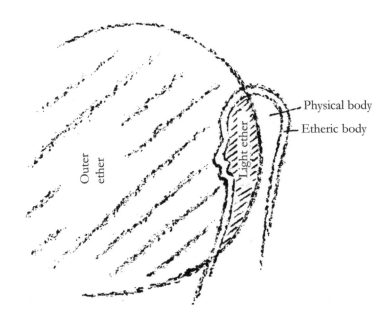

and etheric body, and then in the whole system of the human being the astral body and I are of course part of it. Now let us recall that the etheric body of the human being of course consists of various types of ether which we have learnt about. The types of ether we have learnt about are the warmth ether, the light ether, the chemical ether, which communicates the music of the spheres, and the life ether.

Let us consider the light ether today. Certainly, the whole of the etheric body consists of an intimate connection or an organized intimate connection between these four types of ether. But our intention today is to concentrate particularly on what is light ether in the etheric body. Let us now shade the part of the etheric body that we call light ether. Now I have frequently emphasized that human beings actually obtain a consciousness of things because they are basically in those things with their I and astral body. Only when awake during the day are the I and the astral body in the physical body and the etheric body in respect of those of their parts which are not in things. If we take this into consideration, we can say that the reason why we have sense impressions is because things are first revealed to the human I and also the astral body unconsciously and that this revelation is then reflected in the sensory tools and their nerve extensions in the physical body. We have repeatedly discussed these things.

So today let us ask: how does the memory work? How does it happen that we have memories of various things, of objects but also of experiences we have had? Let us consider this question. Let us consider it today quite empirically, through observation.

Take the case that we meet a person today whom we saw five days ago for the first time. We remember that we saw him five days ago and that he told us his name at that time, and that we spoke with him. We say that we recognize that person. What happens in us when we recall a person and our meeting with him some time later in this way?

Well, the following must be considered to begin with. While we met the person five days ago, our etheric body performed certain movements. We are now always talking about the light ether. The other parts—the warmth part, the chemical part, the life part—are also active but today we will consider the light part of our etheric body. So I will even call it light body to begin with. Our etheric body performs certain movements, because the thoughts which are stimulated by the person whom we have met reveal themselves to our light body as inner light movements. Apart from seeing the person with our senses, we therefore also have something with regard to the impressions which do not come from the senses to the extent that our light body performs movements. The whole meeting with the person has therefore consisted of our light body performing all kinds of movements. Imagine that in a quite living way. While you stood in front of the person, while you spoke with him, your etheric body was constantly in movement. What you spoke about with him, what you felt about him, thought about him, all of those things are revealed in the movement of your light body.

So when we see that person a few days later, the renewed meeting stimulates our soul and this stimulus makes the etheric body repeat the movements it performed five days ago while we were standing and talking with the person, purely out of its retentive capacity. So when you meet the person again five days later, this stimulates the etheric light body to perform the same movements it did five days earlier. We are always in the external light ether with a part of our I and astral body during waking consciousness. Sleep happens, after all, because the part of the astral body and I, which is in the physical and etheric body when we are awake during the day, also withdraws into the outer ether. Since we are therefore basically in the outer ether with our I and astral body and the inner etheric body repeats the movements through its retentive capacity which it carried out the first time, we then feel what the etheric body performed as movement at the time. And that is memory. Perceiving inner etheric movements from the outer ether, perceiving the movements of the inner light body from the outer light ether: that is what remembering means.

So consider, for example, two people face one another in front of you. Let's say the one only sees the face of the other. The etheric body makes certain movements because the one person looks at the face of the other person. Then he goes away. The etheric body retains the tendency to carry out these movements again if stimulated to do so. Five days later, the two people face one another again. They see one another—the one whose etheric body made the movements sees the other one first. That stimulates his light body to make the same movement again which it

made when he saw the face. That comes to expression in the consciousness in that the consciousness says: I have seen this face before. In
other words, the consciousness sees from the outer light ether the inner
light movements of the light ether in the person. That is remembering,
that is memory as a pure process of observation. We can say the
movements that the inner light body makes are seen in the outer light.
But they are not seen as light movements. Why are they not seen as
light movements in ordinary life? They are not seen as light movements
because the light etheric body is inside the physical body. That is why
the movements of the etheric body bump everywhere up against the
physical body. And by doing so the light movements of the etheric body
are transformed into memories. We do not see the movements of the
etheric body but the ideas which arise because they bump up against the
physical body. Those are the memories.

Once the physical body has gone, that is, once a person has passed
through the portal of death, then the I and the astral body are of course
initially in the outer ether with much greater intensity until they leave
the outer ether after a few days. Then the inner light body is no longer
stimulated to produce the ideas which are only possible in the physical
body because it bumps up against the physical body. That is why the
deceased see everything they have experienced—which the etheric body
then causes to fluctuate, to run now that it is free of the physical body
and is no longer impeded by it. They see everything in the few days after
death because the etheric body has the constant tendency to produce all
those things out of itself which it has ever performed as movement
resulting from the experiences of physical life. The whole of life is run
through, fluctuates in the etheric body. And we see it in a tableau—it is
projected in a mighty tableau; all the reflected etheric movements are
projected in a tableau overview over the past earth life.

If we now had the possibility to subdue the physical body to such an
extent that we make ourselves independent of the physical body and
thus also liberate the etheric body—we can achieve that through certain
meditation processes which are all part of the processes described in
Knowledge of the Higher Worlds. How is it achieved?—then we could
manage in life already, many manage to do so, not to be bothered by the
physical body so that in remembering we do not see what arises because

the etheric body bumps up against the physical body but we see the fluctuations, the movements of the etheric body itself. We are then in the outer light ether and see the movements of our light body.

Why can't we do that in ordinary life? Why does it not happen when, for example, Miss Scholl approaches Countess Kalckreuth[58] and recognizes her—assuming there is no clairvoyance? Under normal circumstances Miss Scholl would recall the image in her memory, that is her perceptual image of Countess Kalckreuth, and would not perceive what she could otherwise perceive—the inner fluctuation of her etheric body. So that she has the inner experience: ah, so that is how my etheric body kept fluctuating when it approached Countess Kalckreuth. Light would then perceive light, namely the outer, because the I and the astral body of Miss Scholl would perceive the movements, the constantly inclined movements of her own light body and would know to interpret them in the right way. So she would also say: these are the movements which my light body has always performed when I have met Countess Kalckreuth. So we would then have the phenomenon that through being in the ether—something we always do because we are outside our physical body with a large part of our I and our astral body—that through the weaving and undulation of the light ether we perceive our organized piece of light ether and its movement: light from light, the light that is within ourselves.

Why does that not happen in ordinary life? Why do we only perceive the movements resulting from the etheric body bumping up against the physical body? That is so because Ahriman and Lucifer are linked with the earthly world, because Ahriman has chained the physical body so tightly to the whole being of the human being that the etheric body cannot easily free itself, because this Ahriman has merged the physical body so closely with the etheric body, the light body, and because the spirits serving Ahriman are constantly present causing the light body of human beings with its fluctuations to be obscured so that they cannot see it when they are in the light. Demons constantly keep the light body of the human being in darkness. That happens because of what Ahriman has done with the physical body and, incidentally, also with the etheric body. We can therefore say—and I want to write this sentence specially on the blackboard because it is an important one—if it is possible for the human soul to observe the processes of its own light body from out of the light, then this soul has freed itself from the ahrimanic forces which otherwise obscure the processes in the light body.

What, then, might a soul that wants to achieve this beg for, long for? Such a soul could say something to specific powers who are in the spiritual world and whom such a soul acknowledges: O you powers in the spiritual world, let me become knowing in the light world, in the light, from out of my physical body so that I can observe my own light body, and do not let the power of the ahrimanic forces be too strong over me so that they do not make it impossible for me to see what is happening in my light body!

So, let me say once more what such a soul might beg for in prayer out of a longing for certain powers which would be acknowledged by such a soul. Such a soul might say: O you powers, let me consciously in the light look towards the processes of my own light body and subdue, take away the strength and power of the ahrimanic forces which obscure and darken the processes in my own light body! Let me look consciously at my own light from out of the light! Let me look at the light consciously from out of the light and take away the powers who prevent me from seeing the light out of the light!

What I have told you now, my dear friends, is not just an invented prayer but that is what Christ, after he had passed through the Mystery of Golgotha, taught those to pray who could still understand him in the time which he spent with his more close disciples after overcoming the Mystery of Golgotha.

And that is part of the understanding, the Gnostic knowledge which these disciples were still able to bring to Christ at that time and which has disappeared in the way I indicated about the time, about the centuries when the Mystery of Golgotha happened.

These souls which were closely associated with Christ were able to look up to the power which Christ himself was to them in this way to beg Him for the possibility to observe their own light existence from out of the light and to hold back the adversary powers of an ahrimanic nature, so that the vision out of the light was not subdued and obscured in seeing these light movements of the light body. These close disciples

of Jesus Christ learnt in this time what I have indicted here; that is what
they learnt. And they knew about the nature of all the things we have
discussed today. They knew about it. They learnt about it in the time
when Christ kept company with them after the Mystery of Golgotha.

Among the fragments that have remained of the ancient Gnostic
wisdom, I also spoke about the *Pistis Sophia*[59] text. Allow me to read a
section from this *Pistis Sophia* text. The section says: 'I want to glorify
you O Light, because I want to come to you. I want to glorify you O
Light because you are my Saviour. Do not leave me in chaos'—when I
am outside the physical body here—'do not leave me in chaos, save me
O Light in the heights, because it is you whom I have glorified. You sent
me your light through you and saved me. You have led me to the higher
places of chaos'—in knowledge outside the physical body. 'May the
spawn of evil'—Ahriman, but it does not say Ahriman—'which pursue
me sink down into the lower places of chaos. And do not let them come
to the higher places so that they see me. And may great darkness cover
them and darkness on top of that. And do not let them see me in the
light of your strength which you have sent me to save me so that they do
not gain power over me again. And the counsel they have taken to take
my strength from me, let it not succeed, and how they have said words
against me to take my light from me. Rather take theirs from them
instead of mine. And they said they would take all my light and they
were not able to take it because the strength of your light was with me.
Because they took counsel without your commandment, O Light, that
is why they were not able to take my light. Because I have believed in
the Light, I will not be afraid. And the Light is my Saviour. And I will
not be afraid.'

We think of Ahriman with regard to fear as we have seen in one of
the Mystery Plays.

And now let us take this section of the *Pistis Sophia* text. Is it not as if
it has been saved so that we can say: Look here, opponents of modern
spiritual science. This new spiritual science says that the light movements of the light body can be seen from out of the light if the opposing
ahrimanic demons do not prevent it. But there was once a time in which
that was already known. And there is even a physical piece of evidence
from this time in the form of the *Pistis Sophia* text. Because funda-

mentally what I read out to you is nothing other than the workings which I set out for you on the basis of the structure of the light body and the sojourn of the soul in the light body itself. But there is no possibility of understanding this section of the *Pistis Sophia* text without previously having understood what I explained to you earlier. That is why those who pick up the *Pistis Sophia* text should really say to themselves when they read something of that kind that they do not understand it at all. But they are not modest enough for that.

But that is what has to come over us, this great modesty which with regard to this matter can consist of saying to oneself, yes, here we have a section of the *Pistis Sophia* text, 'I want to glorify you O Light, because I want to come to you. I want to glorify you O Light because you are my Saviour.' When I read it like that I do not understand it. But this humility is what we need, this modesty of not wanting to understand it until we have obtained for ourselves the possibilities of understanding. But such modesty does not exist anywhere particularly in our time. And those who pull such texts out of the rubble and ruins are often the ones with the least of such modesty. Either they interpret such texts in the most superficial way possible by saying: 'Well, the light is a nebulous idea, it is all meant as an allegory.' Or, alternatively, they say: 'Those who wrote these things in ancient times were at a childlike stage of human development and we, we have finally made magnificent progress.' You will recall Wagner's words from yesterday! We have finally made such magnificent progress that we can see that these predecessors with all their understanding were just at a childlike stage.

It is not just a matter in our time that a teaching cannot be understood by those who do not want to understand it, but it is a matter that in our time a certain soul mood cannot so easily be produced which is absolutely necessary if true spirit knowledge is to be obtained. This soul mood is the mystery mood which consists of developing a feeling within oneself: 'We cannot understand something until we have prepared the soul so that it can enter into such understanding.' In our time, on the contrary, there is a soul mood that the clever person—and of course every adult is clever today in their own opinion—can make a judgement about everything. But the world is profound and everything connected with the secrets of the cosmos is profound. And because of this belief in cleverness which every adult today has about themselves, people simply pass by the most profound cosmic problems, the most profound secrets of the cosmos. And when these secrets of the cosmos are talked about, they respond to the speaker at most with ridicule and scorn and cast these things into obscure recesses about which they write their vignettes: superstition and mania and fantasy, if not much worse.

The important thing, my dear friends, is to see this situation clearly. That is the important thing, to see clearly how in our time those who have no intention of understanding anything cast ridicule and scorn on the things that can only be reached in modesty and humility of knowledge by the soul prepared in modesty and humility. To begin with it is not just an understanding of spiritual-scientific truths which is missing, but to begin with a mood for knowledge is absent in our time—that mood which produces a true striving for knowledge.

But the world is dependent on some people, and increasing numbers of people, seeing this clearly and making a start by including in their interest and attention that this is where the lever of true progress has to be applied. We have to know to begin with what needs doing. And clearly and without indulging in any illusions we have to see how the effort is being made by those who pour ridicule and scorn over all true moods for knowledge to take control of what is still meant to permeate humanity in its spiritual culture. The aim is to make human beings part of a materialistic culture from childhood. Materialistic culture takes control even of the delicate souls of children in that it forces these delicate children's souls into materialistic schools which make the soul materialistically pliable less through the content of what they teach than through the way in which they do so.

And such action is packaged in the illusion of the times by saying that this is what is required in the age of liberalism and freedom. The opposite of freedom is called freedom in the materialistic age. And things are organized in such a way that people hardly notice that the opposite of freedom is called 'freedom'. And those who have some inkling of what is going on at most want to combat this lack of freedom in turn with the same lack of freedom only from the other side. This or the other should be prohibited, say some of them; or others in turn flirt with those powers who take control of everything which should grow in freedom like the flowers in the fields.

The first thing that is required is that we should be permeated by the attitude which can only be a truly free attitude coming from spiritual science. We have to be clear, above all, that we cannot introduce into the development of the outer materialistic world order the things that are needed to bring up the human soul in childhood. Not being taken in by words is the first thing we should understand. But that requires that we free ourselves from the whole aura of the prejudices which we encounter everywhere, that under all circumstances we really feel the attitude living in our soul which can arise from the nature of spiritual science, that we frequently ask ourselves: what exists in our soul that comes from the nature of spiritual science and what exists in our soul only because we also adopt those forms of thinking which swarm through the world today.

It may well be that we cannot yet do anything in our age against all the materialistic progress of the materialistic mood of the times with its lack of freedom. But at least we have to learn to experience this as a constraint. That is where we have to start. Neither must we indulge in illusions. Because if the world continues on its present course, as it strives to do in the spirit of these materialistic impulses, then we will gradually enter a development in which not only those who do not have title are prohibited from doing anything for human health, but in which every word will be banned which is spoken about anything related to science by anyone other than those who have sworn some kind of oath not to say anything other than what is authorized in the spirit of the materialistic world order. Today it is still much the case that only things are banned so that people do not feel the ban as a coercion. But we are heading towards times in which, just like any kind of unregistered care to heal people, every word will also be banned which is spoken except in facilities which have been guaranteed and granted title by the materialistically evolved powers.

If we fail to see where this development is going, we will travel full steam ahead into the 'freedom' of the future which will consist of laws being made according to which no one will be allowed to teach anything who does not do so within a registered lecture theatre, according to which everything will be banned which even remotely reminds us of things such as are happening here for example. We do not look at these things today because we do not realize where this development is going.

It is certainly true, we have to keep emphasizing this, that we will not be able to do a lot in our age. But these things have to start with a thought, have to start with a feeling for what is at stake. And we have to start from where we are.

However these words may be received, my dear friends, I have to say them to you at this turn of the year because its celebration is a kind of symbol in our time for the course of the ages as such. Because it is best, when we celebrate the turn of the year, if we draw attention to what lies in the course of the ages. We simply cannot do enough to keep making clear to ourselves how dependent human beings are today on judgements which are swarming all around us, on judgements, specifically, which are swarming all about because they are recorded in the papers with smudgy ink; and this smudgy ink is an infinitely effective magic potion with regard to all the things that people believe in the world. It is interesting, then, to see the occasions when these gentlemen of the press are not quite in agreement among themselves because, you see, there is that which floods all minds, that which is magicked onto the dirty paper with smudgy ink and which exercises such an incredible magic on the whole of humanity today. But there are of course always a few who think that we should believe what it says on this dirty paper using smudgy ink in this or that particular way, and others who want to proclaim as irrefutable truth what is magicked on paper in different words written in smudgy ink. They are at odds with one another. And so people could see where the actual error and harm lies. Except that the person who comes from the right in the newspaper office merely says it is the fault of the person who of course finds their belief on the left. And so it is of interest to call up some words before our soul which for example a certain Dr Eduard Engel[60] has written in the *Türmer* of 1911. It was headed: 'On the psychology of the newspaper reader'. I do not want to say too much myself about these things so I want to show you what people sometimes say when they judge one another among themselves.

So in 'On the psychology of the newspaper reader', *Türmer* 1911, page 230, it says: 'The newspaper reader is a very complex being. But his numerous less important characteristics are overshadowed by two others: he believes everything and he forgets everything. The whole secret of the incredible development of the daily papers is based on these two main characteristics which are present in each newspaper reader. He believes everything and he forgets everything. The papers are one of the essential features of the modern cultured person. The vast majority of readers read only one newspaper and believe what they read. Their view of the world in the evening is the one which they scooped out of their newspaper in the morning. If they meet a person who reads another newspaper and holds forth about his, that is his newspaper's, view, that man appears insane or at least paradoxical to them. Newspaper editors who have a particularly subtle understanding of the soul of their readers nurse their delicate belief in the papers with anxious attention. A newspaper will never print a correction for the great masses of what it has told its readers. Even in the not infrequent cases in which an erroneous report has presented the opposite of the truth and complete nonsense, they guard against shattering the belief of their readers in the infallibility of newspapers. But now and again they are forced to report the truth a few days later. Here they are assisted by the second indispensible characteristic of the newspaper reader, his forgetfulness ...'

If we consider the power which the papers have gradually acquired in the nineteenth century and into our day, and the part which the belief in the papers plays in the whole declining part of our culture, it is necessary occasionally to take a look at the whole miserable situation.

It is this which sometimes also makes one uncomfortable that there is such great demand to transform the form of communications which we have chosen, which should be something different, into a form of printed storage. And it cannot be different, of course, because the black art is a fact of life and the 'white art' too has to take account of this black art which comes to expression on printed paper. Of course we have to have books and lecture cycles. But we should be truly aware that we must act in such a way that the matter which has now been entrusted to the printed page should under no circumstances travel through the world like the things which habitually swarm through the world today, let me use the expression, 'on the wings of the papers out into the minds of the people'.

I wanted to give a clear impression that things are serious. That is why I permitted myself yesterday and today to append to the great mysteries such as those of the human year on earth and seeing the light in the human being out of the light, to append to these great mysteries of existence these contemporary observations also as a kind of New Year's reflection.

LECTURE 9

It rests with me to say something about the differences in the way of thinking and conception between our fifth post-Atlantean epoch and the fourth post-Atlantean epoch. Specifically, I wish to indicate today which elements of thinking and perception have changed a great deal from the one period, the one cycle, into the other cycle. And I wish to show specifically to what extent certain ways of conception and perception have descended to a deeper sphere, as it were, in order then to show what in particular is required in the fifth post-Atlantean epoch, the one we are in ourselves, so that humanity can start to ascend once again.

Now I have long tried to investigate how the matter can be presented in the clearest way and want to try today on the basis of those investigations to present the matter in a pictorial way. For this reason I want to start by telling you a number of things in, let us say, a kind of novelistic form which I have compiled.

The story I want to tell is of a family which lived in the not too distant past and was close to another family. And because all kinds of events in the one family were of great interest and importance to a member of the other family, the member of the other family tried to get to the bottom of these events. Let us assume that there was a young girl in the first family—as I said, the matter already lies a little in the past—who was still some way away from entering her twenties. The father of this girl was a soldier and the time which we are specifically looking at was in advance of a bigger war which the father of the girl had to fight

in. But the girl was virtually engaged to another soldier who also had to
go to war and she was very fond of him so that she was deeply unhappy
that he had to go to war. And as she thought that her father had been
partly responsible for the outbreak of the war, resentment towards her
father built up inside her although she gave no outward sign of it. And
the more the time approached, the more the thoughts and feelings of
this young girl became confused. She could not bear losing her beloved.
And because these feelings were so deep-seated, her image of her father
became totally distorted. Her anger kept growing. The war came. But
what had taken hold of the soul of the young girl kept expanding into a
kind of confusion of soul, the kind of confusion of soul which doctors
today diagnose as mental illness. And so as war broke out this young
girl had all kinds of experiences of a kind which were close to mental
illness: visions and similar things. She had one strong vision in particular: her beloved would be killed in the war and everything that she
would have been able to do in the world in association with her beloved
would become impossible with his death and she would actually become
a victim of war with all her intentions. The mental illness kept growing.
It got to the stage that the doctors found it best to take her far away to
the country where she was well looked after and where she was also able
to do things which were beneficial through a certain manner of the souls
around her, as can happen with people who suffer from that kind of
illness. But there was no hope that the full extent of the mental illness
might not emerge again if she were removed from these circumstances
and placed somewhere else. And so she spent many years there.

The war had long finished and other awful things had happened in
the family which I do not want to discuss in detail here, all kinds of
awful things which included that after a good number of years the
brother of this girl was also affected by mental illness. Now the peculiar
thing happened that, following various other decisions, the brother who
had transformed the girl's mental illness into male form was taken by
wise people to the place where the girl was. And lo and behold, it
happened strangely that the brother, although he was also considered to
be mentally ill, had a positive effect on the girl. In the loneliness which
she suffered among the other people, they had nevertheless met in their
surroundings, recognized one another although they had not seen each

other for many years and caused each other to return to health. So the girl was able to return home and founded a kind of refuge which was organized in such a way that ill people of the kind which the two of them had been could be mentally healed through an understanding of the reasons for the illness. The refuge she founded had a deeply religious character.

Now I said that another family was close to the family in which these events had occurred. A member of the other family was very interested in these remarkable events and said: we have to investigate this strange case. The events which I now tell must be thought of as lying only a few years back. He therefore approached a medical scientist, a physician, whom he knew and who called himself a psychopathologist because he pursued psychopathology. Let us call this psychopathologist Lövius, Professor Dr Lövius.[61] He began by telling the doctor what he knew about the two children, about the way the girl's illness had come about through her resentment against her father; how he had been able to observe her, what he had seen of the affair. Prof. Dr Lövius listened attentively, made a deeply serious face, reflected profoundly and said: that must to a great extent be due to a hereditary affliction. That is undoubtedly a hereditary affliction, we are dealing with an hereditary affliction. We have to look carefully in the family papers, have to look at everything in detail.

And lo and behold, a whole lot of material was collected from the family papers. It happily turned out that the characteristics, the qualities of previous generations could be investigated as far back as the grandfather, the great grandfather and even the great-great grandfather. Professor Dr Lövius studied this case for a long time and he increasingly found confirmation that this was an extraordinary case of a hereditary affliction, as it is called—indeed, a typical case of a hereditary affliction, a textbook case of an exceptional kind. Professor Dr Lövius, who had already investigated the psychopathy of Conrad Ferdinand Meyer, Viktor Scheffel, Hebbel and others,[62] found this textbook case exceptionally interesting and collected all the data which could explain such a textbook case.

Let us begin by trying to follow the man diagrammatically. From what we know about the case, we are to begin with dealing with the

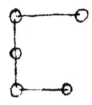 daughter of the soldier and her brother—those are the two individuals to begin with. If we go further back, we come to the father. Professor Dr Lövius began by setting his sights on the father, found that there was something extraordinarily violent in his character and that he was a very ambitious man—but also a man with a great deal of initiative. He had characteristics which could be found again in his brother as characteristics which had been transformed into strengths—we have to look at the whole family structure in these cases—only here they were present in a much more benign form, a weaker form. But the father of the two siblings was a highly ambitious man with exceptional initiative.

Such excessive ambition, drive, also a certain resistance against the world must of course be traced back further in the family. So the father of the father was looked at. Thus we come to the father of the father who in turn had a brother. There we find the extraordinarily interesting fact that the brothers through two generations had certain similarities and differences. Because here there was the father of the father, that is the grandfather of our young girl, who—while the father was only an exaggeratedly ambitious and energetic man—was already a kind of violent man. That characteristic had weakened in the father. But the brother was a type of man who was almost pathological in his kindness, almost abnormal. They were both abnormal in the earlier generation—that is the similarity—but the one through violence and the other through kindness. And then Professor Dr Lövius discovered that the violent man, that is the grandfather of our young girl, was always out to cause dissent and mischief in his brother's family. And Professor Dr Lövius concluded that this violent man really did manage—we are dealing with the grandfather here—to completely ruin the sons of his brother. He turned the one into a gambler and he ensnared the other one in another way. In short, he thoroughly ruined his brother's sons. That is what could be learnt from the family papers. All kinds of bad things had happened. Not everything was altogether clear but this was certain: the man finally behaved in such a way towards his brother, the other man, that actually the whole family, all the sons degenerated and only one remained who decided to revenge his father on the brother.

But this act of revenge in turn brought misfortune on the families, namely into the family of the father of our girl. All kinds of unfortunate events happened.

And now Professor Dr Lövius said to himself: we have to go even further back in the line of descent, because this young girl had quite strange visions at the start of her madness. She kept dreaming about far distant regions where she had never been as a girl but which had a strange resemblance to a certain locality. Professor Dr Lövius discovered in a family diary that something lived in these visions of the region in which the great grandfather and the great-great grandfather had once lived. Oh, said Professor Dr Lövius, this is a particularly interesting textbook case. Here heredity crops up in her thinking as visions; great-great and great grandfather came from another region than the one in which their descendants ended up living. And the experiences of earlier generations had been passed down the line of heredity in such a way that the great granddaughter, or great-great granddaughter had visions about it in her madness. That was something exceptionally interesting for the professor, of course. So he discovered that the grandfather in turn had a father who—as I said, according to an old family diary—had emigrated from a quite different foreign region where the culture was very different. I won't name any locality because that is so unpleasant at the moment. Nations are fighting one another and if we now name localities that immediately arouses feelings. So the great grandfather and the great-great grandfather came from a foreign region. Well, the diary revealed that the great grandfather was also a strange man. He had done all kinds of mad things in this remote region, was also a violent man who sometimes fell into violent rages. As he had committed all kinds of things in his violent rage, he could not stay in the region; he had to emigrate and went to the region where the descendants were. But he also caused trouble in the region where the descendants were, although later he became a very well-respected man. In the region where his descendants were, he had caused trouble simply because he was in love with a woman and when her father refused to permit him to marry her he killed the father in a duel. That is how he obtained the daughter. The affair was swept under the carpet, as we say, and he was able to become a respected man.

Now, thanks to the family register, Professor Dr Lövius was able to get as far as the great-great grandfather. And this great-great grandfather was an especially strange man. He lived in a very exotic region, he was a person who had obtained a kind of deeper insight into the secrets of history. He was a spiritual person. But, said Professor Dr Lövius, someone who exaggerates the spiritual to such an extent as the great-great grandfather has done is not quite right in the head in any case. And when he researched further in the family papers, he also found that this great-great grandfather had retained certain human characteristics despite his thorough knowledge of spiritual things. Above all, he could not stand anyone who had obtained spiritual knowledge in some other way than his own. They were a thorn in his flesh. And playing a trick on them was something which he saw almost as being a spiritual delicacy. What I am relating now is an event which already goes back approximately to the 1760s. But things keep repeating themselves: Eduard von Hartmann[63] subsequently did something similar with the philistine people of the nineteenth century, something I have often talked about. This great-great grandfather once published a kind of work—he did not put his name to it but published it anonymously—in which he thoroughly refuted everything contained in his own teaching. He presented everything as confused and stupid and foolish and always in such a way that the others could take great pleasure in it because he always used their arguments, the kind of things they might have said. These were tasty morsels for the others; he played a great trick on them by doing that.

So Professor Dr Lövius said to himself, well, it is all very obvious. Even in the time of the great-great grandfather we can see at work in the line of heredity what has come to such terrible expression in the descendents. Even the good side of the great-great grandfather, his spiritual gifts, appear again in his great-great granddaughter who founded a kind of spiritual refuge. We can see that all the good and bad characteristics in this textbook case are 'hereditary afflictions' to the greatest extent! So Professor Dr Lövius was extremely interested in this story. He had, of course, decided to write a fat book about this typical textbook case and on one occasion explained it to a colleague. And as it happened, someone was listening on this occasion who did not really want to but could not avoid hearing it. Someone who not only had a knowledge of the human being but who also had cosmic knowledge relating to the development of humanity. That person listened and all kinds of thoughts came to him while Professor Dr Lövius recounted his case. So let me present a version of these thoughts to you—the actual version is not very important—while always building on this family tree, on the family tree of Professor Dr Lövius' textbook case.

So the following thoughts came to the person. There was once a respected family in the course of human development. The fate of the founder of this family, Tantalus, who had to suffer punishment in Tartarus, is well known. He is initiated into the secrets of the gods. The Greeks give expression to it by saying that a person who is initiated into the secrets of the gods may eat at their table. But there was something in him which spurred him on, which made it like a delicacy for him to deceive the gods, the officially recognized gods. And so—you know the story—he served up his son, whom he had cut into pieces, as a delicacy for the gods. And the gods, who committed an error in their omniscience, ate of it and also drank of the blood. As punishment, Tantalus was thrown into Tartarus where he had to suffer the torments of Tantalus which are related in the Greek myths. Through a series of crimes which occurred from one generation to the next, the revenge of the gods was passed down to the last descendant. To begin with, Pelops, the son of Tantalus, was thrown out of heaven where he had been taken by the gods. He wandered through Asia Minor to Greece and won Hippodamia as his wife by vanquishing her father.

This is the thought which came to the listener when he heard the story Professor Dr Lövius was telling, namely that the former had a duel with the father and obtained his wife in that way. The grace of heaven had by no means yet been withdrawn, as his luck proved. But soon he made himself so unworthy of this grace through various actions that the blessing departed from his house. His marriage with Hippodamia produced two sons, Atreus and Thyestes, who fled to Argos guilty of murder where they inherited the throne of this kingdom from their cousin Eurystheus. There the siblings committed new atrocities, so that the royal palace of Mycenae was the scene of a blood feud which from child to child destroyed each generation of both families. The worst crime was the so-called meal of Thyestes. For Atreus, who had learned that his wife had been seduced by Thyestes, invited the latter and his two sons to a banquet. Conscious of his guilt, Thyestes followed the lure and came to the banquet.

This reminded this person, who knew something about human nature, very much of the dispute between the grandfather and his brother, who had lured his sons away and got them into all kinds of trouble which led them to perish, as the family papers said.

The atrocity happened. Atreus served up for this brother his secretly slaughtered pair of sons. The latter drank from the blood. That, too, is really an 'hereditary affliction'—ancient Tantalus had already done that to the gods, now his grandson was doing it! This was a crime from which Apollo turned the steeds of his sun chariot away with a shudder when he looked down on Mycenae. They were revenged by a son of Thyestes, who was born later on, called Aegisthus. Aegisthus, told about the hideous deed, first killed his uncle Atreus and then also lay in wait for his children.

Atreus had two sons with his wife Aerope, Agamemnon and Menelaus, called the Atridae or sons of Atreus. Aegisthus, the last son of Thyrestes, hatched treacherous plans of revenge towards them. But he could not break cover until the two related brothers had undertaken the great campaign of Troy. Once they had departed, he knew how to beguile the passionate queen. Clytemnestra had borne her husband three daughters and one son—the daughter in which we are mainly interested is called Iphigenia and the son Orestes. Iphigenia, the eldest daughter was sacrificed on the altar of Artemis, of Diana, because this goddess had greatly taken against the departing Greeks and had to be mollified with the daughter. The mother hated her husband and responded to the thoughts of murder whispered in her ear. Now we know that Iphigenia was removed to Tauris and awoke in the grounds of a temple. We know that she was taken to a rural area, an environment in which she was harmless, a fate similar to the one of our great-great granddaughter. We do not need to go into the further events in the family. But now the myth still records the following. After Orestes had found his sister Iphigenia again in Tauris and she had healed him of his madness, he took her back to Greece. Then the story further relates

that Iphigenia, when she returned to Greece, established a kind of
oracle, a sacrificial site for Diana of Tauris—which, translated into
Greek circumstances, would be roughly the same as when someone now
established a kind of refuge for ill people in accordance with the kind of
spiritual-scientific principles that I have mentioned.

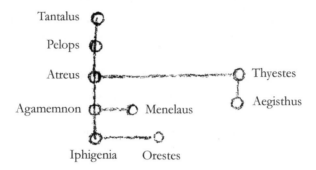

All I wanted to say with that is that we can imagine a similar process
in ancient Greece and in modern times. It happens whatever the times.
Because you can see that the process from the eighteenth and nineteenth
centuries which I related first could have occurred exactly as I related it.
No one will be able to cast doubt on the smallest detail. Neither will
anyone be able to cast doubt on all the trappings I developed. But there
is nevertheless a certain difference, namely the way we feel about this
case, how we think about it.

We have seen how in the nineteenth, twentieth century Professor
Lövius reached the conclusion: hereditary affliction! Textbook case! The
Greeks said to themselves, when something like that happens such an
event expresses precisely the deeper forces at work in the history of
humanity and they turn it into myths. There was no Professor Dr Lövius
in ancient Greece, but there was a poet who in a deeper sense understood these one, two, three, four, five generations [see diagram] and
wrote a poetic work about them which poets continue to use as
inspiration up to and including Goethe's wonderful *Iphigenia*. And the
difference isn't even that great. Because just consider, you only need to
take one of the psychological or psychiatric books to hand by one of the
many scientists which deal with psychology and spiritual forces; you will
find that all of them say the following. The healthy person as such is

exceptionally difficult to study in his mental characteristics. But at the sickbed and in hospital and through the departments of psychiatry a lot can also be learnt about the normal course of the healthy soul and a great many conclusions about the healthy soul are drawn from the sick soul. I only remind you that, for example, the speech centre, the location in which speech is concentrated, was thought to have been found by studying it in sick people lacking the power of speech. So people say to themselves: we can learn about how health works from that which is not in order.

If we imagine these things not in the nineteenth century but in the language of the Greeks, it would sound like this: if we want to know about the forces at work in the progression of human development, we must not go to the people and study them who only display their healthy side in their soul life and all that they are, but we have to go to all kinds of people who have abnormal characteristics in relation to what is normal. How the Greeks became what they are—that is what the Greek poets sought to understand, and at the same time in a certain sense they were still sages because wisdom and beauty were connected with one another. Thus it happened that these Greek poets presented the destiny of the Greeks in these abnormal generations.

But the Greeks took a more differentiated view. The great difference between what Professor Dr Lövius says and what the Greeks said is that the Greeks knew something about the secrets of the human soul. There is a great difference between what awakens in the soul through the extraordinary myth of the Atridae, Iphigenia, Tantalus and Pelops and everything that arises in our soul as ideas when we hear the bespectacled Professor Dr Lövius who says 'It's all hereditary affliction!' Because 'hereditary affliction' is what makes the textbook case in every shape and form in accordance with modern science, in accordance with the knowledge of the fifth post-Atlantean epoch. That is where the difference lies to a person who is still fully immersed in the culture of ancient Greece. Imagine a Greek who wanted to describe how Iphigenia, after she had experienced what the Greek told about events in Aulis, was removed to a foreign land, to Tauris, experienced being reunited with Orestes there and so on; imagine what that Greek would have told, think how that is taken up again in Goethe's *Iphigenia*! Put yourself in the moment when King Thoas in Tauris stands before Iphigenia, in Goethe's work, where he woos Iphigenia and where Iphigenia feels obliged to speak the words: 'Behold! I am of Tantalus' house'—'Calmly you speak momentous words.'[64]

The whole of Greek culture comes to life again in what the Greek, or the resurrected Greek, had to say in the context of such a soul life: 'I am of Tantalus' house.' And then it seems, after those words have been spoken, as if Professor Dr Lövius appears giggling at a small window screen: 'He he he! Hereditary affliction!' There you have the difference in its entirety between what was presented by the fourth post-Atlantean epoch and what the fifth, our post-Atlantean epoch has to offer. Because the two things may indeed be compared. I have not exaggerated in the slightest but only given a very factual account. The two things may be compared with one another, and that is so because the composition of the Greek myth, the meaning of the Greek myth, has been replaced by the teaching of hereditary affliction, even in literature. After all, we only need to compare Sophocles or Aeschylus[65] with Ibsen[66] and we have exactly the same contrast in literature, with the difference that for the Greeks science and literature did not diverge in this way. You only need to read what I have said about the mysteries and the origins of art and religion in the mysteries to understand that there was neither a Greek Ibsen nor a Greek Professor Dr Lövius—they would both be one and the same. But they would be the ones who composed the myth, that which as myth contained the truth. Because health, the physician's skill, the skill of Mercury with his staff, that was not presented in ancient Greece in any form other than in stories just like the story of Tantalus' house and Iphigenia. It was not customary at that time to speak in abstract terms but in images. And images were used to present the truth. And the things which filled Greek soul life, which completely organized the Greek soul inwardly, relate to the things which today are accepted as truth, as the archetypal character of truth in the way that 'Behold! I am of Tantalus' house' relates to 'He he he! Hereditary affliction'.

It is this, my dear friends, which we should inscribe in our soul about something that has descended from the culture of ancient Greece to the present day on a downward path. It can give us an indication of the things that need to be developed if we are to start ascending again. That would take us too far today. I will continue these reflections tomorrow for those who still want to hear them.

LECTURE 10

I attempted yesterday through certain pictorial presentations to draw your attention to the great difference in the soul state of people in the fourth and the fifth post-Atlantean epoch, with us being in the latter. This is a difference to which people today, in our present time, indeed show little inclination to pay much attention. Let us just consider what an average person of the present who is 'clever', that is, who has taken in the prevailing fundamental ideas of the present time, might have to say about what we considered yesterday. He will say roughly the following. It is all well and good what the ancient Greeks developed in their imagination about the sequence of generations from Tantalus to Iphigenia, and it is all well and good the way that Iphigenia is placed in an aura of destiny at work. But none of it is more than imagination. That is the standpoint which is generally adopted by clever people today. Koridan, whom we have just seen in the Palatinate shepherds' play, does not say that right from the start, but Mops does say it: 'It's just imagination!' But it is roughly the Mops (apologies!) standpoint[67] with regard to these things.

Now let us just look at how enormously convincing this point of view is for the people of our time, how impossible it is for people of our time to imagine that someone might step right into our midst who—instead of providing information about such a personality, 'hereditary affliction', which I told you about yesterday—might produce something similar to the Iphigenia-Tantalus myth. And if he did produce it, everyone would of course say: fiction! Everything is allowed in fiction, but it has no connection whatsoever with the truth, with real knowledge. And that, basically, is the point of view which people today adopt towards all of art. Current humanity wholly takes the point of view that truth can only be reached through concepts, through theories—through such concepts, through such theories which are taken from external, physical reality and everything else is simply fiction, however good. People in the present time cannot imagine that any other point of view is justified, or indeed possible at all, and that someone might take another view without actually being bonkers. Just imagine for a minute that someone were even just to suggest—I can dare to say it here but am well aware that it is only possible to say it among us—just assume someone would hit on the idea of saying: in medical lecture theatres there should be less talk of hereditary affliction and suchlike and things should be clothed in something similar to a Greek myth. If the person concerned were to say that as if he meant it seriously and it was not a bad joke, then the least that would happen to him in the current culture is that he would be sent to an asylum. Anything else is hardly conceivable, is it! The conviction is firmly rooted in the present time that any other point of view is not possible from this one: truth can only be found in the way that is officially approved and everything that human beings sought in earlier times through their soul was childishness, was a myth, was fiction. It was not truth. But because we have finally come so 'magnificently far',[68] we can also be certain—that is what contemporary people think—that souls in future periods of the earth will never see anything else as the concept of truth than what has just been explained. We can be quite certain of that. If we succeeded in the future in transforming airships into etherships, and ether as understood by physicists today really existed in space, and a balloon was designed which sent some of our clever earth inhabitants, who were never so stupid as to join a spiritual-scientific society, to Mars, and on Mars different opinions were to be revealed to those which have just been indicated, people would say: naturally, those Mars people are making it up! They have not yet understood how real truth can be found.

That another perspective might be possible is a view which might also be taken seriously by a person who does not take the point of view of spiritual science. But then, if he is serious about that, he might well face a dreadful fate. One such person was Nietzsche[69] who attempted to apply a different measure and even berated truth in his book *Beyond Good and Evil*. But he meant the truth which alone is recognized by the present and he wanted to assert a different standpoint, namely the standpoint of life, the standpoint of the life of the soul above everything else. He could not find access to spiritual science and so he had to pay for his standpoint with his mental health. Another standpoint, for example, might be to ask: how do such concepts as are worked into the Greek myths work on the human soul? And how do such concepts as are worked into the present in the form of 'hereditary affliction' work on the human soul? How do these concepts work on the human soul, on the whole life of the human soul? What effect do they have? And there is indeed a huge difference. A person can summarize a number of generations such as from Tantalus to Iphigenia in this way, be it from scratch (like Nietzsche), be it that he or she can believe in such a summary as something real: anyone who can bring to life such ideas, the feelings associated with such ideas, in their soul will bring a vitalizing element into their whole soul life. But those who only work with concepts such as hereditary affliction introduce a deadening element, a withering element. And this withering element is gradually effected under the influence of one-sided physical, biological and so on knowledge, a withering, a deadening element. Never will this physical, chemical or biological science of the present be able to produce anything that can contribute to the inward fulfilment of the life of the soul.

Anyone who wants to can observe that even in outward things. Try it out. Buy the booklet *Naturphilosophie* (Natural philosophy) by Oswald[70]—it is published by Reclam—and try to get by with this booklet when you are seeking nourishment for your soul. See for yourself what an excellent chemist has to say about all kinds of aspects of nature, which is discussed over very many pages, but how what is intended to serve the soul is squashed into a few pages and is marshalled in such abstract terms that it cannot have any effect on the soul other than to make it wither. And development is not such that these biological, physical and chemical directions would contain any promise of providing food for the soul in the future. That is not the case at all. On the contrary, the further the individual sciences progress, the less they will be able to offer anything which is similar in any way to food for the soul. And when the time comes in which the connection of the individual souls with the ancient religious ideas is completely broken, then souls will no longer have any nourishment, then adult souls—perhaps one might for a little longer preach all kinds of things to children which one no longer believes oneself—then the souls of adults would just spend their day by starting with breakfast, slurping at the newspaper between each spoonful. But the newspapers will contain ever less of the spiritual goods of humanity but more and more of the other. Then people will go to work and perform those of their duties which are necessary for the material supply of humanity. Then they will have lunch, will do something similar in the evening, and if there are people who have the time, they will kill it with amusements because it cannot be filled with any thoughts of any real value about a spiritual world. So what will they do in the evening? It might still be acceptable that people go to watch a play or something like that, which they don't really believe in anyway. Some will read a book, perhaps about such things which were produced in the 'childlike' stages of humanity, which were nice, but were produced like the paintings of Raphael or Michelangelo. And we can be quite clear in our minds: it might all be quite nice but it has nothing whatever to do with values of reality.

We should be under no illusion that our time is heading towards the withering and deadening of the life of the soul. If we now look at what the things I spoke about yesterday can teach us, we find that they contain something immensely bleak. Because what is the meaning of the rise of our fifth post-Atlantean epoch out of the fourth post-Atlantean epoch? The meaning resides in the fact that in the fourth post-Atlantean epoch, in the times of ancient Greece for example, people were not as isolated in their souls as today, that there was still an inner connection between the souls, but also that they still perceived this inner connection of souls in certain last remnants of visions, of inspirations from Diana, as they were conceived at the time, of inspirations from Diana, from Artemis, from what came up out of the unconscious depths of the soul. That really did appear to people in images. We can say that they still had a residue of inner, visionary images about the connections between people, about social life, and they took their guidance from them. It is quite nonsensical to believe that the Greeks would have invented something in the way we invent something like this in our time. It is quite nonsensical to believe that. When the Greeks undertook the Trojan campaign and prepared for such a campaign, it would have been quite impossible for them to start such an undertaking for reasons which can be acquired through the intellect or are given life through the feelings as happens today. They knew when they undertook something of that kind that they were placed in the greater context of humanity and the world and that what had to live in their souls could not be anything connected with the ordinary feelings occurring on the physical plane. They saw the deeper reasons and applied them in imaginative perceptions. Certainly, they said, there was a competition between the three goddesses Aphrodite, Hera and Athena, and Paris was to be given the competition's prize, Helen. It was an image, but in this image the Greeks felt and sensed great spiritual connections going through the world.

People in our time may imagine that the Greeks went to war against Troy for similar motives as exist in the present time and that then someone sat down and thought up the whole myth to explain the Trojan war poetically. That, once again, is to think of it in the external ideas of the present. The myth was seen in a vision; it was the imaginative perception of the deeper forces that were at work there. Now I could of course, if that did not distract us too much from the present task, explain how Helen was the representative, the imagination for the whole relationship between Greece and Asia Minor, how the whole competition between the three goddesses showed what the impulse of the Greek soul life was and how the Greek soul life had to work towards what it later represented in the world. But as I said, consideration of this myth would take us too far away from our present task.

Let us consider this, that residues remained of a visionary clairvoyance which went by the truth of the images and that its poetic expression was not like it is today, where it is presented as something that has been thought up. It was a visionary experience which then came to expression in outward forms and which was not faced by a dry, pedantic, purely theoretical science which would have been as proud of its concept of truth as the current theoretical science is. The connections between people were still looked at. That has been lost completely. It had to be lost because individualism had to arise. Human beings would never have arrived at the individualism for which the culture of the fifth post-Atlantean epoch has to be the teacher and which will gradually develop during the fifth post-Atlantean epoch. Human beings had to lose every last residue of the old clairvoyance to be completely removed—each one individually—from what can still be perceived of this connection. Human beings had to be constricted, we might say, in their soul experience with regard to their individual forms of existence on the physical plane. They had to be constricted. That could only happen if they lost everything that took them beyond their own body, they were completed enclosed in their own body. If you have a vision of what connects you with other people, then you have a perception of the social life. Human beings in the fifth post-Atlantean epoch were not supposed to have that any longer. They were completely thrown back on what they can experience within their own skin. And that is how the first stage of the individualistic concept of human beings arose, what we might call the most brutal stage, where in a certain sense they still are.

If people today want to feel what they really are, the first thing they think of—whatever other nice theories they might have—is what is within their body, within their skin, really within their skin. It is difficult to get a clear idea of this, in particular, because it is true and no one believes it in our time, because people like to develop all kinds of idealism to hide the fact that basically they only believe in themselves in so far as they are enclosed in their own skin. But this transition had to occur. It had to occur because human beings gradually have to realize that in a certain sense and within certain limits they have themselves prepared out of karma what is inside their skin. The thing which was Greek destiny was not prepared by people themselves; it linked them with the sequence of the generations before them. What people will experience as their karma in the future will connect them consciously with other people. People will have to experience their karma consciously as something real. As you can easily imagine, experiencing their karma consciously is still incredibly difficult for people today. It is accepted in theory, but experiencing karma as something conscious, that really is still very difficult for people today. As I once said, let us assume that someone gives us a slap in the face. Outwardly, of course, in so far as we are enclosed in our body and are beings between birth and death, we have to defend ourselves against that. But a higher perspective has to be applied beyond that: who was it that gave you the slap in the face? Who put the person who gave you the slap in the place where he could do that? He would not be standing there if you had not put him there through the way you are connected with him through karma. Just think how incredibly difficult it is for people today to think that. Christians believe that they are people of the present, but truly very few of them follow the one who counsels them: if someone strikes you on the left cheek, turn the other one also[71]—in thought, outwardly it is not possible. People do not yet differentiate in this way between the what is inward and outward. It becomes incredibly difficult for them to live in karma in some way.

And yet, as we enter life from the embryonic period through birth, through early childhood, then that which helps to form our body is our karma. Between our last death and our present birth, we have gone through, and have even taken an interest in going through, how we should experience karma and what kind of body we should have so that we can live out our karma. In this way we work on kneading, in a manner of speaking, our body through the soul forces. We even act in a localizing way in that we place ourselves at the location in the world where we can live out our karma. We thus act on our personal destiny with the consciousness which we have between death and a new birth.

That is the complete opposite of the Greek idea of destiny. But in order to reach that idea in a living way, human beings have to pass through individualism, have to grasp themselves as an individual in a very brutal way, I might say. And human beings are on the way to grasping themselves as individuals. But they have had to accept something, let me say, truly accept something for that, namely that they have to live out the experience: I am enclosed within my skin and my flesh. Human beings have had to accept something. It is that they became the slaves, the soul slaves of their physical body. They allowed themselves to be enslaved by their physical body and the body to begin with became the ruler over a new, believed destiny. An Iphigenia felt at the age to which I referred yesterday—every single sentence in yesterday's account is correct: I roughly indicated how many years she still had to go to the age of 20—an Iphigenia who had visions going back as far as Tantalus, visions which are today interpreted as reminiscences caused by heredity, such an Iphigenia is no longer possible in that direct form today. An Iphigenia who above all expresses in moral and ethical terms what lives in her family right back to Tantalus, 'Behold! I am of Tantalus' house!', that is no longer possible today. Because today the physician will step up to her and explain: hereditary affliction. Your father, your mother, your grandfather, your grandmother and so on suffered from this and this condition, hereditary affliction. And that is the cause of everything. But that is an expression of the way the soul today wheezes along under the yoke of the physical body, wheezing also in perception, in its feeling.

Basically, my dear friends, we can see the soul wheezing along under the physical body when we look at what has happened to the human being in respect of a certain world view of the nineteenth century. People only looked at the physical body and, because they only looked at the physical body, came to the conclusion that the human being originated from the animal world. Scientifically, too, human beings are wheezing along under what ties them to their physical body. And it will hardly be easy to draw people's attention to what underlies this. Because people can come, if we draw their attention to all these things, and they can say: do you really believe you can refute the justified aspects of Darwinism? It has all been well proven. Certainly, it is well proven—it is indeed well proven, but that is not the issue. The issue is that our feeling for truth has changed. These things can be rigorously proven in the context of such a changed feeling for truth, naturally. We do have to be out of touch with today if we cannot experience what the issue is here.

But all of these things have their practical consequences. Outer culture is steering with incredible vehemence towards implementing its thinking in practical life and no longer allowing the impulses of the soul and spirit to apply within practical life. And how close are we already today to applying such things for example in education, the methodology of teaching and upbringing. How close are we to applying them to the upbringing of small children. Just think what will happen when we get to the stage that not just the things are required which are required today of small children but quite other things, when we get to the stage that, once a child has reached a certain age—which will be determined by scientific statistical data—all parents will be obliged to have their child examined by a materialistic physician for his or her hereditary characteristics. In the meantime, the school system will have been divided into various streams and after the medical examination by the materialistic physician parents will have to put their child in this or that school depending on his or her 'hereditary affliction', perhaps even into a specific kindergarten.

Today people are still surprised when such a perspective is raised. But such surprise is the awful thing. We should not be at all surprised about these things because if the form of Darwinism that is being theoretically espoused today were to become true, then it would have to be done like that. That is the key point: then it would be the only way and it would be unconscionable of people if they did not do it like that. The small matter might come up, the small matter that let us say someone might have hoodwinked the physician in some way and the physician issued a certificate which is not correct in the view of others, but that is not their official job. Whereas the child should have been taken to department two, where there are certain 'hereditary afflictions', the child might have been taken to department five where according to the medical certificate the future geniuses are. And then it might have turned out that the child was more clever than those who examined him or her. But that could then only happen through an 'error'. That something like that could be possible is no great surprise, is it?

This is only intended to give you an impulse to obtain a view of the tendency which underlies the direction which is mostly still theoretical today. Today it only represents the globules of fat floating on the soup, but these globules of fat will keep growing in power. More and more materialistic fat will be added and then in the end the whole bowel will be full of such materialistic fat and humanity will have to spoon it up. But it is here that people will have to reach a point through a conception of the world as a result of which they will overcome the great dangers which lie in the practical implementation of the current theories. Once the content of our spiritual science has come inwardly to life in a great number of souls, then people in whose souls the spiritual-scientific truths have inwardly come to life will not be persuaded by all kinds of talk about 'hereditary afflictions' but they will say: 'However much you prove to me what was wrong with my father, my mother, my grandfather, my grandmother and so on, I know that as well as what I carry in my hereditary impulses I have a soul which has nothing to do with these hereditary impulses because in the time in which the hereditary, the previous generation was here, this soul was in the spiritual world between death and my present birth. I carry these forces equally in me and we will see whether I will not defeat this "hereditary affliction".' True, for as long as people believe in the theory of heredity and for as long as the truths of spiritual science do not pass into the flesh and blood, in that time it will not be possible to defeat heredity. It will only be possible to defeat it when the spiritual-scientific concepts truly come to life in souls and pass over into flesh and blood. But many other things still have to happen for that.

We can certainly believe that the spiritual-scientific truths will grow ever more persuasive for those who can comprehend them, but a number of other things will also have to happen. That is why I started today by presenting an aperçu about art. Consider how far what is called truth today has become distanced from art and literature since Greek times, how in the fifth post-Atlantean epoch a divide has arisen between what people call truth and what they call art. But this has a great deal to do with the attitude to art in general of current humanity. And here there is truly some value in taking a look at the way in which people today see art in general. There is one art in which—because it is primarily relevant for the fifth post-Atlantean period and its consequences—in which mistakes of world-historical importance cannot be made, in which people are still forced today to look at the artistic element: that is music. In music alone are people today inclined to recognize the artistic element because they are forced through the nature of music to see it as more than a reflection of external reality. Because the artistic element can only be misconstrued in the furthest reaches of what is musical. If someone tried here or there only to listen to see whether music was imitating the rushing of waves or the whispering of the wind or something similar, we would know that what imitates the rushing of waves or the whispering of the wind or something similar is only of minor importance in music, that something quite different is of importance, namely the inner structure which in reality cannot be observed outwardly on the physical plane. Thus music is protected through its inner nature from being drawn too deeply into the tendencies of the fifth post-Atlantean epoch.

The present time has less facility for poetry. There things can occur which lead from the artistic into the non-artistic and in some fields of poetry these things occur particularly strongly. How many people today can still have a real feeling for the artistic in poetry in the way that we have to have a feeling for the artistic in music? Most people when faced with something ask: does it accord with this or that model in reality out there? Indeed, we have a whole art of naturalism which judges all poetry only by whether it accords with outer, physical reality whereas it is an irrelevance in poetry whether something accords with outer, physical reality. It has just as little value in a poem whether a person in it is drawn accurately in an outer, physical sense as it does whether a musical work imitates the roar of the wind or the play of the waves. So that we can say that current humanity has less of a facility for poetry than for music. In truth it is not important whether I describe something in four verses which accords with some reality or other but it is important how the second verse arises from the first, the third from the second and so on. In a sonnet the important thing is not to express something or other but how the four and four, three and three lines intertwine. The four lines, how are they intertwined? What inner impulses live in them—like melodies or harmonies, but here transferred into the sphere of mental images, the field of sounds? There is very little feeling for that.

A woman, a very intellectual and witty woman, once handed me a novella—this happened a long time ago, about 30 years ago—and asked me to read the novella and tell her what I thought about it. This novella was of a nature—she was a very intellectual and witty woman—that something was recounted in the way that we tell an outer event so that I was forced to say: the whole thing requires that you give it a structure, that you work out three novelistic stanzas, as it were, a first novelistic stanza (I was speaking metaphorically), a second and third one, and that there is an inner framework, an inner structure of an artistic kind. You should have seen the face of the lady concerned—how dare I ask for something like that! What—she asked—I should create three stanzas? That was her ironic response to my suggestion.

Then the next art, for which current humanity has even less of a facility, is painting—painting as it arises from form and colour, as it must look at the artistic element and not at how what is depicted accords with some external physical reality or other. There can also be something artistic in a physical similarity, for example in portraiture or similar things, but then something quite different is important from creating a pure replica. Then it is important that the artistic element comes out through the way that the subject is treated. And terribly little of that is present in humanity at the moment. What people judge first in painting today can be compared with comparing the form of a melody or suchlike in music with something outward in nature.

The descent from music to poetry is also noticeable in another way, can be noticed in another way in the present time. Someone may consider themselves to be a musical genius but they still have to learn something, whereas poetical geniuses today consider it as something quite terrible if they are meant to have learnt something about the finer aspects of technique. And there is almost a similar tendency with regard to painting and suchlike.

But we descend even further in respect of the understanding of people in our time when we turn to sculpture. Almost nothing else is considered here, when people make their judgements, than what would result if a sequence of tones was heard and they then spent the whole night searching for the natural phenomena to which it accords. Most judgements which are made about sculpture are actually of this kind, and we can see particularly in sculpture that an understanding of sculpture will only occur when spiritual science can be sought in the human personality in a living way. You will recall some of the things which I spoke about here[72]—and intentionally had to speak about here—about the way we can feel our way into space upwards and downwards, to the right and left, backwards and forwards; you will recall everything we examined. You will recall my examination of the left and right side of the human being, and remember how much that can be developed—the experience of the human etheric body, which is the thing that structures the physical forms—an experience which the Greeks had instinctively and which has been lost in the fifth post-Atlantean epoch and has to arise anew. We can truly say: the time has to come in which sculpture will be grasped in such a way that every-thing will be abandoned which today makes people reach their judge-ment and everything will be applied which people today only bother about with regard to music.

Let alone in architecture! Because if people today were not forced to put their chairs somewhere in a room next to a table and required to put a shelter around that, and if they were not forced somehow to enter a room and look outside, then today we would be totally incapable of finding the forms which in any way indicate architectural design. Because what do architects actually do? They study Renaissance forms, classical forms, that is, they imitate because you cannot simply put up mere cubic shapes or polyhedral or similar cartons or boxes. Whether or not architecture will once again be able to give birth to forms will depend entirely on whether people will learn to experience again how the creativity of the world flows into the forms, because that had to be lost in the time of individualism. And so it is necessary to bring that back to life; it is necessary that what should bring life back into the ideas of the human soul is supplemented by an understanding of the artistic, that the artistic plays an essential part. That is why it is good that a number of our dear friends have not just heard theoretical lectures about art within our spiritual-scientific endeavours but were also actively involved in the creation of certain forms[73] and other artistic things, even if what can arise in that way is only the beginning of something that belongs to the future.

I must say, the last refuge which the people of the present world conception have chosen is what they call 'reason informed by outer experience'. People have built the current materialistic world conception with such reason informed by outer experience and the purely mechanical and biological, physical and chemical concepts are increas-ingly intended to determine our world conception. There is no incli-nation to go into the extent to which these concepts are filled with life, the way in which they can vitalize the soul. I have expressly emphasized that the great progress brought about by scientific research must be recognized by our spiritual science, that we should not expose and embarrass ourselves by constantly ranting against scientific progress. Furthermore, we will only rant against it for as long as we do not know it. When we get to know it we will see some impressive results. And we should really let ourselves be told that we should not rant against science because we belong to spiritual science if we have no understanding of any kind of a single science. But we should take another look at the philosophical values in current science, or rather the way in which the current scientific concepts can become important philosophical values. We live in a difficult, a sad time today. We see the infinitely sad way in which death covers great swathes of territory. We see how pain and sorrow are spreading, an image which every soul today should face up to. It is particularly sad in our present time when souls look away from the great world events and concern themselves with their own, personal affairs to such an extent. From this perspective, my dear friends, it caused me infinite sorrow for example in the last year that so much of a personal nature came to light particularly in our ranks in a time in which the great interests of humanity could approach our souls in such an intensive way. But I do not want to talk about those things at all, I just want to draw your attention to them.

How do people of the present time face up to such overwhelming contemporary events? There are those people who say: 'Are we not aware to such an extent of the transient nature of the physical, particularly in this time in which thousands and thousands of deaths are occurring across the earth, that human beings have to bring to life within themselves what can arise as an idea of the eternal powers of the human soul? Are not these events, in particular, appropriate for guiding human thoughts towards the eternal powers of the human soul?' And so we might think that perhaps someone who was already very inclined to surrender completely to Ahriman, that is to materialism, might be urged by the power of the current impression of transient superficiality, of the withering of all that is transient, to turn their gaze to the eternal. We might think that. But let us look at some of the things which happen in reality, let us take one of the most excellent scientific people of the present and his world conception. Let us take Ernst Haeckel.[74] What is the approximate content of Ernst Haeckel's 'idea of eternity'?

He says, we can see in the present time how innumerable people are going through death, how an inexplicable destiny is breaking into the physical earth life of human beings—I say these things now in our words. Can we not see from that the absence of any meaning in the idea of the eternity of the human soul when we see how human beings can simply be mown down like that? Is that not proof that the scientific world view is correct when it says: there is nothing which has meaning beyond purely physical corporeality? Is what we are experiencing now not proof that those are wrong who speak about an eternal human soul?

We cannot say that someone made aware on the basis of contemporary events of the forces of eternity in the human soul would be more logical than someone who says: 'We can see people dying through what I can only describe as chance. How can I believe that there is real meaning in human development or that there are eternal values?!' We cannot from a contemporary perspective say that the one is more logical than the other. You cannot find the one thought logical and the other one illogical if you apply logic seriously to your considerations. Because anyone who argues like that reminds us of what lies in current scientific achievements. We can truly infinitely admire them. We can say: what magnificent things have been achieved by this science of chemistry, by this science of mechanics! It has perhaps achieved wonderful things when it is a matter of a contribution to human progress, but it has used its wonderful achievements equally to create very brilliantly terrible instruments of murder. The one thing is just as possible in this science as the other. This science can be completely neutral. It can produce the most wonderful instrument for investigating the secrets of nature and by the same achievements the most terrible instruments of murder. That is what this science as such is like. It can prove out of shocking events that human souls are more than transient but also that these events specifically show—it can prove that equally well!—that the human soul is only transient. This science is completely neutral.

Something positive has to come; the message, the news, the revelation of the spiritual worlds has to come and these spiritual worlds must work through their inner power. You know that what comes through revelation is not in contradiction but in harmony precisely with the achievements of science but it cannot come from the latter. That is why those who claim that scientific concepts can lead to a satisfactory world conception are talking nonsense. Scientific concepts have to be supplemented with spiritual research and that is the path by which we can get out of the great dangers of the present time. We have to see that the path of decline is the one which is associated with the greatest progress and that the ascending path is the one which has to come from the revelation of spiritual life. In this fact of world events alone, we have to be completely radical. That is what matters. Only spiritual science will be in a position to say something in turn about more profound secrets.

Truly, my dear friends, it is not easy for an understanding of karma to enter souls. That will only happen when a larger number of people is in a position to grasp the narrowness of such concepts as 'hereditary affliction', the invalidity and unproductiveness of such concepts, and to look at what lives in souls. Then, when people come and see a child of which the physical physician has said, 'It manifests like this but nothing can be done about it because the father was like this, the mother was like this, the grandfather was like this, the grandmother was like this,' and so on, we have to be resigned to that. If that is what the physical physician says, then people have to learn to sense that it can also be true that there is a soul contained within that, a soul which has prepared for quite different things from what the physical physician believes on the basis of heredity, for something quite different between the previous death and a new birth, and that above all those things must not be allowed to lie fallow but that these forces must be developed. These spiritual findings must find a voice in the world so that we will experience it as unconscionable if we fail to look at the soul and spiritual aspect. It will have to be understood that these spiritual characteristics will remain latent if they are left out of consideration in education. Because at a certain age the physical side has come to full expression and the spirit can no longer penetrate it and then it will remain lying fallow for the rest of the incarnation concerned, something that should have been noticed.

This is where spiritual science acquires practical importance. This is what we would wish for, that this practical meaning is understood. These are the things which I wanted to place before your souls still in connection with what we said yesterday.

LECTURE 11

BERN, 9 JANUARY 1916

FUNDAMENTALLY, all of spiritual science ultimately aims to understand human beings in their essence, in their tasks and endeavours, in their necessary endeavours in the course of development. The misunderstandings to which we often have to refer and which spiritual science encounters from outside are largely due to humanity at present still being little able to familiarize itself with certain basic truths which simply have to be recognized, which simply have to be comprehended if we want to come to any kind of understanding of life and the nature of the human being.

What, actually, is the basis—let us begin today by touching on this question—what, actually, is the basis for the scientific approach whose great, important triumphs of the last four centuries should be fully recognized, particularly fully recognized by spiritual science? It starts from what it perceives in its physical environment, what is revealed in the environment of physical existence. Now it is of course self-evident that we begin by having trust in what we perceive as so-called reality in our surroundings and that we try to explain this reality on the basis of what is contained in this reality itself. It is of course difficult to be clear from the beginning that this reality itself might contain appearance, that this reality itself could be deceptive. This cliff must first be surmounted by anyone who really wants to understand spiritual science. They must learn to comprehend that reality as it surrounds us can be deceptive, that it can indeed mislead us, can be interpreted in the wrong way. And many of the things we have learnt in spiritual science in the course of the years has been able to convince us that the reality which directly surrounds us can be deceptive. Today let us start from a very specific point, from a point which, however, can only be obtained from within spiritual science. That is what spiritual science is like, that we have to understand things and then, once we have understood them, we can find what we have understood confirmed in reality. The most important things in particular must first be understood in spiritual science before we can look at them. It could easily be set out that this is a method which is also frequently applied in the external world, and specifically in the world of external science. But we will not spend time on that today. We cannot always develop everything from first principles.

One such fact which is eminently suitable for deceiving us about external reality as a result of appearance, as a result of the physiognomy of that reality itself, is about the differences, the different characteristics of people on earth. When we look at people as they inhabit earth, we say to ourselves: there are basically no two people who are the same in the physical field. People in the physical field are all different from one another. And then it is quite natural that we accept the differences between people on earth as a fact—I am now talking about the difference in the physical body—and that we then proceed to find out in some way from the facts of life on earth why people are different, why they look different.

But now spiritual-scientific observation shows something quite different. It shows us that if we only take account of the observation of the shape that the physical body on earth can adopt through the earth forces, human beings cannot be different on earth but they would all be the same, all have the same shape. The forces which exist on earth to give human beings their physical shape are such that all people would have to have the same outer shape if nothing but the formative forces of our earth acted on them. This happens because the physical human body has been sufficiently prepared. We know that it has been prepared through the Saturn, through the Sun and Moon periods. Everything is prepared through forces which were at work in these three periods so that the earth forces cannot act on the body in any other way than to give it a homogenous shape across the whole earth, precisely if we only take account of this earth. Let me put it this way: because of what was incorporated in their physical body as forces during the Saturn, Sun and Moon period, human beings are so armoured against all differences in the earth forces that they would have to be the same across the whole earth if they were only subject to the earth forces. Spiritual science must therefore assume that a homogenous shape is predetermined for human beings through the earth forces.

If we now also look at the differences between male and female, then what has just been said also applies to this difference between male and female. Because this difference has not either been caused by what earth forces form in the human being but by quite different forces which we will speak about shortly. So we can assume a certain sum of earth forces which have a formative action on human beings and which seek only to produce absolutely the same human shape across the whole earth. So we can of course ask ourselves why it is that human beings are nevertheless so different.

We know that we are not only dealing with the physical earth body of human beings but that behind the physical earth body there is the etheric body. Now spiritual-scientific observation shows us that—even if all human beings should actually be the same with regard to their physical earth body—they have to be different with regard to the etheric body. And this is so for the reason that the etheric body is not just affected by earth forces. It is a completely mistaken belief that only earth forces act on the human etheric body. Forces from out of the cosmos, the universe act on the etheric body of human beings which form and shape them. Therefore we have to distinguish between the earth forces acting in a homogenous way across the earth, which would make all human shapes the same, and the forces acting on the earth out of the universe which make the etheric bodies of human beings differ-ent. We can follow the differences between human etheric bodies through spiritual-scientific observation. There are human etheric bodies which might be described as being at their outer limit, which have strong forces, etheric bodies in which one can observe that they almost retain their form like a physical form. That is one kind of etheric body.

A second kind of etheric body is the one in which the etheric body is very flexible, is flexible like what I might describe as something completely in motion, fluttering, is flowing and flexible in contrast to the firm shape. These two forms of etheric body are revealed such that they can be described as being inwardly pretty uniformly shaded. Another type of etheric body is the one which is inwardly shaded, is inwardly shaded in a shimmering way, which is not uniform in its colour but inwardly shaded, inwardly tinted. A fourth type of etheric body is the one which, although it has a basic colour throughout its whole sub-stance, if we can describe it like that, changes its colour over the course of time without it being possible to say that it is changed by anything other than from something within. So it is not shimmering, not shaded in different colours, but it is such that it is uniform but changes its colour over the course of time, a chameleon-like etheric body. Then there are etheric bodies which have a strong tendency to be inwardly illuminated, clarified, which at certain moments become lighter and lighter. Other etheric bodies have a very strong ability to reproduce the music of the spheres. And then we can observe etheric bodies which occur particularly in inventive, brilliant people, such etheric bodies which already show forces within themselves which are alien to and rare on earth. While the six preceding types of etheric body show that they are of a kind which can be found in human beings, even if they are the average person, the latter type of etheric body produces the kind of person who has strong abilities of which we say that they are not 'of the earth'—poets, artists and suchlike.

It is not because of some arbitrary assumption of the figure seven that we distinguish between seven such forms of etheric body in human beings. We simply have to count them. We find no others than the ones which I have now presented as the typical ones and that is why there are seven types of etheric body—there is no other reason. There are really seven different types of etheric body in human beings. We have forces in the etheric bodies which are not earthly in a certain sense, which come from the cosmos. But now the etheric body has a formative influence on the physical body and so it happens that, whereas human beings would all be the same with regard to their physical body through the earth forces, they are shaped differently through the etheric body. Indeed the differences between male and female bodies, for example, are only effected by the astral body, are only developed through the forces which are not developed by the astral body until it passes between death and a new birth—which is the time in which human beings prepare for the gender which they must have in accordance with karma in the next incarnation.

But let us stay with our consideration of the etheric body. So we can say that whereas the physical body is predisposed to be the same across the earth if we only take account of the earthly forces, human beings would be divided into seven groups across the earth because their etheric bodies are predisposed in a different way from the cosmos, from outside the earth—because they have a different structure, a different substance throughout. That is the situation, that is what we gradually find if we attempt to investigate through spiritual science the reciprocal relationship of the human etheric body with its physical body. Now this difference that occurs is connected with the characteristics, with the differences between the races on earth. Basically the races can always be reduced to this number seven because of these differences in the etheric body. Even if some typical forms die out, and if external science distinguishes fewer than seven basic races, there are in reality seven differences between the basic races in the whole of humanity. But they are actually caused by the etheric bodies and do not have their origin in the earth forces during our development but they have their origin in cosmic forces.

If we now follow the development of the earth backwards to the Atlantean and the Lemurian period, we can see that originally characteristics and impulses existed through which the physiognomy which the human physical body has received through the power of the etheric body—that is, the differences which took shape—should not actually have happened on earth in accordance with the original characteristics as it did. It should not have happened like that, but if everything had happened in a certain way—we will shortly see in which way—the seven-coloured etheric body of the human being would have caused differences in the way the human form developed. But it would have happened consecutively in such a way that through the etheric body a certain shape of human being would have existed in the fifth Atlantean epoch, a second in the sixth Atlantean epoch, a third in the seventh Atlantean epoch, a fourth in the first post-Atlantean epoch, a fifth in the second post-Atlantean epoch, a sixth in the third post-Atlantean epoch, a seventh in the Graeco-Latin period, the fourth post-Atlantean epoch: various human types would have arisen consecutively. In a sense, human beings would have developed in such a way that there would have been human beings in the fifth Atlantean epoch in whose body shape one form of etheric body would have acted particularly strongly, in the sixth Atlantean epoch the second of the forms described and so on up to the fourth post-Atlantean epoch. That was actually the disposition.

Lucifer and Ahriman resisted that, they did not want it to happen like that. It was the continuing developmental trend in the regular progress of human development. Lucifer and Ahriman resisted it. They caused these developments to be shifted so that—whereas the actual development had been organized such that essentially one form of human being should have appeared in the fifth Atlantean epoch, and this should then have gradually been transformed into another form of human being—Lucifer and Ahriman preserved the form of the fifth Atlantean epoch into the sixth, and again from the sixth Atlantean epoch into the seventh and in turn across the flood of Atlantis. So that actually something whose form should have passed away was retained. And instead of the differences between the races having developed consecutively, as should have happened, the old forms of race were retained, remained stationary and the new ones inserted themselves, as it were, so that they developed alongside one another instead of con-secutively as was actually intended. And that is how it has come about that such physically different races inhabit the earth and inhabit it into our time, whereas the development should have taken place as I described it. We can indeed see everywhere, when we look at what arises from the development of the etheric body, how Lucifer and Ahriman play their role in the earthly development of humanity everywhere.

Now we have to ask ourselves: how was that actually intended in the world context, that human beings should develop consecutively in this way up to the Graeco-Latin period? After all, we know in turn that roughly at the time which I have described as the Atlantean period souls gradually—that is, starting with the fifth Atlantean period—descended from the planets to which they had ascended. Remember from my *Occult Science* how it is set out there that the souls ascended and then descended again, that from the time when they descended life on earth really started as an incarnated life. We can thus see that the human Is, the actual individualities, would then have passed through these various forms in the consecutive periods. Our Is would have passed through one human form in the fifth Atlantean period, would have passed through a different human form in the sixth one, through another one in the seventh, through another one again in the first post-Atlantean period and so on. We would have gradually completed these consecutive human types, human shapes. And so it was actually planned that human beings would have completed in this way what was necessary to train the human individuality, what was necessary as a passage through various etheric shapes which then would have had different effects on the physical shape, that all those stages would have been passed through. A human type could have appeared on earth which was the result of seven consecutive developmental periods which each would have added something to completeness. And it would have happened in the fifth post-Atlantean epoch that a harmonious human type was intended to exist across the whole earth.

Lucifer and Ahriman thwarted that. The only thing that was possible was that the Greeks dreamt of an ideal, extra-human type of form which they sought to shape in various ways—in the Apollo way, the Zeus way, the Athena way and so on. They did not encompass it completely because it did not exist in reality. But we can feel, if we have a sense for Greek sculpture, how Greek culture dreamt of what was to arise as a harmonious, perfect human type. That it did not happen in this way was prevented by Lucifer and Ahriman in that they preserved the forms of race once they had been created so that a consecutive development turned into a parallel one.

Thus human development in the fourth post-Atlantean epoch, the Graeco-Latin period, faced the fact that through the influence of Lucifer and Ahriman it could not be achieved what had actually been intended for the earth in relation to the outer form by the gods whose impulses determined the earth. The spirits from the hierarchy of form had intended that through the collaboration of the various hierarchies of form the perfect human type in terms of physical shape could really have arisen. Thus the Greeks could only dream of it and bring it to expression in their art. There is something deeply moving when in the course of spiritual-scientific research we reach the point at which we say: why was it, that the Greeks created such perfection in sculpture? Because they captured through what I might describe as a divine-spiritual tool the disappointment which Lucifer and Ahriman had prepared for the good divine spiritual beings who wanted to achieve something different with humanity than was then able to arise. That which could have arisen through the good divine spiritual beings—that lay in the soul of the Greeks and that is what they at least wanted to put into form after it could not arise in outer reality. It has a powerful and harrowing effect when we look at these inner forces of human development, forces which occur here in artistic forms, which want to capture what could not be achieved in outer reality. We look at Greek art in quite a different light in this context which in that age developed in such a unique form and will never be repeated.

But the time had also come in which humanity had reached a crisis point through the influence of Lucifer and Ahriman. Lucifer and Ahriman had managed to achieve that the races assumed life not living one after the other but alongside one another. But at the same time all those forces were paralysed which the forming spirits, the spirits of form would have originally poured into the development of humanity on earth. They could not do anything more than fertilize the Greek imagination in such a way as I have explained. The spirits of form faced the necessity, as it were, to say to themselves: shall the human race now develop in such a way that human beings will never ever converge in earth development? Because that is what would have had to happen. If earth development had simply continued from the fourth period, the Graeco-Latin time, it would have fallen apart into a sevenfold division caused by luciferic and ahrimanic forces—into seven groups of human beings on earth which would have split apart because they were as different as the various animal groups which have split apart. Just as the individual animal groups do not understand one another but see each other as separate beings, in the same way the view would have had to develop towards the end of the fourth cultural epoch, the Graeco-Latin period, and from the fifth epoch onwards in which we live—we would still be in the middle of it, it would not yet have fully reached completion what actually in this context means the greatest imperfection, but it would have gradually happened on earth—that seven groups of human beings would gradually have formed on earth who would have looked at one another as completely separate beings. The term 'human being' for all human beings on earth would not have been right but there would have been seven designations for seven different groups of beings on earth, not a homogenous designation for human beings across the earth.

What happened was this, that in the fourth post-Atlantean epoch, the Graeco-Latin period, measures were taken in the cosmos so that the development which threatened to occur could not happen, so that the moment would not occur in the future—once the earth has reached the goal of its development—in which there were seven groups of beings living on earth with different names, like the different animal species are given different names, who do not see themselves as equal and who would at most have inherited some kind of imitation of Greek forms such as the figure of Zeus, the figure of Apollo, which would have been perceived as something alien, as something that could never have existed on earth. Something had to be done to prevent that happening. But physical development had already progressed too far for anything to be changed in it. So measures had to be taken with regard to the etheric body of the human being. An impulse had to enter the etheric body which countered the division of humanity on earth into seven groups. And the impulse which was intended in the cosmic plan to counter such a splintering of humanity, this impulse which was intended to ensure that the term human being retained a real meaning across the whole earth and would grow in meaning, this impulse is—and here we reach a new aspect of this matter—the Mystery of Golgotha. The first attempt as it were, which had been made with humanity on earth before the luciferic and ahrimanic impulse had intervened in earth development, was to create unity across the earth in humanity. This attempt by the spirits of form failed. It failed because of the influence of Lucifer and Ahriman. But it was not allowed to fail in its totality; something had to be provided for which in turn could paralyse what Ahriman and Lucifer brought about. It was no longer possible to have such an effect on the physical body as was originally intended. But the etheric body was to be affected. And that happened in that the divine-spiritual being of whom we have talked so often, the Christ being, united with the human form at the time of human development in which the possibility still existed to keep a hold of the archetype of humanity.

What period is that in human development? All the forces which counter the originally identical shape of the physical body are active in the human being such that they can work in the first seven years in which the physical body is primarily in a soft stage of development. At that time they do not let it become identical but vary it from inside out. They can also still do so in the second septennium until puberty. They can even still do so in the third and fourth seven years during the development of the astral body and the sentient soul. But when we get to the middle of the intellectual or mind soul, that component of human development which has particularly developed in the fourth post-Atlantean, the Graeco-Latin period, that is when the extraterrestrial forces can least approach the human being and they do so with the greatest difficulty in the middle, that is, in the period of the human being which lies between the ages of 28 and 35, and there in turn in the middle. If we add two years beforehand and leave away two years afterwards, we have the period from the age of 30 to 33. Afterwards we get to a time in which extraterrestrial forces have a greater influence once again; indeed then human beings have become such that extra-terrestrial forces have the greatest influence on them. But now—from the age of 30 to 33—it is the case to the greatest extent that only earth forces continue to act on human beings. And in this period, in these three years—even if the developmental differences from younger years were retained and supplemented by what comes in later years—if the only thing which acted on human beings was what acts on them in the period from the age of 30 to 33, human beings would have much greater similarity on earth.

Christ now had to use these three specific years—they are three particularly separated years—in order to enter into community with the earth forces in human beings in which the earthly in human beings has been retained to the greatest extent. That was prepared through the two bodies of Jesus,[75] as we have discussed, until the age of 30 the Christ body, and then, from the age of 30 to 33 Christ took possession of that body. In the location where the earth forces were most strongly at work and where deformation was able to occur, that is where there was no longer any development, that is where physical death occurred. So the Christ Sun being entered the sphere of the earth in reality and then united with the whole of the etheric body of the earth in the way I have often described, entered the aura of the earth where He now continues to work. But for human beings it has to work in such a way that they increasingly understand that in Christ they were sent that divine spirit to earth through whom what was separated through the opposition of Lucifer and Ahriman against the original impulses of humanity—what was split up—was reversed again from the inside out.

The good spiritual beings work together with Lucifer and Ahriman in the outer nature of human beings. But the thing which was prescribed to humans from the physical beginning of the earth as something they should have externally—equality across the whole earth, the possibility of the name of human across the whole earth—that was now to be brought by the Christ spirit from out of the innermost nature of human beings. That was one of the many-layered meanings of the Mystery of Golgotha, that something was given to the earth with the Christ spirit which, if understood in the right way, once again makes the name of human possible across the whole of earth humanity. When the true content of Christianity, which has already partly been revealed through Christianity, which those will discover who search in the spiritual world with regard to Christ what the latter continuously reveals in accordance with his words, 'I am with you always, even unto the end of the world,'[76] when it gradually emerges further what humanity can be told in the name of Christ from the inside out, then what Lucifer and Ahriman have managed to do in humanity on earth will gradually be balanced out.

We can, nevertheless, ask: is there any sense in this detour having been made? And this, let me say, childish question is very frequently thrown up by people who want to be cleverer than the cosmic wisdom—and there are many people who want to be that. Particularly those people who want to be cleverer than the cosmic wisdom say: if we are to believe in powerful divine beings, could they not have excluded the luciferic and ahrimanic influence from the beginning of earth development so that their work was not spoiled? That is certainly human wisdom, but in the sense of Paul's 'For the wisdom of this world is foolishness with God'.[77] It is certainly human wisdom.

We simply have to look at things in our considerations in the way that we do. In that context the things which arise through the adversary, which arise from the other side through the opposition of Lucifer and Ahriman do not of course appear as something absolutely evil. For let us also consider the other side of the matter. Imagine that the original divine cosmic plan for the earth had been fulfilled; the Graeco-Latin period would have approached in the proper way as I indicated and that beautiful, harmonious human type of which the Greeks dreamt would not only have been created by Greek sculptors but would have walked among people and would have spread further and further across the earth. All other human forms would gradually have disappeared and only that which lived in the disposition of the Apollo type, the Zeus type, the Diana type, the Athena type would have walked the earth and would have called itself human because it would have recognized itself in its outer perception. The name of human would have been possible and the feeling of the equality of all human beings would also have become possible. We might say that a human culture in Greek beauty would gradually have spread across the earth and in our time we would have seen human beings tending increasingly to an ever closer approximation to this Greek, beautiful human type which would have achieved its fullness when the earth reached its goal in the seventh post-Atlantean epoch and progressed to another stage of existence. But human beings would have come to such human community with a lack of freedom—that has to be understood. Human beings would have been forced to see themselves across the whole earth as the same being. Everything that has come among human beings so that they see themselves as unequal, that they do not regard one another as being like themselves, that they do not love the other like themselves, all that has become possible because such a shape did not come about. Perhaps you can feel that if it had really happened that human beings became like one another externally, as should have been the case in line with the original divine-spiritual forces without the luciferic and ahrimanic influence, the feeling would also have developed that one had to love one's neighbour like oneself; it would not have been possible to do anything else. Any other feeling would have been nonsensical, a nonsensical feeling, a nonsensical sentiment. But that element which was not allowed to come from outside because it would have turned human beings into someone who loved automatically, into people who, although they loved the other like themselves, would not have known which power drove that love—that element which would have come in unfreedom, in fact turned into freedom because the adversary was allowed. The permission of such opposition is therefore part of the original wise plan. We can even say: if we go further back in earth development, the opposition to the regularly progressing divine-spiritual forces is in fact created so that this opposition can then be there and induce freedom.

Here we have reached a point at which we have to appreciate that concepts have to change as soon as we rise from physical considerations to higher considerations. Some of you might be aware that in philosophy we talk about antinomies,[78] that Kant even showed that it is equally possible to prove that 'the world is limited in space' and 'the world is unlimited in space'; 'the world has a beginning in time' and 'the world has no beginning in time'.[79] The one like the other can be rigorously proven. Why? Because logic stops when we reach those things which can no longer be physically grasped. We finally have to learn to recognize that human physical logic stops not only with the things which philosophers have come to know but that it stops altogether when we take a look at forms of existence other than physical ones. We cannot stand there and look at the opposition of Lucifer and Ahriman in the way that we look at the opposition of a good and bad person on earth. The error consists of constantly transferring the earthly aspect into the transcendental one. Most people imagine Lucifer and Ahriman to be evil beings, only much enhanced, infinitely enhanced. But that is not what this is about; we have to understand that certain nuances of physical feelings which we associate with concepts lose their meaning when we get beyond the earthly. So we cannot say that on the one side here we have the good gods, on the other side we have the evil gods Lucifer and Ahriman—and then demand that judgement should be held in the cosmos. In that case a particularly highly qualified cosmic lawyer would have to seat himself on the cosmic bench and lock up Lucifer and Ahriman once and for all; they should actually be locked up so that only the good gods can influence earth. True, it might make sense in earthly life that someone is locked up. In the cosmos that would not make any sense because such terms lose their meaning there. The good gods once created that opposition themselves, albeit in a previous time, so that in this way they could deploy their full strength for the course of development I have outlined. The luciferic and ahrimanic element was incorporated so that freedom could arise, so that human beings could not come to an unfree love through their outer shape, so that human beings would come to understand the name of human in a united way across the earth from the inside out. They first allowed human beings to, let me say, splinter through the opposition so that once their physical bodies had splintered they could return to unity in the spirit, in Christ.

And that is also one of the meanings of the Mystery of Golgotha, the conquest of the unity of human beings from inside out. People are becoming more and more different in respect of their outside and that will cause not unity but difference across the earth. That will cause human beings to have to use all the greater strength from inside to achieve unity. There will always be setbacks with regard to the unity of human beings across the whole earth. We see such setbacks occurring. What was actually intended for an earlier epoch is retained in a later one. That which was destined to cause diversity in a specific period stands in parallel. Human beings form various groups, and while they conquer their unity across the earth through the Christ name, through the Christ impulse, the variety remains as a throwback and will always remain in that human beings will only gradually be able to conquer their unity for themselves and in the meantime the individual groups of human beings will fight one another to the death with regard to all outer life. Throwbacks exist from earlier times which basically run counter to the Christ impulse and not with the Christ impulse.

We nevertheless come to understand a very profound meaning of the Christ impulse. We can say from true knowledge: Christ is the saviour of humanity that stops it from splintering into groups. That this cannot yet be fully recognized by all of humanity is due to the old things having been preserved in parallel. When we see today how little one of the nerve centres, the communality of life in the Christ impulse, is understood by humanity,* then this is connected with the fact that such an understanding has to come from the innermost nature of the human being. We have to be clear about the way that in the almost two thousand years that the Christ impulse has worked in the earth's aura this Christ impulse has worked without being understood. Because it can only be fully understood, as we have often emphasized, through what spiritual science opens up for us. Only when a number of people increasingly understand, think and feel what has entered human earth development in this fourth post-Atlantean epoch will an understanding of that grow. We cannot yet demand it in full from present humanity. Because consider how few people today are inclined to recognize that this fourth post-Atlantean epoch, the Graeco-Latin period, has such a fundamental, such a great significance in the whole of human development. Consider how few people today are inclined to recognize such a post-Atlantean period at all and to put the Graeco-Latin element at its centre. That requires one to have assimilated the ideas of spiritual science. Otherwise it is impossible to understand; in other words, we cannot understand what is happening in respect of the development of humanity if these concepts have not been assimilated.

Then it is necessary to understand the full meaning of the spirits of form, how these spirits of form wanted to develop a homogenous human race which they however wanted to develop in seven consecutive stages. And how this homogenous human race was splintered through Lucifer-Ahriman and how the Christ impulse enlivened from the inside that power which despite all outward differences wants to spread the homogenous human name meaningfully across the whole earth until the end of the earth period.

Understanding how Christ stands in between Lucifer and Ahriman, what His meaning is with regard to Lucifer and Ahriman—that is the

---

* Editor's note: This should probably read: 'When we see today how little one of the nerve centres [of the Christ impulse], the communality of life in the Christ impulse, is understood by humanity...'

main task of the immediate future. That is why what we call Lucifer and Ahriman will have to keep recurring in human consideration and the Christ impulse as battling them, as that which saves the earth from the one-sided luciferic-ahrimanic impulse. That will have to be represented in this form with increasing frequency.

That is why the representative human being is being placed in the most prominent location in our Dornach building, his disposition and how he is to be newly created from inside out through Christ, and the luciferic-ahrimanic aspect surrounding him. That will be the importance specifically of this statue[80] at the centre of our building in Dornach. When we look at this central figure, we can say: yes, that is what the good gods wanted. It was initially splintered, Lucifer and Ahriman appear, but the Christ impulse appears in victory restoring from the inside out, from the inside of human beings outwards, what was originally predisposed from the outside, thus returning their freedom.

That which is to be achieved in terms of an understanding of human development will be set before humanity through our building and what it contains. What is most necessary for humanity in the immediate future—that is the purpose of this building so that we can hear and see from human development what is most necessary in the immediate future and that this is placed there.

It is true that many objections can be made. Such objections have already been made. When we look at the pictures, the works of sculpture in our building, several people have said: a real work of art is only one which everyone can understand directly when they look at it, which does not first require an explanation. When people go in there they first have to have things theoretically explained to them. That is what people normally say. If people would only think just a little bit! Imagine for a minute a person who is completely Turkish and does not understand anything other than what it says in the Koran, who has never heard anything about Christ other than that he has to fight Christianity, imagine such a real Turk. I don't even want to say a Chinese, but a Turk and take him to see the *Sistine Madonna* and simply present it without any explanation, imagine that! Of course someone can only understand a work of art who lives in the whole spiritual stream out of which the art work has been created. Thus our ideal form with Ahriman and Lucifer will only be understood by those who are within this stream. But that is something which the art works of all periods have in common, that they are only comprehensible for those who are within that spiritual stream. They can only be true works of art within that spiritual stream but the spiritual direction has to be within them. Just as someone who understands the *Sistine Madonna* or, let us say, the *Transfiguration of Christ* by Raphael has to know something about the spiritual stream from which these pictures have arisen, in the same way the person who has looked at something in our building of course has to have in their soul, their heart that which belongs to our spiritual stream. But once that is in the soul, the work of art has to speak for itself, then no one needs to write anything further on it in explanation, a name or something like that.

So a person may look at one of our glass windows[81] and see a coffin at the bottom with a dead person in it and further up see next to a winding path, something he recognizes as a winding path, an old man, for example, a youth, a virgin and a child. If he has assimilated our spiritual stream then he will see that this is the review. Once we have passed through the portal of death we see our earth life in review. We have to know that of course. But then the picture will work through what it contains just like the *Sistine Madonna* works on the person who knows the story of Christ through what is contained in the picture but it will not work on the Turk. Equally what appears in our building cannot work on those who have not assimilated this spiritual stream. We have to look at these things in the right way.

That is what I wanted to make clear, that Christ is the spirit from the cosmos in the course of earth development who brought in a spiritual way what had to be predisposed in the outer shape but which could not be completed in this outer formal way because otherwise human beings would have become robots of love and human equality. It is a basic law on the physical plane that everything has to work through opposites, through polarities. It was not possible, as childlike human wisdom might say, for the divine to send down Christ right at the start of earth development because then this contrast of outer splintering and inner collection would never have arisen. But humanity has to live under this contrast, this polarity. Then we approach Christ with the right feelings so that He can increasingly become the being who fills the innermost recesses of our own I if we recognize Him as the saviour of humanity on earth from dispersion. Everywhere where we are really able to comprehend this unification of humanity across the earth through Christ there is Christianity. It will matter little in the future whether that which the Christ is will still be called Christ, but much will depend on seeking Christ as the unifier of the whole of humanity on a spiritual path and that we come to terms with the thought that the outer multiplicity will keep growing in the world.

But we will also have to come to terms with the fact that many setbacks against such a spiritual grasp of the Christ impulse will still come. That which happened in parallel instead of consecutively will still unfold its forces on earth for a very long time, will fight against a spiritual grasp of human equality across the earth. That will still produce many, many terrible storms and the purpose of most of these storms is to maintain the luciferic-ahrimanic battle against the Christ impulse. And it will be one of the greatest, most beautiful, most important achievements if in our time already we can be at least a small group of people who have an understanding of this unification idea for all humanity, an understanding that luciferic-ahrimanic residues on earth seek to achieve particular things in individual groups of people to the exclusion of other groups. It is really difficult to say anything final about these things today already. A last word spoken about these things would tend to have a shock effect, human hearts being what they are, and would provoke resistance, maybe even hate and abuse rather than working in the spirit of the Christ impulse. But as much as can be said about this principle in the Christ impulse, that humanity will be saved from physical dispersion through spiritual unification, that must be said because that has to take effect to an ever greater degree within the development of humanity. We must be able to face the multiplication of human nature with calmness and courage because we know we can carry a word into all the human differences which is not just a word of speech but a word of strength. Groups which fight one another may arise on earth, we may belong to one or another of these groups, but we know we can carry something into each of these groups which can say, 'Not I, but Christ in me,'[82] and that which is 'Christ in me' that does not lead to groups forming, that enables the glory of the name of humanity to spread in reality across the whole earth.

That is one of the practical sides, one of the moral-ethical sides of our spiritual-scientific endeavours, that the following can come to life through the understanding of our spiritual science: no matter into which of the fighting groups of human beings we carry our I, we carry the strength into these fighting groups of human beings which arises from the words 'Not I, but Christ in me.' In that way we introduce something which belongs to the whole of humanity, not one single group, and that is the thing which alone can lead to the true spiritual understanding of Christianity.

Great spiritual-cosmic paths always come to expression in that ultimately they are framed in simple words. Let us see, then, in what simple words basically the sum total of almost two thousand years of Christianity as it has penetrated the world can be spoken. But these simple words are only achieved on the basis of broad developments. They were not there immediately, these simple words in which Christianity can be framed, they first had to be achieved. Well, we can be very clear about one thing: we belong to those who are working on the task that in the future very, very simple words will have to be found which summarize in an incredibly primitive way the truths which we have to develop and disseminate today. But without this development what is simple would never be able to arrive. We can be certain of one thing: even if we are not yet in a position today to be able to form the words in some language which summarize our spiritual-scientific endeavours on, let us say, a quarter of a page, so that they can illuminate all human spiritual striving, as can really happen in Christianity, in Christianity as it arose two thousand years ago, there will nevertheless be something in these simple formulations of what I tried to indicate to you today—something that might turn our spiritual gaze towards the development of humanity, towards the importance of the Graeco-Latin period, towards the occurrence of the Mystery of Golgotha in this period, towards the opposition, the polarity of Christ and Lucifer-Ahriman.

That which can be recognized in all of these things will be compressed into a few words which will then act on future humanity in the same way as for example when we say today, 'Thou shalt love the Lord thy God with all thy heart, and with all thy soul, and with all thy strength, and with all thy mind; and thy neighbour as thyself.'[83] Just as something is contained in these words which had to be achieved in a long development, in the same way these things will be summarized later in simple words. Then they will be obvious to people.

But our spiritual work is necessary to that end because the simple things in the spiritual development of humanity only arise if people have decided to familiarize themselves with the details over a longer period of time. That is what you are called upon to do, to be involved in this development which will then lead to something appearing before humanity in simple, lucid clarity which cannot yet be expressed today because we do not yet have the words in the languages for it—but which has to be what our spiritual science is moving towards. If you feel part of such a spiritual stream and are happy to be in such a spiritual stream because you recognize it as being a necessity within the development of humanity, then you are in this spiritual movement with the right attitude; you are part of this spiritual movement in such a way that you look at the greatest thing towards which this spiritual movement is moving in the right way out of an ever better under-standing of the opposition between Christ and Lucifer-Ahriman and the necessity of this opposition.

That is what I wanted to set before your souls today. After all, it is connected with the question as to the meaning of the whole of our earth development. It is the case, after all, that when spirits from other planets look down at the earth and ask, 'What is the meaning of earth development?' they will recognize the meaning if they learn something about the Mystery of Golgotha. Because everything that happens in the course of earth development only acquires its meaning through the Mystery of Golgotha. That rays out into cosmic space and gives meaning, central meaning to everything else that rays out from the earth.

LECTURE 12

DORNACH, 15 JANUARY 1916

Tomorrow I would like to return to the spirituality of the early periods of Christianity and sketch out in a few strokes its continuing effect. On that basis we will then be able to deepen what arose in the public lectures of the last few days.[84] Today I want to give a kind of philosophical introduction to that to familiarize you with some of the historical aspects, because it is a good thing if within the movement of spiritual science we know something about how others in the world are striving to approach the riddles of the world, what the thoughts and feelings are in respect of these riddles of the world.

When we look at the textbooks about the history of philosophy up to the present day, we basically only ever find certain philosophical streams discussed, philosophical streams which are the popular ones among most current philosophers. But we would be completely wrong if we considered what we normally find to be the only philosophical research in the present time. So for example most of you will know that in the course of the nineteenth century, particularly in the second half of the nineteenth century and very particularly towards the end of the nineteenth century up to our day, there was an active philosophical life within the Catholic Church, that within the Catholic Church scholarly priests fostered, and many still foster, a very specific philosophical direction diverging from the rest of philosophy in the world. Hence there is a wealth of literature in this field, or at least as much of a literature as there is for other directions of philosophical activity. And this literature is termed the literature of neo-Scholasticism.

It was due to a peculiar circumstance that the school which flowered in the high Middle Ages, which basically started with Scotus Eriugena and then lived via Thomas Aquinas into the time of Duns Scotus,[85] reappeared in the nineteenth century, even if out of a very specific desire for knowledge tinged with faith. We see this direction of neo-Scholasticism appear in Catholic circles particularly in the second third of the nineteenth century. Book upon book is written in all central and western European languages in an effort to understand what lived in Scholasticism. And when we try and investigate the inner reason why Scholasticism was revived we actually have to take a wider look. And that is what we will discuss a little today.

I repeatedly emphasized in the lectures I gave in recent days that the path to spiritual-scientific knowledge consists of a very special treatment of the thinking, the concepts, of logic, that people under the influence of the exercises which lead to the development of such thinking manage to think no longer with their physical body but with their etheric body. As a result they do not think just with the dead logic of concepts but live where the thinking is activated, that is, they live in the movement of their etheric body, as we call it technically. It is an entry into the life of the etheric body in which logic itself comes to life, in which—as I described it in popular terms—the statue which we can use as an image for the logic at work in ordinary life[86] comes to life, in which human beings themselves come to life in their etheric body—that is, concepts are no longer dead concepts but those living concepts arise of which I have said for years that the concept takes on life as if we were in something that is alive with our soul. This living entity which is the truth of concepts and ideas has basically been lost to humanity in external philosophy for many centuries. I tried to point to this fact in the first chapter of my *Riddles of Philosophy* which I added to the new edition.

Even towards the end of the philosophical periods of Greek culture, humanity actually no longer knew anything about the possible aliveness of concepts and ideas in philosophical terms. Bear that in mind. To begin with, the Greeks—you can read about this in my *Riddles of Philosophy*—had concepts and ideas in the way that people today have sense impressions, a colour, a tone or a smell. The great Plato, up to Aristotle, and even more so the more ancient philosophers did not believe that they had developed the concept, the thought inwardly but that they came to them from things in the same way that we have red or blue, that is the sensory images, coming in.

Then the time came—I have described how this progresses in cycles—in which there was no longer an inner feeling that it was the things which gave one the concept but people only felt that the concept arose in the soul. And then people did not know what they should do with the concept, the inner idea of which the Greeks still believed they came from things. That is how those Scholastic problems arose, those Scholastic riddles: what does the concept mean in relation to things, in the way that a colour belongs to a thing? The Greeks could not ask such a question because in their consciousness it was the things which gave them the concepts, so the concepts belonged to the things, like a colour belongs to a thing. That ceased as the Middle Ages arrived. There people had to ask: what is the relationship between something that arises in our spirit and the thing? And also: the things out there are multiple, manifold and individual, but concepts are general, a unity. We go through the world and see many horses; from these many horses we form the uniform concept of horse. Every horse accords with the concept of horse.

Today many people, who know even less what to do with the concept than the medieval philosophers did, who saw it as an acute problem, say: well, it is simply that the concept is not in the things themselves.

I have repeatedly referred to a comparison which my friend, the late Vincenz Knauer,[87] who was very knowledgeable about medieval philosophy, often used for the people who say: it is only the material part of the animal which is out there, the concept is produced in the soul. Good old Knauer would always say: people say that the lamb is out there but what is really there is only matter, the wolf is out there but what is really there is only matter; it is the soul which produces the concept of lamb and the concept of wolf. And good old Knauer would add: if it were really just matter and the wolf were locked up and were given nothing but lambs to eat, then finally, once it had replaced its previous matter, it would only be lamb because it only has the matter of lambs within it—but astonishingly it remains a wolf so something else has to be there apart from matter.

A significant problem, a significant riddle arose for medieval Scholasticism at this point. The Scholastics said to themselves: the concepts are the universals because they comprise many individual things. And they could not say, as people today like to say, that these universals were something that had only arisen in the human spirit, had nothing to do with things. These medieval philosophers distinguished between three types of universals. The first, they said, was the universals *ante rem*, before the thing, before what we see out there. So the universal 'horse' is thought before all possible sensory horses, as a divine thought. That is what medieval Scholasticism said.

Then there is the universal *in re*, in the thing in the sense of being the essence of things, the part which matters. The universal 'wolf' is what matters and the universal 'lamb' is what matters. They are what stops the wolf turning into a lamb if it eats lots of lambs.

And then there is a third form of universal: that is *post rem*, after the thing, as it is in our spirit when we look at the world and have detached it from the thing. The medieval Scholastics placed great value on these distinctions. This protected them from the kind of scepticism, the kind of quibbling according to which we cannot get to the essence of things because such scepticism considers the concepts and ideas which people obtain in the soul through things to be merely fabrications of the soul and does not imagine them to be anything which could be of relevance to the things themselves.

A development of this scepticism can then be found in the one form in Hume[88] and in the other form in Kant. There concept and idea have totally turned into something which the human spirit creates in the form of ideas. Human beings can no longer get to the things through concepts and ideas.

A very particular difficulty now arose, and will always arise, for the theologians who also wanted to be philosophers, who wanted to penetrate theology with philosophy—because theologians are obliged not just to see the things in the world but to think of them in a certain relationship with the divine archetype. And they get into difficulties if they cannot themselves place the concepts and ideas which they obtain from the things—and which form the content of the only knowledge of the spirit unless we progress to spiritual science—into some relationship with God, that is, conceive of them as universals *ante rem*, as universal concepts before the thing.

Now there is something very important connected with what I have said. There will always be people who cannot see anything in the concept which is connected in some way with things, who simply see matter in the things out there; and on the other hand there are those who see something real in the concepts which is connected with the things themselves, which is in things, and which the human spirit extracts from things again, which the human spirit turns from universals *in re* to universals *post rem*.

Those who accept that concepts have a reality outside the human spirit were called realists in the Middle Ages and beyond, and particularly in Catholic philosophy. And the view that the concepts and ideas have a real meaning in the world is called realism. The other view, which assumes that concepts and ideas are only fabricated in the human spirit, as words as it were, is called nominalism and its representatives are called nominalists.

You can easily see that the nominalists can actually only perceive what is real in its manifoldness, its diversity. Only the realists can see something real in the all-encompassing, the universal. And that is where we reach the point where a particular difficulty arose for the theologians who were also philosophers. These Catholic theologians had to defend the dogma of the Trinity, of Father, Son and Spirit, the three persons in the Divinity. In accordance with the development of church theology, they could only say: the three persons are individual, self-enclosed beings, but at the same time they must be a unity. If they were nominalists, the Divinity would always be separated into three persons. Only the realists were still able to conceive of the three persons under one universal. But in order to do so, the universal concept had to have a reality; that required a realist. That is why the realists were better able to cope with the Trinity than the nominalists, who were in great difficulties and who finally, when Scholasticism had already degenerated into scepticism, hid behind saying: we cannot understand how three persons are supposed to be one Divinity, but that is precisely why we have to believe it, have to do without knowledge; something like that can only be the subject of revelation. Human reason can only lead to nominalism; it cannot lead to any kind of realism. And this is basically the teaching of Hume and Kant which via the detour of phenomenalism has become pure nominalism.

The central dogma of the Trinity, the three divine persons, was therefore dependent in realism or nominalism on the one or other view of the nature of universals. You will therefore understand that there was a reaction in Catholic circles when Kant's philosophy increasingly became the philosophy of Protestant circles in Europe. And this reaction consisted of saying that the old Scholasticism would have to be re-examined in detail to fathom precisely what the Scholastics had meant. In short, the attempt was made—because there was no new way to obtain an understanding of the spiritual world—to reconstruct Scholasticism. And a wealth of literature was created which solely set itself the task of making Scholasticism accessible to people again.

Of course this literature only lived among the Catholic scholarly theologians, but among them it was widespread. And for those who are interested in everything which happens in the intellectual culture of humanity, it is certainly not without benefit to look a little into this comprehensive literature which made its appearance. It is useful occasionally to take a look into this neo-Scholastic literature, if only because one can get an idea how black and white can live alongside one another in the world—please, no pun intended! The whole way of thinking, the whole way of looking at the world is different in the advancing stream of philosophy which picks up from Kant, Fichte, Hegel or previously Descartes, Malebranche, Hume, to Mill and Spencer.[89] That is quite different research into ideas; that is a quite different way of thinking about the world than comes to expression for example in Gratry[90] and the numerous neo-Scholastics who were writing everywhere, in France, in Spain, in Italy, in Belgium, in England, in Germany, for there was a wealth of Scholastic literature in all countries. And all the orders of the Catholic priesthood participated in the discussion. The study of Scholasticism became particularly active starting in 1879 because that is when the *Aeterni patris* encyclical of Pope Leo XIII appeared. This encyclical made the study of Thomas Aquinas virtually a duty for Catholic theologians. Since that time a wealth of literature based on Thomism has arisen and the philosophy of Thomas Aquinas was studied and interpreted in detail. But the whole movement had already started earlier so that we can fill libraries today with the many brilliant things that have been written in this renewal of Thomism.

You can, for example, inform yourself in a book such as *The Origin of the Human Reason* or from many a French book[91] or, if you prefer, from numerous works of the Italian Jesuits and Dominicans about the brilliance with which philosophy was once again pursued. A lot of brilliance was used in all countries in the study of Scholasticism—a brilliance about which the people, including those who are studying philosophy today, have no idea because they do not have the necessary interest to turn their attention to all aspects of human endeavour. The need had arisen from this side to respond to Kantianism which had pulled the rug from under the feet of Catholic theology in that it had turned into pure nominalism, particularly in the second half of the nineteenth century.

I am speaking now in purely historical terms, not to place a value on anything, not even to refute or agree with anything, purely historically. And here we can see that people in this area have basically endeavoured to the present day to discover what the concept, the thinking is about. People today cannot do anything at all with concepts in the old sense. They have to be given some life if people want to make some progress; attempts will have to be made for a long time to obtain a theoretical understanding with a mere pictorial concept of the importance of thinking with regard to the Divinity.[*]

Others tried in other ways. A very important movement arose, for example, which is even very close to Catholicism and has been promoted by Catholic priests but which did not find the approval of the Catholic authorities to the same degree as Scholasticism. It had been made a duty of Catholic theologians in the *Aeterni patris* encyclical to renew the philosophy of Thomas Aquinas, to resurrect it. Another direction which was not viewed with such benevolence by the Catholic authorities was the direction of Rosmini-Serbati[92] and Gioberti.[93] Rosmini in particular, who was born in Rovereto near Trento and died in 1855 in nearby

---

[*] Editor's note: There are gaps in the note taken by the stenographer here. The sentence should probably read: '. . . attempts will have to be made for a long time to obtain a theoretical understanding, [not just] a mere pictorial concept, of the importance of thinking [for a comprehension of] the Divinity.'

Stresa, brought his endeavours to expression particularly in works which were not published until after his death. It is interesting how Rosmini wanted to make progress by investigating the real value of the concept. Rosmini realized that human beings have the concept present in their inner experience. Those who remain pure Nominalists stop there, that they experience the concept internally, and pass over the question where the concept exists in reality. But Rosmini was brilliant enough to realize: even if something reveals itself inwardly in the soul, that does not mean that it only has reality inwardly in the soul. And so he knew, by starting specifically from the concept of being, that the soul, when it experiences concepts, at the same time also experiences the living inner being of things that lives in the concepts. And so Rosmini's philosophy consisted of a search for inner experiences that were experiences of concepts for him, but in doing so he did not fill them with life but merely came to a diversity of concepts. And then he sought to specify how the concept can live simultaneously in the soul and in things. That was expressed with particular clarity in the posthumous work[94] of Rosmini's called *Teosofia*. Others also took this view in Catholicism but Rosmini was one of the most brilliant.

Now a direction such as Rosmini's is somewhat inconvenient for Catholic theology and causes it discomfort because it is difficult for this side to combine the concept of revelation with this theory of the concept. For the concept of revelation basically says that the highest truths must be revealed. They cannot be experienced inwardly in the soul but must be revealed outwardly in the course of human history. Human beings can only approach reality with their concepts up to a certain degree, and beyond this sphere of the concepts there rises the sphere of revelations. That is the standpoint of the Scholastics. That also coincides better with what Catholicism today sees as its nerve centre than the concepts experienced in Rosmini's way, because if we have experienced concepts then it is actually God who lives in us—and Catholic theology basically has a dread of that, when people claim that God lives in human beings. That is also the reason why Pope Leo XIII decreed in the 1880s that Rosmini's theory was heresy[95] and prohibited Catholic theologians from studying and teaching Rosmini's philosophy without permission from their superior authorities. Because that is how they do things among the Catholic theologians. I don't know whether that is absolutely complied with. In any event, the publications of Catholic theologians from all camps carry the seal of the superior episcopal authorities. That means that Catholic theologians are allowed to study such a work. There are certain exceptions for those who are university teachers but things are handled very strictly, at least in theory.

So we can see here, too, an attempt to work one's way through to an understanding of the role of thinking in the world.

I would like to interpolate something of a quite different nature here. Such interpolations are sometimes necessary. Many of our friends believe they are doing something particularly good for our movement when they tell Catholic theologians for example that we are not anti-Christian at all and that we are seeking an honest concept of Christ. And in their credulity our friends go so far as to tell one or another Catholic theologian about the way we characterize Christianity. Because our friends then believe in their—excuse me—naivety that they can convince these theologians that we are good Christians. But as Catholic theologians they can never admit that. My dear friends, they will be much happier with us if we do not seek Christ, if we do not concern ourselves with Christ. Because it is not a matter—we always have to be aware of that—of someone having this or another concept of Christ, but it is a matter of the rule of the Church. And particularly if there was a good or better concept of Christ outside the Church that would be combated to the greatest possible extent. So those of our friends do us the most damage in their credulity who go to Catholic theologians and want to convince them that we are not anti-Christian. Because they will say: it is very bad if a concept of Christ can establish itself outside the Church. We have to judge the things in life in accordance with the circumstances of life and not in accordance with naive opinions. We will be particularly severely attacked if the theologians should discover that we somehow understand something about the inner existence of Christianity which could make a convincing impression on a larger number of people.

So we can see that it has become necessary to obtain a deeper understanding of the concept and its relationship with reality. And here we do have to say: among the most brilliant things that have happened in this direction at all in modern times is what is contained in the writings of Rosmini. He worked through it in all fields and it can be of particular value if we study Rosmini's concepts of beauty, the aesthetic concepts.[96] Rosmini's aesthetics is something particularly valuable which we should study to see how a modern intellect works his way up until he stands before the gates of spiritual science but is unable to enter. That can be studied exceptionally well in Rosmini.

Thus we will find that there really are spiritual streams that want to work towards an understanding of the concept but do not get as far as to see that we now live in the time in which the concept must be filled with life if we want to enter reality.

So the concept has a certain history behind it. I discuss this history in part in my book *Riddles of Philosophy* in the chapter I mentioned. But I still want to refer to something else here. We can say that the concept continues to develop. There was a time in which the concept was perceived, like colour and tone are perceived. This was the case with the Greeks. Plato is the last one to speak of concepts in such a real way that we can see that there is still some understanding in him of such an apprehension of the concept. It has already changed in Aristotle. Then we come to the Middle Ages where the concept is seen in purely rational terms and where people investigate its behaviour as a universal and where the structure of *ante rem, in re, post rem* is found as a bridge. Then the time comes in which the concept is conceived of in purely nominalist terms. That carries on into our time. But there is a reaction, the ancillary movements that seek the concept as an inner experience, like Rosmini does. From this point [see diagram: Rosmini] we could come to the life or an experience of concepts. The concept would be chained to the physical body, as it were, in this time [see diagram: before Plato to the Middle Ages] and now be transferred to the etheric body. The concept would lead to a clairvoyant experience of the concept. But here we would have to say that the concept as perceived at a very early stage, as well as the concept of the nominalists and realists, has developed from an atavistic clairvoyance. And now the way in which the concept is experienced has to be a conscious way whereas in earlier times it was more subconscious. And indeed, if you go from Plato, from the Greek philosophers who had the concept as something they perceived, back to the remains of Zoroastrianism, then you have this atavistically understood—or perhaps we should not say 'atavistic' because this expression has only obtained validity today—this dreamlike clairvoyant experience of the concept.

	Physical body			Etheric body
Concepts experienced in a dreamlike clairvoyant way	Concept perceived	Concept rational	Concept nominal	Experience of the concept
Persians	before Plato	Middle Ages	Rosmini ⟶	

Thus the philosophies of Asia Minor presented the concept as something which they experienced pictorially. Persian philosophy sees a being in the 'horse in general' which takes specific, differentiated form in the individual horse, something still living. The Persians called that *feruer*. That becomes abstract and turns into the Platonic idea. The *feruer* of the Persians become the Platonic idea.[97]

Abstraction increasingly gains ground because the thinking is only experienced in the physical body. We have to return to a conscious experience of the concept. You can see a wonderful cycle occurring in this field from the ancient clairvoyance of the concept through what the concept had to become in the age of physical experience: the only rational concept, the only conceived concept, the only logical concept.

I have often emphasized that logic first arose through Aristotle when the concept was no longer understood as anything but a concept. Previously, no logic was needed for the concept as an experience. And now logic comes to life, the statue of logic passes over to life.

This one example of the concept illustrates once again what can otherwise be seen in general on a large scale. Thus we also have to study the whole course of human development in detail because then we will gain an ever better understanding of the meaning which underlies the spiritual movement to which we belong. And we will become ever more objective through these things, something that is also necessary. Where would we be if the objective side were not understood and our dear friends were dragged ever more into what is personal. Working objectively—that must be our task and the purely personal has to recede ever more into the background.

LECTURE 13

WE attempted yesterday to put ourselves in mind of the way that the formation of concepts and ideas develops, how concepts about the world and ideas come into being, and we saw that a certain development can be observed here too: that from a certain clairvoyant type of experience of concepts something developed which was the Platonic ideas, and that gradually that abstract way of thinking developed which has existed into our day; but also that the times are pressing for the introduction of the vitality of life into concepts in a conscious way once again in order to be able to enter living spirituality at all, so that we achieve once again in a conscious way what was left behind as the dreamlike clairvoyance of concepts.

Now it is a matter of looking more precisely at the way in which in quite a different way the highest concerns of cosmic existence could be grasped in a time in which there was still something of an echo of the old, clairvoyantly perceived concepts and how the highest concerns of humanity had to be approached in quite a different way once conceptual thinking had already become intellectually and rationally abstract. Because the questions we discussed yesterday, which were such an important concern for medieval Scholasticism, these questions could naturally only develop in an age in which there was uncertainty about the relationship between the world of concepts and the true world of reality. In a time which preceded, say, Greek philosophy something like the teaching of the universals *in re, post rem, ante rem*, which we discussed, would not have been thought up because the livingly owned concept led into reality. People knew that it placed them in reality and it was not possible to raise the questions we discussed yesterday. They simply did not arise as riddles that need to be solved.

Now there was certainly something of an echo of the ancient clairvoyant world of concepts existing in the first period of Christian development and we can say: when the Mystery of Golgotha occurred during the development of European humanity and humanity in Asia Minor, many people were still capable of grasping in echoes of clairvoyantly conceived concepts the things which actually can only be understood spiritually and which relate to the Mystery of Golgotha. That is the only way we can understand that everything which developed in the first Christian centuries as concepts to understand the Mystery of Golgotha had to become incomprehensible for later periods. When the older Christian teachers still used the echoes of old clairvoyant concepts to understand the Mystery of Golgotha, the actual core of these clairvoyant concepts remained incomprehensible for later centuries and basically what we call gnosis is nothing other than the echo of old clairvoyant concepts. People sought to understand the Mystery of Golgotha with old clairvoyant concepts and the clairvoyant concepts were later no longer understood, only abstract concepts. That is why what gnosis actually wanted was misunderstood. Now we would see the matter in a very one-sided way if we were simply to say: there was gnosis, it used old clairvoyant concepts which still extended into the first, second and third centuries after the Mystery of Golgotha, and then there came these ignorant people who were not capable of understanding the Gnostics. It would be very one-sided to think like that. Working with clairvoyant concepts in a certain perfect sense belongs to a much older time than the time in which the Mystery of Golgotha falls, a much older time. And these clairvoyantly understood concepts were already very much luciferically infested. In other words, the old understanding using clairvoyant concepts was luciferically penetrated and this luciferic penetration of the old clairvoyant system of concepts—that is gnosis. As a result there had to be a kind of reaction against gnosis because gnosis was the dying old clairvoyant world of concepts, the old clairvoyant world of concepts infected by Lucifer. We have to understand that.

Now I want to start with a man who in the first centuries of Christianity attempted to stop the Gnostic stream which had turned luciferic and who wanted to understand the Mystery of Golgotha from this perspective. That is Tertullian.[98] He came from North Africa and was knowledgeable in the affairs of heathen wisdom. At about the end of the second century after the Mystery of Golgotha, he converted to Christianity and became one of the most erudite theologians of his time. Now it is particularly interesting to examine him a little because he still had something of an inner understanding of the ancient clairvoyant world of concepts as a result of his study of ancient heathen wisdom, and because, on the other hand, he completely had the Christian impulse within him—the story of his conversion shows that—and in a certain way wanted to combine both things in such a way that Christianity could fully persist as a result. To that end he had to drive back what he felt to be luciferically tinged gnosis in Basilides,[99] Marcion[100] and others. So certain questions arose in him. These questions arose in Tertullian for a very specific reason. You see, in starting spiritual science today, we talk very frequently about the structure of human nature, about the way in which human beings first obtained their dense physical body which can be seen with the eyes and grasped with the hands—how we then have the etheric body, an astral body, a sentient soul and so on. In other words, we try above all to recognize the constitution of human nature. But if you look into the historical development of spiritual life in the centuries since the Mystery of Golgotha, you will not find anywhere to the present day that the constitution of the human being is observed in such a way as we do. That was lost, and had already been lost, when the Mystery of Golgotha occurred. Those who came into contact with the impulse of the Mystery of Golgotha no longer had any knowledge of this structure of human beings. But that caused a particular difficulty for them. In order to identify this difficulty, my dear friends, try connecting with your own heart, your own soul in order to ask yourself something. You know we have tried in a variety of ways to make clear for ourselves the way in which Christ intervened in the development of the earth through Jesus. But try seeing how you would have coped with understanding this whole matter, how Christ penetrated the component elements of Jesus, if you knew nothing about the whole constitution, the nature of the human being. How Christ penetrates these bodies as a kind of cosmic I becomes comprehensible only because you know something about these bodies. Anyone seeking in future to obtain an understanding of Christ will require knowledge of the way the human being is structured as an essential preparation.

In ancient times, when there were still dreamlike clairvoyant concepts, people knew something about this structure of the human being; and something had passed to the Gnostics, even if in distorted form. That is why the Gnostics tried to understand the entry of Christ into Jesus of Nazareth with the last remnants of the concepts about the human constitution. But the others, to whom Christianity was to come and who were taught by their Church teachers, knew nothing about this structure of the human being and their Church teachers did not either. And thus the great, comprehensive question arose: how is it actually as regards the way that the nature of Christ and the nature of Jesus come together? How is it possible that Christ as a divine being can occupy Jesus as a human being? And it was this question which occupied people like Tertullian. Because they did not have the prerequisites for understanding the matter, the problem arose for them once more posthumously, as it were—and through Jesus Christ they were prompted to ask: how are the spiritual and physical and the soul actually combined? They did not know how they are combined in human beings as such but they had to find out in some way how they were combined in Jesus Christ. Now because the gnosis of the time had a luciferic tinge, they of course no longer found the right answer there either. If you recall certain lectures which I have given here recently,[101] you will find that I said that people on the one hand get to materialism and on the other hand to a one-sided spiritualism. The one-sided materialism has an ahrimanic, the one-sided spiritualism a luciferic tinge. The materialists do not get to the spirit and the luciferic believers in the spirit do not get to matter.

That is what the situation was with the Gnostics: they did not get as far as physical existence, as material existence. And if we now look at a person like Marcion, we can see he had a more or less clear concept of Christ, but he could not understand at all how this Christ was contained in Jesus. Hence the whole process became etherized for him. He got as far as understanding Christ as spirit, as an etheric being which had assumed a body for appearances. But he could not understand the proper way in which Christ was in Jesus. Marcion finally reached the point where he said—he in particular reached the point where he said—that Christ descended to earth but everything which Jesus experienced was only experienced for appearances; Christ was not actually involved but He was only there like an etheric being which, however, remained quite separate. That is why Tertullian had to turn against Marcion and against others who thought similarly, Basilides, for example. And the great riddle arose in him: how was the divine nature of Christ combined with the human nature of Jesus? What actually was the God-man? What was the Son of God? What was Son of Man? He attempted above all to bring clarity into these concepts. And so he began by developing a concept which was very important and continues to be important today, which has to be understood if we want to gain an insight into the many opportunities there are for people to err.

Tertullian developed a certain way of thinking. He had to get out of the old clairvoyance, he had to achieve clarity about the concepts and their relationship with realities, also with higher, spiritual realities. I will interpolate an episode here from which you will see not what Tertullian became conscious of but what was at work in his thinking. I want to interpolate a purely intellectual episode but which I ask you to consider thoroughly. I will do the following. I will write the number

1	and then double it	2
2		4
3		6
4		8
5		10
6		12
7		14
8		16
9		18
10		20

And now imagine that I never stop, I continue writing to infinity. How many such numbers would I have then written? An infinite number, don't you think? But how many have I written here? Did I write a number on the right for each number on the left? Undoubtedly, I wrote as many figures on the right as I wrote on the left and if I continued to infinity there would always be a number on the right for a number on the left. But now imagine that each number on the right here is also on the left there. But that means that I have as many numbers on the right there as I have on the left, but at the same time I only have half as many numbers on the right as I have on the left. Because it is quite obvious that a number must always lie between two numbers which are doubled, I have to have only half as many numbers on the right as on the left. There is always one left out, that is clear, so I can only have half as many on the right as on the left. That is not difficult to understand. But remember that there is always one missing, that 1, 3, 5, 7 and so on are missing, in other words, half the numbers are missing on the right. So I only have half has many on the right as on the left. Yet I have exactly as many numbers as on the left. That means that as soon as I get to infinity, half is equal to the whole. That is quite clear: as soon as I get to infinity, half is equal to the whole—there is no way round that. As soon as we move with our concepts from the finite to infinity, it emerges by itself that half is equal to the whole. You can write all the numbers here on the left and their square on the right:

$$
\begin{array}{ccc}
1 & — & 1 \\
2 & & 4 \\
3 & & 9 \\
4 & & 16 \\
5 & & 25 \\
\end{array}
$$

Of course there is a square for each number but as true as it is that many numbers are missing here, only some of them can be here. Remember, it is only ever the squares.

The same thing can also be illustrated in another way. I will draw two parallel lines here—I have demonstrated this many times before. How

big is the space between these two parallel lines? Infinitely large, of course. That is shown in mathematics, as you know, with the symbol: ∞. But if I now draw a vertical line and draw another parallel line at the same distance, then the present space is precisely twice as large as the previous one, but still infinite. In other words, the new infinity = twice the previous infinity. You can see that illustrated here:

You can see here with the simplest methods of thought that the thinking only applies in the finite. It is without foundation or results as soon as it leaves the finite. It cannot do anything with its inherent laws once it has moved from the finite to the infinite. But you must not imagine infinity just as very large or very small, but you also have to think of the infinite within the world of qualities.

This is a triangle, this is a square, this a pentagon [see drawings], I could continue and make a hexagon, a heptagon, an octagon and so on and the further I go the more similar it becomes to a circle. If I then draw a circle, how many corners does that have? It has an infinite number of corners. But when I draw a circle which is twice the size— that too has an infinite number of corners, but twice as many corners! So the concept of infinity is also contained within boundaries so that our thinking can come to grief through infinity, through intensive infinity also where it encounters boundaries. In other words, the thinking

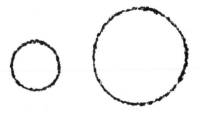

always has to be aware that it is helpless and flounders about when it tries to move into infinity out of the finiteness of the sphere which it has initially been given.

We have to draw practical consequences from that. We truly have to draw the practical consequences that we cannot just start thinking without rhyme or reason, that we can come badly unstuck if we just start thinking without rhyme or reason. And among the many negative things which can be ascribed to Kant there is the positive one that he thoroughly rapped people over the knuckles in relation to this nonsense: the way they wildly flail about with their thinking. If we flail about wildly with our thinking we can prove that space must have a limit somewhere, that the world is finite; but we can equally prove that it is infinite because the thinking starts floundering about as soon as it leaves a certain sphere. And so Kant compiled the so-called antinomies:[102] how one thing can be proved just as well as its opposite because the thinking is floundering about and only has relative value. Someone can think quite correctly in relation to a point; but if he is not in a position to extend that to something that might be alongside, then he will err if he just launches into thinking or even just observation. We can really see in this field how little people are aware that we cannot just simply flail about with our thinking or our observation and the way we take in some of the things out there.

It might appear that I will now combine something very meta-physical and epistemological with something very mundane. But it is precisely the same riddle; it is just a pity that we do not have the time to discuss epistemologically in what respect it is the same riddle. Some days ago, Mr Bauer[103] drew my attention to something lovely in this context. You know that Pastor R.[104] in his lecture in which he slaughtered our spiritual science pointed out that if someone walked up to our building they would be reminded of old Matthias Claudius[105] by all the incomprehensible things that were erected there for people. What Pastor R. wanted to say was that dear good old Claudius would have stood there and said: the anthroposophists are at work up there and want to know what cannot be known. Human beings simply cannot know it. And so he quotes Matthias Claudius:

> We proud human beings
> Are poor vain sinners
> Who do not know a lot;
> Creating flights of fancy
> Seeking many arts
> In straying further from the goal.

So we are supposed to be hurt by that because old Matthias Claudius has told us that human beings are all poor sinners and should not turn their gaze towards the incomprehensible and impenetrable. Now, good old Matthias Claudius then still goes on to say by implication that Pastor R. is such a clever man who knows that human beings are all sinners and do not know anything about what cannot be visible to the outer eye. Mr Bauer, then, who did not stop at simply listening to these words from Pastor R., opened Matthias Claudius and read the 'Evening Song' which goes like this:

> The moon it has arisen,
> The golden stars resplendent
> In heaven bright and clear;
> The forest black is silent
> And from the meadow rises
> The white mist wondrously.
>
> How much the world is silent
> And in the covering twilight
> So homely and so fair!
> A quiet room for resting
> Where all the daytime sorrow
> In sleep you shall forget.

See where the moon is standing?
While half of it is darkened
And yet so round and fair!
That is like many matters
Which cause us confident laughter
Because we do not see.

We proud human beings
Are poor vain sinners
Who do not know a lot;
Creating flights of fancy
And seeking arts a plenty
While straying further from our goal.

It looks like it is Pastor R. who is straying further from the goal! He seems to have forgotten that the fourth verse is intimately connected with the third one!

As you can see, the important thing is that we should try to be somewhat more rounded. Of course one can draw the exact opposite conclusion from the fourth verse when it relates to Pastor R.—when Pastor R. identifies himself with all modest human beings—than one would draw if the third verses were added. This last trivial example is not totally without connection to the more metaphysical and theoretical aspect which I discussed. It is necessary for human beings to be clear that when they look at something like that and start flailing about with our thinking it may happen that the precise opposite sets in from what is really true. And that is what we encounter in particular measure when the transition is to be made from the finite to the infinite or from the material to the spiritual or something similar.

Well, a person like Marcion says out of his luciferically infected gnosis: the process of becoming human and so on which takes place here on earth cannot be gone through by a god because a god must be subject to other laws which belong to the spiritual world. He did not find the connection between the spiritual and the material, the sensory. Now there was a dispute which has been lost—Marcion can be identified outwardly, physically only through his opponents, for example Tertullian—that the whole outer story of Jesus of Nazareth is not appropriate for the divine world order; the way that God can be on earth is only appearance, is all without meaning. Christ had to be understood purely in spiritual terms. Tertullian says: you are right, Marcion—that is what it says in Tertullian's writings—you are right when you construct your concepts as you do, they are very comprehensible clear concepts, but then you also have to apply them only to what is finite, to things which take place in nature; you must not apply them to the divine—other concepts are needed for the divine. And in that context finite reason might consider absurd what is the rule, the law for the activity of the divine.

So Tertullian faced—I do not want to say consciously but in his feelings and unconsciously—the great riddle how far the thinking can be applied that is appropriate for nature, the natural phenomena. And he pointed out to Marcion: if we only use the thinking that appears plausible for human beings, then we can claim what Marcion says. But with the Mystery of Golgotha something has entered world development to which this thinking cannot be applied, for which other concepts are needed. Hence he coins the phrase:[106] these higher concepts, which relate to the divine, force us to believe what is absurd with regard to the finite. In order to do justice to Tertullian, we must not merely quote his sentence: I believe what is absurd, what cannot be proven. But we have to quote this sentence in its whole context which I wanted to make comprehensible just now. That was the main problem which now occupied Tertullian: how is the divine Christ nature linked with the human Jesus nature? And here he was clear that human concepts are not suitable for grasping what happened in the Mystery of Golgotha. Human concepts always mean that the spiritual which has been understood about Christ cannot be linked with what must be understood as earthly history in relation to Jesus. But as I said, Tertullian lacked the possibility to understand the problem out of the constitution of the human being as we try to understand it once again today. As a result he only managed to begin with to find what I might describe as a surrogate for that concept which we form when we want to understand something in a specific place in our spiritual-scientific knowledge.

Remember a place in our spiritual-scientific knowledge which you can find, for example, in my *Theosophy*. There you will see that we start by talking about the physical body, etheric body, astral body, then sentient soul, intellectual or mind soul, consciousness soul, and finally the individual connections with the Spirit Self. There are various discussions about how the Spirit Self works into the consciousness soul. But that is also precisely the place which we have to consider when we want to look into the sojourn of Christ in the human being Jesus, if we want to understand that. That is the prerequisite, that we know how in humanity in general the Spirit Self enters the consciousness soul; that is the prerequisite for understanding how the Christ nature as a special cosmic Spirit Self entered the consciousness soul of Jesus of Nazareth. Tertullian only found one surrogate for that and we can understand the concept he developed similarly to when we say today: there is no mixing—according to Tertullian—between Christ, corresponding to the Spirit Self, and Jesus, corresponding to the consciousness soul and all the associated lower components of the human being, no mixing but only an association. And humanity will only get to know such an association when the Spirit Self will in future be properly here. At the moment we are living in the age of the consciousness soul. Every human being will have a much looser connection once the Spirit Self will be ordinarily developed in the sixth post-Atlantean epoch. Then people will also understand better in what a different way the Christ nature was tied to the Jesus nature from, say, the consciousness soul to the intellectual soul. The consciousness soul is of course always inwardly mixed with the intellectual soul. But the Spirit Self is united with the consciousness soul but not mixed with it. And Tertullian really did develop this concept. He said: Christ is not mixed with Jesus but united with him. In this way he perceives the one God-man, Jesus Christ, in order to show through Him once more in the age in which the old conceptual clairvoyance no longer existed how the divine and the soul and physical part of human nature were connected with one another. Christ appears before Tertullian rather like the representative of general humanity. He used Christ to study the constitution of the human being in order to understand Jesus Christ. Christ became the focus of all his thinking which could now no longer be applied to human nature. And because Tertullian had clearly realized that Christ is not mixed with Jesus but united with him—he could not say, as we would say, like the Spirit Self with the consciousness soul, but he said not mixed but united—that made it clear to him that he could say: everything with which Christ has united Himself comes out of the spirit of the world; that is the Father principle in the world. The Father principle became for Tertullian what belonged to the earthly appearance of Jesus as it were. That is where the Father principle, the creative principle in nature lies, that thing which causes everything in nature to appear. The Christ principle, the Son principle united with that. That is what it became for Tertullian, and through the Father and the Son, through catharsis of what is external and natural through Christ, the Spirit is created in turn which he calls the Holy Spirit.

Thus what we see at the time of the Mystery of Golgotha as Jesus Christ proceeded as Jesus from the Father principle like everything in the world proceeds from the Father principle. Thus, because He bore Christ within him, this Jesus Christ was the Son proceeding from the Father principle who had simply come later, the bringer of the Spirit— the Spirit which in turn came from Him. In this way Tertullian sought the path from the individual human being out into the cosmos: to the Father, Son and Spirit principle.

Jesus	Father
Christ	Son

Holy Spirit

Now he faced the great difficulty of how to make it comprehensible that there can be three in one and one in three. In ancient times, when there were still clairvoyant concepts, it was not particularly difficult to imagine that. But in the period when concepts made everything fall apart and nothing could be properly connected any longer, this difficulty arose. Tertullian needed a nice comparison in order to make clear how one can be three and three one. He said, take a spring. The spring produces a stream and the stream produces a river. If we ask about the river, we say it comes from the spring through the stream, from the spring through the stream. Or let us take, he said, the root, the shoot and the fruit as a comparison. The fruit comes out of the root through the shoot. Tertullian used a third comparison in that he said: the flame comes out of the sun borne by the cosmos. This is how we must imagine that the Spirit comes out of the Father through the Son. And as little as the trinity of spring, stream and river contradicts the unity which the river is in reality, as little the fact that the Spirit proceeds from the Father through the Son contradicts the uniform development of Father, Son and Spirit.

In this way he tried to clarify for himself how three can be one: just like root, shoot and fruit, like spring, stream and river. And he also tried to obtain a certain formula. He did so by thinking with regard to the Father principle—that is, the principle which is always that part from which the Spirit principle proceeds through the Son—that he thought with regard to the Father principle: what is natural, externally created, externally revealed; with the Son principle, what penetrates what is externally revealed; and in the Spirit principle, what is then brought by both for earth development. In that way he developed a teaching which was, however, basically only a single symptomatic expression for what developed in people in the first centuries of Christianity—people who on the one hand still had something of gnosis within them but at the same time went through all the suffering and sorrow because the gnosis had to be lost, and who at the same time tried to come to terms with what Jesus Christ was, what he had to be for the goal of the Mystery of Golgotha. Tertullian was only a particularly brilliant one, but he was a representative of what people thought in these initial periods of Christianity in order really to penetrate spiritually what had happened.

Now what you know as the creed,[107] the Apostles' Creed, developed out of Christianity and then became established in the third and fourth centuries and was laid down by the Councils. If we study it in the way it was at the time, we can indeed discover that it was basically a defence against gnosis, a rejection of gnosis because people sensed the luciferic factor in gnosis. The gnosis had a tendency towards Lucifer, that is, a one-sided spiritual perception. It can therefore not gain an understanding, an appreciation of the Father principle. The material becomes something which it must reject, something it does not need. In opposition to this, there was a need to specify: I believe in one God, the Father almighty—the first part of the creed. This first part of the creed is framed to counter the contempt of what is material, is framed in such a way that the external, which can be seen with the eyes, is conceived of as something divine, and specifically something divine which proceeds from the Father principle.

The second thing was: to lay down in opposition to gnosis that there was not just an etheric Christ at the time of the Mystery of Golgotha but that this Christ was really united with the human being Jesus of Nazareth, not mixed, but united. So it had to be laid down on the one hand that Christ was connected with the spiritual and on the other hand that Christ was connected with Jesus of Nazareth, the natural development on earth, and that when all the suffering, the dying, the resurrection and everything had been fulfilled what was still to happen after the Mystery of Golgotha, this was not something in which Christ had no involvement but that He really suffered in the body. The Gnostics had to deny that Christ suffered in the body because He was not united with the body; it was just pretend suffering as far as the Gnostics were concerned, at least certain Gnostics. In contrast, it was to be laid down that Christ had really been united with the body in such a way that He suffered in the body. So all the events which took place on the outer physical plane were to be linked with Christ. Hence: I believe in Jesus Christ, the only-begotten Son of God, incarnated of the Holy Spirit and of the Virgin Mary, who suffered under Pontius Pilate, died, rose again on the third day and ascended into heaven. That means: became spiritual again—sitting on the right hand of the Father to judge the living and the dead.

We can say that the Gnostics still came closest to that spirit which should be seen to begin with as something purely spiritual. But it is something spiritual to the extent that, although it shows itself as something spiritual now, it must gradually realize itself in human coexistence, in the social structure that will arise during the Jupiter, Venus and Vulcan period in which the Holy Spirit incarnates—not now in the individual person but in the whole of humanity, in the con-figuration of society. But right now it is only at the beginning. But the Gnostics were best able to understand that something only has a spiritual existence and does not intervene in the material. As a result the god of the Gnostics was closest to the Holy Spirit. But the Christianity which wanted to establish itself on earth, which did not want the spirit to be lucifericized, to be seen only as something spiritual, this Christianity now also had to lay down the belief in the Spirit as something that is connected with matter: I believe in the Holy Spirit, in the Holy Church. That is now contained in the Apostolic Creed and says that the Church is a great physical body of the Holy Spirit. This Christianity was not allowed to consider life in the Spirit as something purely inward but had to realize the Spirit outwardly through the forgiveness of sins in that the Church itself took over the office of forgiveness of sins as well as the teaching of the resurrection in the flesh: I believe in the Holy Spirit, in the Holy Church, in the forgiveness of sins, in the resurrection in the flesh.

This is the creed, say, in the fourth century. So it was a whole lot of barricades against gnosis; and the way that these three parts of the Apostolic Creed are framed is closely connected with something like this: the river has arisen out of the spring through the stream; or, the fruit out of the root through the shoot. We can see an incredible striving in that time with regard to how the spirit is connected with the material aspect which is spreading in the world, how the spirit can be thought as being connected with matter, the Trinity can be thought as being connected with external matter as it spreads. That is what is sought, intensively sought. But if we consider all the things that live in the Apostolic Creed, which today has become totally incomprehensible, we have to say: in it there still lives an echo of the old clairvoyant concepts which is dying out and so the matter does not acquire the old living forms which it could have acquired if the Trinity and the Apostolic Creed had been understood with the previous clairvoyant concepts, but it represents a start in grasping matter together with the spirit.

There are many people today who say: why do we bother with this old dogma? People only pondered all kinds of airy-fairy concepts out of which no one can make any sense, they are all flights of fancy. But if we look more closely, we can see that behind these flights of fancy there is a mighty struggle going on to understand what had just happened in the world through the Mystery of Golgotha on the one hand and through the loss of clairvoyant knowledge, the gradual ebb of the old clairvoyant knowledge, on the other.

Now development continues and something similar happens as

already happened in more ancient times when out of the single root of the mysteries, in which art and religion and science were still one, these three things developed separately. The thing contained in the common root which was sought to be understood through the Apostolic Creed in turn strives apart into the Trinity. I will now attempt to present this further development in the way it can be presented today without causing too much offence. Because if I were to say the things which can be said about it without further ado, many a mind would take fright.

The thing which started from a unity now developed in three separate streams within western culture. That is, one stream was particularly suited to comprehend the Spirit, the Holy Spirit, one stream the Son to a greater extent and one stream the Father to a greater extent. And the peculiar thing is that the Holy Spirit stream, the Christ stream and the Father stream increasingly develop in separate directions but in a one-sided way. Because of course they can only be comprehended in a comprehensive way if they are all three together. If what should be understood as a Trinity develops in such a one-sided way, then difficulties arise in that development; then some things are left out and others degenerate. Now the following happens. The common development gradually separates in such a way that there is a clear continuation of a developmental stream which is primarily directed towards the Holy Spirit, not as the chronologically first (the chronologically first is of course the association), and that is the one which today is still essentially incorporated in the Russian Orthodox Church. As strange as it may seem, it is an essential characteristic of the Russian Orthodox Church that it especially fosters the Holy Spirit. And you will see from the way that Solovyov[108] for example talks about Christ that he is primarily concerned to grasp Christianity from the aspect of the Holy Spirit. It does not matter whether he speaks consciously about Christ or not but what spirit is at work in him, what meaning he associates with things. What matters is the inner attitude, particularly the way in which he considers the outer social order of the church to be indivisible from what is taught and is the cultus. That comes wholly out of the nature of the Holy Spirit. The early church however wanted to avoid this pure knowledge out of the Holy Spirit in that it set up the Trinity in the creed and added Christ and the Father to the Holy Spirit.

But these three must—and that is also Solovyov's ideal—find their way back to some kind of synthesis.

The second stream is the one which developed more in the direction of fostering Christ. It brought all kinds of things about the Holy Spirit but essentially it fostered Christ. It is the Church which in the West spread out from Rome and had the tendency to concentrate on fostering Christ. Consider that in relation to all the fields in which this Church was active it basically wanted to foster Christ. Wherever you look: Christ. Wherever you look, this Church takes a lead in fostering one-sidedly the middle article of faith in the creed. It is only in recent times that this Church has tried also to comprehend the Father principle. But because there is no knowledge of the actual inner connection, it is not possible to come to a proper relationship between Christ and the Father. And all of this failure properly to understand the relationship between Christ and the Father is what has caused all the debates in modern Protestantism. There is a push from Christ to the Father. We can observe that once again particularly in our time. The sad events of the present have also led individual souls, or rather many souls, to be imbued with a religious awareness by these events; that can be shown. But there is very little of Christ in this flaring up of religious consciousness; it is rather the Father principle, the general principle of God with which the Father principle is meant. Anyone who can observe things properly in the world will notice that. Let me just describe one small symptom. During our last stay in Berlin, a dear member died[109] who was cremated in Berlin. I made it a condition—that was necessary because of the prevailing circumstances—that a pastor should speak. He was a very dear man who agreed wholeheartedly that I should say a few words afterwards. And lo and behold, he gave a truly very moving address and one had the feeling as he spoke about God the Father that he spoke from the depths of his soul. And all the time that I listened to him I noted: that is actually a confirmation of something which spiritual science shows us in general; it was Christ who was fostered, but now confusion has arisen. When we speak of the religious life, we now come to the Father principle. Many letters from the front whose writers enlarge upon religion speak little about Christ but everywhere about the principle which has to be considered the Father principle. Anyone who studies this can see it. And then in conclusion, because Christmas was just around the corner, the pastor mentioned Christ. It was a bit artificial because he felt as a Christian that it might make sense to refer to Christ. There was no rhyme or reason to it. And such phenomena are becoming more and more frequent.

There is still a third stream in which the Father principle is fostered in a one-sided way. And now you can imagine that the two pillars which were erected in the Apostolic Creed against a one-sided fostering of the Father principle, Christ and the Holy Spirit, must be left out if the Father principle is fostered in a one-sided way. On the other hand, the Father principle was included in the Apostolic Creed to indicate that the material world is also a divine one. The one-sided Father principle, very one-sided, is fostered in the spiritual stream which builds on Darwin,[110] on Haeckel[111] and so on. That is the one-sided development of the Father principle. And however much Haeckel might resist that he is born out of religion, he is simply born out of religion in a one-sided formation of the Father principle, just as other religious streams were born out of the one-sided development of the Holy Spirit or Christ principle.

And it basically appears quite superficial if people keep saying that the first Councils had merely grappled with dogmatic concepts. These dogmatic concepts are not just dogmatic concepts but the outer symbol of profound contrasts which live in European humanity, of the contrasts which live in those people who are primarily predisposed as Christ people, predisposed as Holy Spirit people and predisposed as Father people. This differentiation is deeply ethnographically founded in the nature of the European world. And to the extent that in the first centuries of the proclamation of Christianity people looked at the whole of Europe, they established a creed which takes account of the Trinity. Every one-sidedness can of course bring the other side with it but it does not have to. But humanity has to go through many a test, must go through many a one-sidedness to find its way to totality, to wholeness from out of its one-sidedness. And then we also have to have the good will to study these things in their deeper content, in their deeper essence.

If we study the three layers of European spiritual life which I have characterized in the way I have just done in their deeper essence, we will see that this differentiation has entered deeply into the grain of the soul of human beings, and we will learn to understand many things which, if we do not understand them, will face us like a painful riddle. We might say: in the way that the unity presented itself in the trinity for Tertullian, there lived in the way that the One came to symptomatic expression in the Three, the three main needs of European humanity in so far as they were determined by religious life. And something like the formation of the schism[112] between the western Roman and the eastern Roman Church, the Roman and the Greek Orthodox Church, is only the outer expression of the necessity which lies in the impulse which has to fork in various directions.

In this sense spiritual science will make many things in human life comprehensible. It is of course still very little understood today in the way that it tries to throw an ever deeper light on the situation of humanity, on the situation within the whole of human development. Because the time is increasingly developing with ever greater clarity in which the world does not want to know anything about spiritual science, a time in which a deeper understanding also of historical events is no longer wanted, in which everyone only pursues what they want to believe as true in their subjective opinion, in their personal sympathy or antipathy. Of course spiritual science has to be there in such times in particular because the pendulum of development will also swing in the other direction. But it is just as self-evident that spiritual science will be much misunderstood in such a time. And we have to be very clear how much lives in our time which means that people do not seek objectivity or an overview but that they make quick judgements on the basis of their inclinations. It really is the case that basically there would be a profound necessity, on the one hand, to say a great deal from out of the spiritual world, but that it is exceptionally difficult to make oneself understood particularly in our immediate present time. Never as much as in our present time have people lived in the general aura, as it were, of which they are not at all aware. I am deeply convinced when I say this, that much in our time must remain unsaid. There will be many who will find it obvious that they are suited to hearing, perhaps in smaller groups, what cannot otherwise be said. But this opinion is quite wrong.

It may well be that many have the longing to hear something of the things it might only be possible to tell humanity in years to come. But we have to be clear that we live in an age today when judgements are not made once a word has revealed its meaning to our soul but when the judgement is made before the word has reached our soul. The way in which words are received is already mostly completed in our time as soon as the word sounds in the ear and has not yet been taken in by the soul. People no longer have the time to ask about meaning—the passions, the emotions of people are currently so troubled through the depressing events into which we have been placed—and some words could only be tolerated because they were spoken in our context.

We can do nothing other in our context than always make clear to ourselves that the important thing is that a number of people can be found who stand firmly on the ground of what we have been able to obtain through our spiritual science, who stand firmly and loyally on that ground, and who may have the hope that standing firmly and loyally on the ground of spiritual science in this way can become important and essential for the development of humanity in a certain time. The time will undoubtedly come in which—now that many passions have already been aroused—something like a great question will pervade the atmosphere which lives in our spiritual-scientific stream. That question will not be clearly heard but it might have clear effects. The answers, too, will not be given in clear words but they might be very clear in respect of outer events. Things like the following will whisper through the spiritual-scientific stream without being framed in words: 'Shall I go along with it or shall I not go along with it?' And the response will reflect what has driven people from out of feeling, out of sympathy with the general feelings which come from spiritual science. Many subsidiary feelings will lead to the answer which will not be clearly framed, which will not simply be expressed by saying: 'I liked spiritual science, now other feelings have intervened. Now I no longer like it'—but people will put on masks and seek all kinds of reasons which will be set out in many ways. But the essential thing will be that a person previously liked spiritual science and now no longer likes it, which has a lot to do with infatuation, with sensationalism, with all kinds of feelings of emotional sensuality and so on. In a certain sense something like the following will increasingly arise particularly from the emotions of the present time, 'I will go along with it'—and, 'I will not go along with it.' Yet inwardly our spiritual science is unconquerable, wholly unconquerable. And what we have to focus on is that there are at least some people in whose hearts it is firmly attached, but attached not from sympathy and preference, from delight and sensationalism, from vanity and infatuation, but because the soul is connected with it because of its truth and because the soul does not shy away from any difficulty in entering the core of truth in the world. Some things will fall away completely. But maybe what remains will be all the more important and secure. That is what we have to consider when I keep emphasizing that—until more peaceful times return to our civilized countries—we have to do without many things which might perhaps be useful for an understanding of the present time but which really cannot be put before humanity in the present time as I have characterized it.

I want to say these words in explanation of the fact that some of the things in recent lectures could only be hinted at. But I still want to add one thing. Particularly if it is true—and it is true—that we live in a time today in which the word is led to judgement before it has reached the soul, many people can learn a lot from the events of the present time with the tools which spiritual science has already given them. A lot can be learnt in particular from what is happening around us if we consider it more deeply , if we consider how outer humanity today has almost no possibility of making any kind of objective judgement, how emotions underlie the judgements which pervade the civilized world. And when we investigate the reason why this is so, when we see this reason swarming in the human aura of the present, and then know how the word has already become judgement before it enters the soul, then we can learn much from the events of the present time particularly with the instrument of spiritual science. And we should learn if we want to reach a situation in which we become a tool in reality—as a society for spiritual science. The example I gave today in which a person who wanted to insult our society quoted the fourth verse but left the third one out—well my dear friends, when you look for the reasons for the opposition which arises against us: they can be found everywhere. They must be sought everywhere in the superficial attitude, in the quite terrible superficial attitude. A fourth verse has happened everywhere, as it were, and the third one is overlooked, metaphorically speaking. The only thing is that many among us still do not believe it. Many among us still believe that they are doing good if they go to some person and tell him: 'I have become so spiritual through our spiritual science that I can even read to my husband on the front and I know that it helps him.' Then people will of course turn against us. Or if we tell people something that came to our ears, the 'Nathaniel story' which was taken out and so on. That such things occur at all, that things really are taken outwards from our midst, appears to happen to begin with out of good will, but out of a good will which is combined with naivety—a naivety which is boundlessly arrogant because it does not and does not want to recognize itself as being naive. It takes itself so seriously as a person that it thinks there is nothing more important than to convert some person about whom it would know, if it were not so naive, that there is nothing doing there. It is infinitely important to be able to recognize that sometimes naivety feels in infinite arrogance that it is on a mission. And no one as a rule takes greater umbrage than a naive person who believes he is doing the very best when out of a certain infatuation he does something totally absurd.

And it is necessary, when we consider the matter, that we gain at least this from spiritual science that we are modest in our thinking. When the thinking really can go wide of the mark in the way I sought to make clear today, why should we then always when something has wormed its way into our brain, why should we then always believe that it is the irrefutable truth? And why should we then directly trumpet it out into the world as if we were on a mission? Why should we not decide first to learn something real and acquire a certain impulse of vitality from spiritual science other than the one we obtain if we just take little sips from it? Hence we cannot appeal often enough to the seriousness, the profound seriousness which must pervade us and which always has to tell us: however much you may believe in your judgement in any respect, you have to examine it because it could be wide of the mark. If we take all these things into consideration and some other things too—we cannot always mention everything—then we will increasingly become a group of people in whom something lives inwardly which is as impersonal as the most important impulses of our time have to be impersonal if they want to prevail against the merely personal impulses which undulate and flow through the world today.

I wanted to address your souls about such sentiments and feelings as we will not meet for a few weeks now.[113] I also wanted to present you with a larger tableau in these last hours in advance of the weeks in which we will not be able to speak with one another by opening up one aspect of the original development of Christianity and its division into various streams. I am convinced if you continue studying the development of Christianity in the previous centuries that you will have a guide in what I said today which will clarify very many things regarding external phenomena. And external phenomena will, if you really observe them seriously, confirm everywhere what I indicated today. So it would be good if we could use something like this as some sort of material for meditation which can put problems and riddles before the soul which everyone can try to solve according to their ability. Of course some people may only be able to do that with fleeting thoughts, for a few minutes, and others will find it easier to familiarize themselves with something which can bring clarification about the things we have indicated. But everyone can be motivated to try to develop what I might call the undulating thoughts which go through the centuries and which are nevertheless significantly involved in what we see in the present time so that there is the necessity to understand it. I know that in reality no one will understand our present sorrowful time who does not familiarize themselves with all the antagonisms that have arisen in the course of the development of Europe in a quite natural way. But when we compare the judgements which are made today about the world situation with what is objectively correct, which can only be recognized if we know all the forces which have intervened in that development, and which can only arise from an observation of history also in a spiritual respect—if we compare today's judgements with what leads to real judgement, then we get deeply, deeply sorrowful feelings. Not just sorrowful feelings, my dear friends, about what is happening today but the difficulties which arise in getting beyond what is hap-pening today. And we must get beyond what is happening today! And the better you understand that a deep spiritual knowledge of the developmental forces of humanity is required in all fields, without thereby letting our emotions of a personal nature intervene—the more such knowledge of the developmental impulses through spiritual science is sought, the more you recognize the importance of understanding those impulses through spiritual science and bringing them to life in your soul—the better you will belong to those souls who can stand firmly on the ground on which we have to stand firmly today if that is to be achieved, which must actually happen as a result of the inner, necessary demands of the secrets of human development.

I want to address your sentiments, your feelings so that spiritual science can enter these sentiments, these feelings and be firmly anchored within them, so that there may be human beings such as there should and must be if we want to make progress in the development of humanity. We have to think these thoughts in all modesty, but we have to act in such modesty because this is not suitable for turning us to megalomania but is only suitable for generating the need in us to use the greatest possible strength, the greatest possible intensity to penetrate thoroughly those things which want to become spiritual reality in the history of the development of humanity.

NOTES

Text source: These lectures were taken down in shorthand by the professional stenographer Helene Finckh (1883–1960) who later became the official stenographer for Rudolf Steiner's lectures. This publication is based on her text transcriptions. These transcripts belong to her initial, not yet official work and still reveal a number of shortcomings. The lecture of 15 January in particular contains a number of gaps. It was, however, possible to fill in some of them from the transcript of a stenographer whose name we do not know. For the 1981 edition, the complete text was compared with the original shorthand notes and corrected as necessary.

Some orthographic corrections were made for this third edition. Despite some shortcomings, it was decided not to edit the text for style.

A number of unclear places in the text are clarified in footnotes. The endnotes were supplemented and extended.

The individual titles were provided by Marie Steiner for publication in the *Goetheanum* and the *Nachrichtenblatt* or for single editions.

As title for the whole volume, the title of the lecture of 9 January 1916 in Bern was used; it was chosen by Marie Steiner in 1925 when the lecture was published in the *Nachrichtenblatt.*

No blackboard drawings have survived. The drawings in the text were prepared by Hedwig Frey in accordance with the stenographer's note.

1. These and similar words of commemoration were spoken by Rudolf Steiner during the time of the First World War from 1914 to 1918 before each lecture that he gave to the members of the Anthroposophical Society in the countries affected by the war.

2. The lecture had been preceded by a performance of the Oberufer Paradise play. See *Weihnachtsspiele aus altem Volkstum—Die Oberufer Spiele,* single edition 1990, no. 5236–6; also Rudolf Steiner, *Ansprachen zu den Weihnachtsspielen aus altem Volkstum,* GA 274.

3. The legend about the Provenance of the Cross—also called the 'Golden Legend' by Rudolf Steiner—occurs in the medieval collection of legends *Legenda Aurea* by Jacobus de Voragine. See also the lecture of 29 May 1905 in GA 93 as well as the special reference to the Golden Legend in the volume *Bilder okkulter Siegel und Säulen,* GA 284, pp. 185 ff.

4. The spiritual importance of Jesus' dual line of descent as described in the Gospel of Luke (descent from the priestly line, the line of Nathan of the house of David) and in the Gospel of Matthew (line of Solomon) is discussed by Rudolf Steiner in, among others, the following lectures: the cycles on the

Gospel of Luke (1909), GA 114, and the *Gospel of Matthew* (1910), GA 123, and the volume *Spiritual Guidance of the Individual and Humanity* (1911), GA 15, and in the lecture for workers building the Goetheanum of 21 April 1921, GA 349.

5. Matthew 19:14, Mark 10:14, Luke 18:16.

6. 1825–1900, scholar of German, professor at Vienna Technical University, teacher and fatherly friend of Rudolf Steiner. See Rudolf Steiner's *Autobiography: Chapters in the Course of My Life: 1861–1907*, GA 28.

7. 1823–1901, scholar of German, collected *Weihnachtsspiele und Volkslieder aus Süddeutschland und Schlesien*.

8. An epic poem in old Saxon (*c.* 830) paraphrasing the Bible and telling the story of Christ in alliterative verse. Christ is represented as a mighty Germanic king, the disciples as his noble followers.

9. 1834–1919, naturalist. His book *Ewigkeit. Weltkriegsgedanken über Leben und Tod, Religion und Entwicklungslehre* was published in Berlin towards the end of 1915.

10. There is a poem by Eduard Mörike about such a depiction by the Italian early-Baroque painter Francesco Albani (1578–1660):

Sleeping Child Jesus

Son of the Virgin! Heavenly child! On the ground
Fallen asleep on the wood of sorrow
Which the devout master, with meaningful allusion,
Has placed beneath your gossamer dreams;
Flower that you are, even enveloped dawning in the bud
You are still the glory of the Father!
If only we could see the pictures
Painted behind this brow, these black
Lashes, in gentle variation!

11. Rudolf Steiner spoke at the Berlin Architektenhaus about 'Fichte's spirit among us' on 16 December 1915. The lecture is published in GA 65.

12. Johann Gottlieb Fichte, 1762–1848, professor of philosophy in Jena, Erlangen, Königsberg and Berlin. See *Fichtes Werke*, edited by Immanuel Hermann Fichte, Berlin 1845–6, volume 8, pp. 461 ff., second sonnet.

13. The lecture on 26 December 1915 was preceded by the performance of a shepherds' play from the Palatinate and the Oberufer Three Kings play. At the start of the lecture, Rudolf Steiner spoke words of remembrance for the Munich branch leader Sophie Stinde, who had died at the end of November 1915, and who had been particularly committed to the building of the first Goetheanum (called 'Johannesbau' at the time). The words of remembrance are printed in the volume *Unsere Toten*, GA 261.

14. 1182–1226

15. In the two lectures on 26 and 27 December 1914, in GA 156.

16. The three Christmas songs are taken from the chapter 'Christus in der geistlichen Dichtung des Mittelalters' in the book *Jesus im Urteil der Jahrhunderte* by Gustav Pfannmüller, Berlin/Leipzig 1908.

17. By Walafried Strabo, abbot of Reichenau (d. 849).

18. Sequence by Notker Balbulus, abbot in St Gallen, lived from 830 to 912.

19. Twelfth-century German Christmas song from the Codex Manesse.

20. Rudolf Steiner spoke among other things about the 'younging' of the etheric body (as opposed to the ageing of the physical body) in the Berlin lecture of 7 December 1915, included in GA 157a.

21. See note 13.

22. Died after 190, Greek Church Father. A corresponding account can be found in the work, highly thought of by Rudolf Steiner, by Otto Willmann, *Geschichte des Idealismus*, volume 2, p. 5: 'Through keeping alive the memory of the personalities of the apostles, and through constantly refreshing their accounts, the following generations sought to maintain the connection with the visible living presence of the Lord on earth. Thus Irenaeus tells that St Clement of Rome, the fourth pope, still saw the apostles himself and associated with them, and that he still heard their sermons and saw their accounts, and not just he alone because many pupils of the apostles were still alive at that time. Equally, he reports about Polycarp "who was not just a pupil of the apostles and associated with many who had seen Christ, but was appointed by the apostles in Asia as bishop of the Church of Smyrna, and whom we also saw in our early youth because he continued to live for a long time and only departed from life at a ripe old age".'

23. Bishop of Smyrna, died as a martyr *c.* 155.

24. St Ambrose, *c.* 340–87, Latin Church Father, opponent of Arianism; St Augustine, 354–430; Johannes Scotus Eriugena, *c.* 840–77, *De divisione naturae*.

25. They were published by Carl Schmidt in Leipzig in 1905 under the title *Koptisch-gnostische Schriften*.

26. The quotes from the *Pistis Sophia* and the Books of Jeu have been taken from the Pfanmüller collection referred to in note 16. They are reproduced here in the wording given by Rudolf Steiner, i.e. with a number of small improvements which he made to the translation.

27. See note 22.

28. Two figures from the Palatinate shepherds' play.

29. Second-century Gnostic living in Rome.

30. Clement of Alexandria, *c.* 150–217. Greek philosopher and theologian in Alexandria; Origen, *c.* 185–254, Theologian, pupil and successor of Clement of Alexandria.

31. Exodus 3:2 ff.

32. The diagram which Rudolf Steiner presumably drew on the blackboard has not been preserved. It could not be reconstructed from what little information there was in the shorthand note. Rudolf Steiner also speaks about gnosis in the following lectures: Leipzig, 28 and 29 December 1913, included in GA 149, as well as Dornach, 15 June 1923, contained in GA 225.

33. *Man in the Light of Occultism, Theosophy and Philosophy*, 10 lectures given in Christiania (Oslo) from 2 to 12 June 1912, GA 137.

34. Johannes Tauler, *c.* 1300–61; Meister Eckhart, *c.* 1260–1327. Rudolf Steiner

writes in detail about these two mystics in his book *Mysticism at the Dawn of the Modern Age*, GA 7.

35. Rudolf Eucken, 1846–1926, professor of philosophy. Adolf von Harnack, 1851–1930, writes in *Das Wesen des Christentums*, Leipzig 1910, p. 102: 'Whatever may have happened at the tomb and in the appearances—one thing is certain: it was from this tomb that the unshakeable belief in the triumph over death and in eternal life derived its origin.'

36. Rudolf Steiner was a co-founder of the Giordano Bruno League in Berlin and regularly took part in its events in the years from 1900 to 1905. What we know about this is documented in the booklet *Beiträge zur Rudolf Steiner Gesamtausgabe* no. 79–80 as well as the annex to the volume *Über Philosophie, Geschichte und Literatur*, GA 52. No further details are known about the event referred to.

37. This is the Protestant theologian and Goethe specialist Max Christlieb, 1862–1916, a Weimar friend of Rudolf Steiner's at around 1890. In 1892, Christlieb went to Japan for some years as a lecturer at the Theological Academy in Tokyo and did not meet up with Rudolf Steiner again until 1906.

38. *Ecce Deus. Die urchristliche Lehre des rein-göttlichen Jesu* by Benjamin Smith (1850–1934) was published in Jena in 1911. Rudolf Steiner spoke in detail about it in the tenth lecture of the cycle about the Gospel of Mark, GA 139.

39. In the lectures of 10 and 11 October 1911 of the lecture cycle *From Jesus to Christ*, GA 131.

40. *The Spiritual Guidance of the Individual and Humanity. Some Results of Spiritual-Scientific Research into Human History and Development* (1911), GA 15.

41. The lecture was held in the Basel branch of the Anthroposophical Society. Rudolf Steiner's remarks were preceded by an address from Michael Bauer.

42. Genesis 2:16–17.

43. Adalbert Stifter, 1805–68, Austrian writer. The tale 'Rock Crystal' is contained in the collection *Colourful Stones*.

44. In the preface to Adalbert Stifter's *Colourful Stones*.

45. Rudolf Steiner had spoken about the Norwegian folk legend *The Dream Song of Olaf Åsteson* at the 1914 New Year's celebrations in Dornach. This address is published in GA 158 together with other lectures about the *Dream Song*.

46. See the lectures in the volume *The Occult Movement in the Nineteenth Century and its Relation to Modern Culture*, GA 254.

47. Goethe, *Faust I*. Mephisto's words to the student about the law: 'All laws and rights are passed down / Like an eternal disease from one generation to the next, / moving cautiously from place to place. / Reason turns to nonsense, benefaction to plague! / Woe betide you if you are a grandchild. / The rights with which we are born, / To those, alas!, no one makes reference.'

48. Friedrich Albert Lange, 1828–75. *Geschichte des Materialismus und Kritik seiner Bedeutung in der Gegenwart*, Leipzig 1866.

49. Fritz Mauthner, 1849–1923. *Beiträge zu einer Kritik der Sprache*, 3 volumes.

50. In the Dornach lectures *Zufall, Notwendigkeit und Vorsehung*, GA 163.

51. William Shakespeare in *Julius Ceasar*, Act 3, Scene 2 from Mark Antony's speech after Caesar's death.

52. The quote in Mauthner is (loc. cit. Volume 3, p. 526): 'We have come to know our senses as random senses, as random breaches which the world of reality has opened in the random organization of the human individual; and we have no guarantee that magnetic iron ore with its highly developed sense for electricity does not in its way have a better experience of the cosmic mystery than we can have with our seeing eyes and hearing ears.'

53. The writer Gustav Landauer, 1870–1919. In his *Skepsis und Mystik. Versuche im Anschluß an Mauthners Sprachkritik*, Berlin 1903, it says on pp. 12 ff.: 'The world streams towards us and with the few pathetic holes of our random senses we take in what we can grasp and attach it to our stock of words as we have nothing else with which to keep hold of it ... But this world, nature in its voicelessness and inexpressibility, is immeasurably rich in comparison to our so-called world view, in comparison to what we babble about nature as knowledge or language.'

54. Svante Arrhenius, 1859–1927, Swedish naturalist. *Das Werden der Welten*, second volume *Die Vorstellung vom Weltgebäude im Wandel der Zeiten*, translated from the Swedish by L. Bamberger, Leipzig 1909, at the end of the preface, pp. iv ff.

55. Goethe, *Faust I*, Scene 1, Night.

56. Loc. cit.

57. Loc. cit.

58. Mathilde Scholl from Cologne and Pauline Countess Kalckreuth from Munich, both longstanding members of the Anthroposophical Society, were among the listeners.

59. *Pistis Sophia*, Chapter 58. *Koptisch-gnostische Schriften*, Volume 1, edited by Carl Schmidt, Leipzig 1905, pp. 72 f.

60. 1851–1941, writer and journalist, wrote primarily about European literary history.

61. The name is likely to be a play on the name of the Leipzig neurologist and lecturer Paul Julius Möbius, 1853–1907. See the supplementary note to the lecture of 6 January 1916, 'Die Pathographie der Tantaliden' by Wolfgang Groddeck, in *Nachrichten der Rudolf Steiner Nachlassverwaltung*, No. 22, pp. 30–1.

62. Corresponding *Pathographies* had been published by Paul Julius Möbius in the years 1903–7.

63. 1842–1906. His *Philosophie des Unbewußten*, Berlin 1869, was sharply criticized by followers of Darwinism. As a result Hartmann anonymously published the work *Das Unbewußte vom Standpunkt der Physiologie und Deszendenztheorie. Eine kritische Beleuchtung des naturphilosophischen Teils der Philosophie des Unbewußten*, Berlin 1872. After Hartmann's opponents had welcomed this work as a proper refutation of the *Philosophie des Unbewußten*, Hartmann published a second edition under his own name with a corresponding annex. See Rudolf Steiner's essay 'Einheitliche Naturanschauung und Erkenntnisgrenzen' which appeared in *Monatsblätter der wissenschaftlichen Clubs in Wien*, 1892/93, Volume XIV, pp. 89–99, reprinted in GA 30.

64. Goethe, *Iphigenia in Tauris*, Act 1, Scene 3.

65. Sophocles, *c.* 496–406 BC; Aeschylus, 525–456 BC.

66. Henrik Ibsen, 1828–1901, Norwegian poet and playwright.
67. See note 28. 'Mops' in German also colloquially means 'podge' and 'pug'.
68. Words said by Wagner in Goethe's *Faust I*.
69. Friedrich Nietzsche, 1844–1900, *Jenseits von Gut und Böse*, Leipzig 1886. See also Rudolf Steiner, *Friedrich Nietzsche: Fighter for Freedom*, GA 5.
70. Wilhelm Oswald, 1853–1932, chemist, physicist and philosopher. His work *Grundriß der Naturphilosophie* appeared in Leipzig in 1908.
71. Matthew 5:39, Luke 6:29.
72. In the Dornach lectures of 20 to 22 November 1914, *The Balance in the World and Man: Lucifer and Ahriman*, GA 58.
73. See *Wege zu einem neuen Baustil*, GA 286, *Architecture as a Synthesis of the Arts*, 1999; *Der Dornacher Bau als Wahrzeichen geschichtlichen Werdens und künstlerischer Umwandlungsimpulse*, GA 287.
74. See note 9.
75. See note 4.
76. Matthew 28:20.
77. Paul, 1 Corinthians 3:19.
78. Antinomies are described as the contradiction between two conclusions which can both be proven with the same rigorous reasons.
79. In *Kritik der reinen Vernunft,* Riga 1781, pp. 420, 426 f.
80. The nine-metre high sculpture called *The Representative of Humanity*, a wooden sculpture created by Rudolf Steiner which survived the fire of the first Goetheanum and today stands in the new Goetheanum in Dornach. See lecture of 3 July 1918 on the Dornach building, GA 181, pp. 313 ff.
81. *Die Goetheanum-Fenster. Sprache des Lichtes. Entwürfe und Studien*, with quotes from Rudolf Steiner, reports about the work on the windows and etchings by Asya Turgenev as well as a pictorial documentation on the creation of the windows of the first and second Goetheanum. GA-K12, Dornach 1996.
82. Paul, Galatians 2:20.
83. Matthew 22:37–40, Mark 12:30–1, Luke 10:27, Galatians 5:14, James 2:8.
84. Rudolf Steiner had held two public lectures in Basle on 12 and 14 January 1916: 'Wie kann die Erforschung der übersinnlichen Wesenheit des Menschen bewirkt werden?' and 'Die Harmonie zwischen Geistesforschung und Naturforschung und die Missverständnisse über die erstere und den ihr gewidmeten Bau in Dornach'. The two lectures have not yet been published in the complete edition (GA). The lecture of 12 January 1916 was printed in the journal *Die Drei* 1930/31, Volume 10, Issue 12, the lecture of 14 January 1916 in the *Nachrichtenblatt* 1939, Volume 16, Nos. 41–9.
85. Thomas Aquinas, 1225–74. See Rudolf Steiner's lectures 'Die Philosophie des Thomas von Aquino', Dornach 22–24 May 1920, GA 74, *The Redemption of Thinking*, 1983.
    John Duns Scotus, 1266–1308. Scottish theologian, taught in England, Paris and Cologne.
86. In the Basle lecture of 12 January 1916 (see note 84) Rudolf Steiner had said the following: 'The thinking takes on a quite different character under the influence of the exercises that we do. It really does become quite a different force in the soul. And I would like to show with a comparison how surprising

this change in the activity of thinking can be. Let us imagine we have a statue, a sculpture before us; it has a form. Imagine that it happened that this statue, this sculpture started to walk, to live. Then we would have found something that was against the laws of external nature. That cannot happen, of course. I only wanted to use that as a comparison because something happens in our soul life which can quite well be compared with that. In the thoughts which we ordinarily have in normal life and which lead to memories, we primarily have the impression in our own inner experience that these thoughts have to be passive images which depict what is outside, that they do not have a life within us; and if they did have a life of their own, where would our soul life come to expression through our inner life, through the independent life of the thoughts, in the imagination, in dreams, if not in something worse, in hallucinations. In our ordinary soul life the thoughts really do have something which can be compared with the forms of a statue. What takes place as the logic of thinking, in the ordinary activity of thinking of which we are not aware in our own thinking activity, in what combines thoughts, what brings them together and separates them again, this can in a certain sense be compared with the dead statue. But while the statue cannot become active or alive, our inner logic, the inner weft and life of our thoughts can move into the consciousness, can come inwardly to life; the inner statue of 'logic' can turn into an inner living logical being which we then experience as if we were entering a completely different world. From this moment onwards we know: the thing which we first peeled away, separated from the memory, the thinking activity, has separated itself from its dependence on the physical organs.'

87. 1828–94. Priest in the Benedictine order and private lecturer of philosophy at Vienna University. His lectures, printed in 1892 under the title *Die Hauptprobleme der Philosophie in ihrer Entwicklung und teilweisen Lösung von Thales bis Robert Hamerling*, as well as his *Geschichte der Philosophie mit besonderer Berücksichtigung der Neuzeit* were highly thought of by Rudolf Steiner. Knauer's amusing explanation of the concepts of matter and form in Aristotle using the example of a wolf which eats lambs is often mentioned by Steiner. See e.g. the essay 'Philosophie und Anthroposophie' in GA 35.

88. 1711–76, Scottish philosopher.

89. René Descartes, 1596–1650; Nicole Malebranche, 1638–1715; John Stuart Mill, 1806–73; Herbert Spencer, 1820–1903.

90. Alphonse Gratry, 1805–72.

91. The names of the authors quoted by Rudolf Steiner here are illegible in the shorthand note.

92. 1797–1855, important Italian philosopher, Catholic priest. Founder of a religious order. Was vehemently attacked by the Jesuits because of his writings so that individual ones were listed on the Index. He undertook to refound Christian philosophy in the form of an objective idealism which built in a free and creative way on the thinking of St Augustine and Thomas Aquinas. Rudolf Steiner refers to Rosmini, of whom he thought very highly, and his pupils possibly as late as in the lecture of 30 May 1920—although without quoting him by name—as a 'cleric who is working towards a certain

freedom of Catholicism'. (See Rudolf Steiner, *Heilfaktoren für den sozialen Organismus*, GA 198, p. 92). Giancarlo Roggero provides a very good introduction to Rosmini's life and work in his book *Antonio Rosmini, Liebesfeuer aus Wahrheitslicht*, Novalis Verlag Schaffhausen, 2000.

93. 1801–52, Italian writer and statesman.

94. *Teosofia*, 5 volumes, 1859–74.

95. Some of Rosmini's writings had been listed on the Index of Prohibited Books as early as 1849, but were taken off in 1854. At the instigation of the Jesuits, 40 essays by Rosmini were condemned by the Inquisition in 1887.

96. See also Karl Werner, *Idealistische Theorien des Schönen in der italienischen Philosophie des 19. Jahrhunderts*, Vienna 1884. This book—with underlinings—is included in Rudolf Steiner's library (sig. P 1107).

97. About the *feruer*—also *ferouer, fravashi or farvarshi*—see Otto Willmann *Geschichte des Idealismus*, Volume 1, Chapter: 'Die Magielehre', as well as Rudolf Steiner's lecture of 19 September 1909 in GA 114, *According to Luke*, 2001.

98. Quintus Septimius Florens Tertullianus, born *c*. 160 in Carthage, died *c*. 222. Oldest Latin ecclesiastical writer, creator of Latin ecclesiastical language and co-founder of early Catholic doctrine. In his writings he turned against everything that can threaten Christians in a world ruined by the devil; he hated philosophy and fought against Gnostic teachings.

99. Gnostic teacher in Alexandria *c*. 130/140.

100. Marcion of Sinope on the Black Sea was a bishop and belonged to the Christian congregation in Rome, from which he was expelled in 144 as a heretic. His teaching was sharply criticized in Tertullian's diatribe *Against Marcion*. Literature about gnosis from Rudolf Steiner's library: Eugen Heinrich Schmitt, *Die Gnosis. Grundlagen der Weltanschauung einer edleren Kultur*, Volume 1, *Die Gnosis des Altertums*, Leipzig 1903; George Mead, *Fragmente eines verschollenen Glaubens*, translated into German by A. v. Ulrich, Berlin 1902. Rudolf Steiner was personally acquainted with both authors. Also: *Koptisch-Gnostische Schriften (Die Pistis Sophia, Die beiden Bücher Jeû)*, ed. C. Schmidt,Leipzig 1905.

101. The preceding Dornach lectures are printed in the volumes *Die okkulte Bewegung im 19. Jahrhundert und ihre Beziehung zur Weltkultur* (10 October to 7 November 1915), GA 254, *The Occult Movement in the Nineteenth Century*, 1973; and *Der Wert des Denkens für eine den Menschen befriedigende Erkenntnis* (20 August to 11 October 1915), GA 164.

102. See note 78.

103. Michael Bauer, 1871–1929, leader of the Nuremberg branch and a member for many years of the executive council of the Anthroposophical Society.

104. The Reformed pastor E. Riggenbach in Arlesheim had given a lecture in Liestal with the title 'The anthroposophists' colony in Dornach'. The lecture concluded with the words: 'I imagine in my thoughts what the old Wandsbek newspaperman Matthias Claudius might have said when he saw the cupola-crowned temple and the giant chimney which despoil our region in such a stunning way; when he saw the little men and women who try to outdo one another in the novelty of their clothes and hairstyle; when, indeed,

he read the writings of the anthroposophists in which everything that is light is obscured and what is already obscure is obscured even further. What, indeed, would he say about that? I almost believe he would creep up to the temple in the dead of night, armed with a piece of chalk, and there in his graceful hand write the verse on the door which can be found in his lovely evening song: 'We proud human beings ...' (*Basellandschaftliche Zeitung*, Volume 83, No. 293 of 11 December 1915.)

105. 1740–1815, German poet, editor of the magazine *Wandsbecker Bote*.

106. 'Et mortuus est Dei filius; prorsus credibile, quia ineptum est', *On the Flesh of Christ*, 5, Migne 2, 806. Rudolf Steiner deals in greater detail with these words in a lecture of 16 October 1918 (in GA 182, pp. 170 ff.).

107. At the first general Christian Council of Nicea in 325 the creed was laid down which taught that the Son was of one being with the Father (Nicene Creed); it was expanded in 381 at the Council of Constantinople through the addition of 'filioque', meaning that the Holy Spirit also proceeded from the Son. This teaching led to a long conflict within the Church and made a significant contribution to the schism between the Eastern churches and Rome in 1054. See note 112.

108. Vladimir Solovyov, 1853–1900. *Ausgewählte Werke* translated from the Russian by Harry Köhler (Harriet von Vacano), 4 volumes, Stuttgart 1921–2.

109. The reference is probably to Anna Riebensahm, who died on 13 December 1915 (see GA 261, pp. 180–2).

110. Charles Darwin, 1809–82, important representative of evolutionary theory.

111. See note 9.

112. The centuries-old conflict of dogma between the Eastern and Western Church led to a schism in 867 after Pope Nicholas I attempted to assert the primacy of the Bishop of Rome by interfering in the appointment of Photius as Patriarch of Constantinople. The final schism occurred in 1054 when three legates from Pope Leo IX threw the bull of excommunication against Patriarch Michael on the main altar of the Hagia Sophia in the middle of mass. See also Rudolf Steiner's lecture of 1 October 1922 in *Die Grundimpulse des weltgeschichtlichen Werdens der Menschheit*, GA 216, *Supersensible Influences in the History of Mankind*, 1956.

113. Rudolf Steiner afterwards travelled to Germany where he gave lectures in Berlin, Hamburg, Munich, Stuttgart and other cities. He did not return to Dornach until the end of July 1916.

RUDOLF STEINER'S COLLECTED WORKS

The German Edition of Rudolf Steiner's Collected Works (the *Gesamtausgabe* [GA] published by Rudolf Steiner Verlag, Dornach, Switzerland) presently runs to 354 titles, organized either by type of work (written or spoken), chronology, audience (public or other), or subject (education, art, etc.). For ease of comparison, the Collected Works in English [CW] follows the German organization exactly. A complete listing of the CWs follows with literal translations of the German titles. Other than in the case of the books published in his lifetime, titles were rarely given by Rudolf Steiner himself, and were often provided by the editors of the German editions. The titles in English are not necessarily the same as the German; and, indeed, over the past seventy-five years have frequently been different, with the same book sometimes appearing under different titles.

For ease of identification and to avoid confusion, we suggest that readers looking for a title should do so by CW number. Because the work of creating the Collected Works of Rudolf Steiner is an ongoing process, with new titles being published every year, we have not indicated in this listing which books are presently available. To find out what titles in the Collected Works are currently in print, please check our website at www.rudolfsteinerpress.com (or www.steinerbooks.org for US readers).

Written Work

CW 1	Goethe: Natural-Scientific Writings, Introduction, with Footnotes and Explanations in the text by Rudolf Steiner
CW 2	Outlines of an Epistemology of the Goethean World View, with Special Consideration of Schiller
CW 3	Truth and Science
CW 4	The Philosophy of Freedom
CW 4a	Documents to 'The Philosophy of Freedom'
CW 5	Friedrich Nietzsche, A Fighter against His Own Time
CW 6	Goethe's Worldview
CW 6a	Now in CW 30
CW 7	Mysticism at the Dawn of Modern Spiritual Life and Its Relationship with Modern Worldviews
CW 8	Christianity as Mystical Fact and the Mysteries of Antiquity
CW 9	Theosophy: An Introduction into Supersensible World Knowledge and Human Purpose
CW 10	How Does One Attain Knowledge of Higher Worlds?
CW 11	From the Akasha-Chronicle

Public Lectures

Lectures to the Members of the Anthroposophical Society

CW 88   Concerning the Astral World and Devachan

CW 89   Consciousness—Life—Form. Fundamental Principles of a Spiritual-Scientific Cosmology

CW 90   Participant Notes from the Lectures during the Years 1903–1905

CW 91   Participant Notes from the Lectures during the Years 1903–1905

CW 92   The Occult Truths of Ancient Myths and Sagas

CW 93   The Temple Legend and the Golden Legend

CW 93a   Fundamentals of Esotericism

CW 94   Cosmogony. Popular Occultism. The Gospel of John. The Theosophy in the Gospel of John

CW 95   At the Gates of Theosophy

CW 96   Origin-Impulses of Spiritual Science. Christian Esotericism in the Light of New Spirit-Knowledge

CW 97   The Christian Mystery

CW 98   Nature Beings and Spirit Beings—Their Effects in Our Visible World

CW 99   The Theosophy of the Rosicrucians

CW 100   Human Development and Christ-Knowledge

CW 101   Myths and Legends. Occult Signs and Symbols

CW 102   The Working into Human Beings by Spiritual Beings

CW 103   The Gospel of John

CW 104   The Apocalypse of John

CW 104a   From the Picture-Script of the Apocalypse of John

CW 105   Universe, Earth, the Human Being: Their Being and Development, as well as Their Reflection in the Connection between Egyptian Mythology and Modern Culture

CW 106   Egyptian Myths and Mysteries in Relation to the Active Spiritual Forces of the Present

CW 107   Spiritual-Scientific Knowledge of the Human Being

CW 108   Answering the Questions of Life and the World through Anthroposophy

CW 109   The Principle of Spiritual Economy in Connection with the Question of Reincarnation. An Aspect of the Spiritual Guidance of Humanity

CW 110   The Spiritual Hierarchies and Their Reflection in the Physical World. Zodiac, Planets and Cosmos

CW 111   Contained in CW 109

CW 112   The Gospel of John in Relation to the Three Other Gospels, Especially the Gospel of Luke

CW 113   The Orient in the Light of the Occident. The Children of Lucifer and the Brothers of Christ

CW 114   The Gospel of Luke

CW 115   Anthroposophy—Psychosophy—Pneumatosophy

CW 116   The Christ-Impulse and the Development of 'I'-Consciousness

CW 117   The Deeper Secrets of the Development of Humanity in Light of the Gospels

CW 240   Esoteric Observations of Karmic Relationships in 6 Volumes, Vol. 6

CW 243   The Consciousness of the Initiate

CW 245   Instructions for an Esoteric Schooling

CW 250   The Building-Up of the Anthroposophical Society. From the Beginning to the Outbreak of the First World War

CW 251   The History of the Goetheanum Building-Association

CW 252   Life in the Anthroposophical Society from the First World War to the Burning of the First Goetheanum

CW 253   The Problems of Living Together in the Anthroposophical Society. On the Dornach Crisis of 1915. With Highlights on Swedenborg's Clairvoyance, the Views of Freudian Psychoanalysts, and the Concept of Love in Relation to Mysticism

CW 254   The Occult Movement in the 19th Century and Its Relationship to World Culture. Significant Points from the Exoteric Cultural Life around the Middle of the 19th Century

CW 255   Rudolf Steiner during the First World War

CW 255a   Anthroposophy and the Reformation of Society. On the History of the Threefold Movement

CW 255b   Anthroposophy and Its Opponents, 1919–1921

CW 256   How Can the Anthroposophical Movement Be Financed?

CW 256a   Futurum, Inc. / International Laboratories, Inc.

CW 256b   The Coming Day, Inc.

CW 257   Anthroposophical Community-Building

CW 258   The History of and Conditions for the Anthroposophical Movement in Relationship to the Anthroposophical Society. A Stimulus to Self-Contemplation

CW 259   The Year of Destiny 1923 in the History of the Anthroposophical Society. From the Burning of the Goetheanum to the Christmas Conference

CW 260   The Christmas Conference for the Founding of the General Anthroposophical Society

CW 260a   The Constitution of the General Anthroposophical Society and the School for Spiritual Science. The Rebuilding of the Goetheanum

CW 261   Our Dead. Addresses, Words of Remembrance, and Meditative Verses, 1906–1924

CW 262   Rudolf Steiner and Marie Steiner-von Sivers: Correspondence and Documents, 1901–1925

CW 263/1   Rudolf Steiner and Edith Maryon: Correspondence: Letters, Verses, Sketches, 1912–1924

CW 264   On the History and the Contents of the First Section of the Esoteric School from 1904 to 1914. Letters, Newsletters, Documents, Lectures

CW 265   On the History and from the Contents of the Ritual-Knowledge Section of the Esoteric School from 1904 to 1914. Documents, and Lectures from the Years 1906 to 1914, as Well as on New Approaches to Ritual-Knowledge Work in the Years 1921–1924

CW 266/1 From the Contents of the Esoteric Lessons. Volume 1: 1904–1909. Notes from Memory of Participants. Meditation texts from the notes of Rudolf Steiner

CW 266/2 From the Contents of the Esoteric Lessons. Volume 2: 1910–1912. Notes from Memory of Participants

CW 266/3 From the Contents of the Esoteric Lessons. Volume 3: 1913, 1914 and 1920–1923. Notes from Memory of Participants. Meditation texts from the notes of Rudolf Steiner

CW 267 Soul-Exercises: Vol. 1: Exercises with Word and Image Meditations for the Methodological Development of Higher Powers of Knowledge, 1904–1924

CW 268 Soul-Exercises: Vol. 2: Mantric Verses, 1903–1925

CW 269 Ritual Texts for the Celebration of the Free Christian Religious Instruction. The Collected Verses for Teachers and Students of the Waldorf School

CW 270 Esoteric Instructions for the First Class of the School for Spiritual Science at the Goetheanum 1924, 4 Volumes

CW 271 Art and Knowledge of Art. Foundations of a New Aesthetic

CW 272 Spiritual-Scientific Commentary on Goethe's 'Faust' in Two Volumes. Vol. 1: Faust, the Striving Human Being

CW 273 Spiritual-Scientific Commentary on Goethe's 'Faust' in Two Volumes. Vol. 2: The Faust-Problem

CW 274 Addresses for the Christmas Plays from the Old Folk Traditions

CW 275 Art in the Light of Mystery-Wisdom

CW 276 The Artistic in Its Mission in the World. The Genius of Language. The World of Self-Revealing Radiant Appearances—Anthroposophy and Art. Anthroposophy and Poetry

CW 277 Eurythmy. The Revelation of the Speaking Soul

CW 277a The Origin and Development of Eurythmy

CW 278 Eurythmy as Visible Song

CW 279 Eurythmy as Visible Speech

CW 280 The Method and Nature of Speech Formation

CW 281 The Art of Recitation and Declamation

CW 282 Speech Formation and Dramatic Art

CW 283 The Nature of Things Musical and the Experience of Tone in the Human Being

CW 284/285 Images of Occult Seals and Pillars. The Munich Congress of Whitsun 1907 and Its Consequences

CW 286 Paths to a New Style of Architecture. 'And the Building Becomes Human'

CW 287 The Building at Dornach as a Symbol of Historical Becoming and an Artistic Transformation Impulse

CW 288 Style-Forms in the Living Organic

CW 289 The Building-Idea of the Goetheanum: Lectures with Slides from the Years 1920–1921

CW 290 The Building-Idea of the Goetheanum: Lectures with Slides from the Years 1920–1921

CW 342   Lectures and Courses on Christian Religious Work, Vol. 1: Anthroposophical Foundations for a Renewed Christian Religious Working

CW 343   Lectures and Courses on Christian Religious Work, Vol. 2: Spiritual Knowledge—Religious Feeling—Cultic Doing

CW 344   Lectures and Courses on Christian Religious Work, Vol. 3: Lectures at the Founding of the Christian Community

CW 345   Lectures and Courses on Christian Religious Work, Vol. 4: Concerning the Nature of the Working Word

CW 346   Lectures and Courses on Christian Religious Work, Vol. 5: The Apocalypse and the Work of the Priest

CW 347   The Knowledge of the Nature of the Human Being According to Body, Soul and Spirit. On Earlier Conditions of the Earth

CW 348   On Health and Illness. Foundations of a Spiritual-Scientific Doctrine of the Senses

CW 349   On the Life of the Human Being and of the Earth. On the Nature of Christianity

CW 350   Rhythms in the Cosmos and in the Human Being. How Does One Come To See the Spiritual World?

CW 351   The Human Being and the World. The Influence of the Spirit in Nature. On the Nature of Bees

CW 352   Nature and the Human Being Observed Spiritual-Scientifically

CW 353   The History of Humanity and the World-Views of the Folk Cultures

CW 354   The Creation of the World and the Human Being. Life on Earth and the Influence of the Stars

SIGNIFICANT EVENTS IN THE LIFE OF RUDOLF STEINER

1829:   June 23: birth of Johann Steiner (1829–1910)—Rudolf Steiner's father—in Geras, Lower Austria.

1834:   May 8: birth of Franciska Blie (1834–1918)—Rudolf Steiner's mother—in Horn, Lower Austria. 'My father and mother were both children of the glorious Lower Austrian forest district north of the Danube.'

1860:   May 16: marriage of Johann Steiner and Franciska Blie.

1861:   February 25: birth of *Rudolf Joseph Lorenz Steiner* in Kraljevec, Croatia, near the border with Hungary, where Johann Steiner works as a telegrapher for the South Austria Railroad. Rudolf Steiner is baptized two days later, February 27, the date usually given as his birthday.

1862:   Summer: the family moves to Mödling, Lower Austria.

1863:   The family moves to Pottschach, Lower Austria, near the Styrian border, where Johann Steiner becomes stationmaster. 'The view stretched to the mountains ... majestic peaks in the distance and the sweet charm of nature in the immediate surroundings.'

1864:   November 15: birth of Rudolf Steiner's sister, Leopoldine (d. November 1, 1927). She will become a seamstress and live with her parents for the rest of her life.

1866:   July 28: birth of Rudolf Steiner's deaf-mute brother, Gustav (d. May 1, 1941).

1867:   Rudolf Steiner enters the village school. Following a disagreement between his father and the schoolmaster, whose wife falsely accused the boy of causing a commotion, Rudolf Steiner is taken out of school and taught at home.

1868:   A critical experience. Unknown to the family, an aunt dies in a distant town. Sitting in the station waiting room, Rudolf Steiner sees her 'form,' which speaks to him, asking for help. 'Beginning with this experience, a new soul life began in the boy, one in which not only the outer trees and mountains spoke to him, but also the worlds that lay behind them. From this moment on, the boy began to live with the spirits of nature ...'

1869:   The family moves to the peaceful, rural village of Neudorfl, near Wiener-Neustadt in present-day Austria. Rudolf Steiner attends the village school. Because of the 'unorthodoxy' of his writing and spelling, he has to do 'extra lessons.'

1870:   Through a book lent to him by his tutor, he discovers geometry: 'To grasp something purely in the spirit brought me inner happiness. I know that I first learned happiness through geometry.' The same tutor allows him to draw, while other students still struggle with their reading and writing. 'An artistic element' thus enters his education.

1871:   Though his parents are not religious, Rudolf Steiner becomes a 'church child,' a favourite of the priest, who was 'an exceptional character.' 'Up to the age of ten or eleven, among those I came to know, he was far and away the most significant.' Among other things, he introduces Steiner to Copernican, heliocentric cosmology. As an altar boy, Rudolf Steiner serves at Masses, funerals, and Corpus Christi processions. At year's end, after an incident in which he escapes a thrashing, his father forbids him to go to church.

1872:   Rudolf Steiner transfers to grammar school in Wiener-Neustadt, a five-mile walk from home, which must be done in all weathers.

1873–75: Through his teachers and on his own, Rudolf Steiner has many wonderful experiences with science and mathematics. Outside school, he teaches himself analytic geometry, trigonometry, differential equations, and calculus.

1876:   Rudolf Steiner begins tutoring other students. He learns bookbinding from his father. He also teaches himself stenography.

1877:   Rudolf Steiner discovers Kant's *Critique of Pure Reason*, which he reads and rereads. He also discovers and reads von Rotteck's *World History*.

1878:   He studies extensively in contemporary psychology and philosophy.

1879:   Rudolf Steiner graduates from high school with honours. His father is transferred to Inzersdorf, near Vienna. He uses his first visit to Vienna 'to purchase a great number of philosophy books'—Kant, Fichte, Schelling, and Hegel, as well as numerous histories of philosophy. His aim: to find a path from the 'I' to nature.

October 1879–1883: Rudolf Steiner attends the Technical College in Vienna—to study mathematics, chemistry, physics, mineralogy, botany, zoology, biology, geology, and mechanics—with a scholarship. He also attends lectures in history and literature, while avidly reading philosophy on his own. His two favourite professors are Karl Julius Schröer (German language and literature) and Edmund Reitlinger (physics). He also audits lectures by Robert Zimmerman on aesthetics and Franz Brentano on philosophy. During this year he begins his friendship with Moritz Zitter (1861–1921), who will help support him financially when he is in Berlin.

1880:   Rudolf Steiner attends lectures on Schiller and Goethe by Karl Julius Schröer, who becomes his mentor. Also 'through a remarkable combination of circumstances,' he meets Felix Koguzki, a 'herb gatherer' and healer, who could 'see deeply into the secrets of nature.' Rudolf Steiner will meet and study with this 'emissary of the Master' throughout his time in Vienna.

1881:   January: '... I didn't sleep a wink. I was busy with philosophical problems until about 12:30 a.m. Then, finally, I threw myself down on my couch. All my striving during the previous year had been to research whether the following statement by Schelling was true or not: *Within everyone dwells a secret, marvelous capacity to draw back from the stream of time—out of the self clothed in all that comes to us from outside—into our innermost being and there, in the immutable form of the Eternal, to look into ourselves.* I believe, and I am still quite certain of it, that I discovered this capacity in myself; I had long had an inkling of it. Now the whole of idealist philosophy stood before me in modified form. What's a sleepless night compared to that!'

Rudolf Steiner begins communicating with leading thinkers of the day, who send him books in return, which he reads eagerly.

July: 'I am not one of those who dives into the day like an animal in human form. I pursue a quite specific goal, an idealistic aim—knowledge of the truth! This cannot be done offhandedly. It requires the greatest striving in the world, free of all egotism, and equally of all resignation.'

August: Steiner puts down on paper for the first time thoughts for a 'Philosophy of Freedom.' 'The striving for the absolute: this human yearning is freedom.' He also seeks to outline a 'peasant philosophy,' describing what the worldview of a 'peasant'—one who lives close to the earth and the old ways—really is.

1881–1882: Felix Koguzki, the herb gatherer, reveals himself to be the envoy of another, higher initiatory personality, who instructs Rudolf Steiner to penetrate Fichte's philosophy and to master modern scientific thinking as a preparation for right entry into the spirit. This 'Master' also teaches him the double (evolutionary and involutionary) nature of time.

1882:   Through the offices of Karl Julius Schröer, Rudolf Steiner is asked by Joseph Kurschner to edit Goethe's scientific works for the *Deutschen National-Literatur* edition. He writes 'A Possible Critique of Atomistic Concepts' and sends it to Friedrich Theodore Vischer.

1883:   Rudolf Steiner completes his college studies and begins work on the Goethe project.

1884:   First volume of Goethe's *Scientific Writings* (CW 1) appears (March). He lectures on Goethe and Lessing, and Goethe's approach to science. In July, he enters the household of Ladislaus and Pauline Specht as tutor to the four Specht boys. He will live there until 1890. At this time, he meets Josef Breuer (1842–1925), the co-author with Sigmund Freud of *Studies in Hysteria*, who is the Specht family doctor.

1885:   While continuing to edit Goethe's writings, Rudolf Steiner reads deeply in contemporary philosophy (Edouard von Hartmann, Johannes Volkelt, and Richard Wahle, among others).

1886:   May: Rudolf Steiner sends Kurschner the manuscript of *Outlines of Goethe's Theory of Knowledge* (CW 2), which appears in October, and which he sends out widely. He also meets the poet Marie Eugenie Delle Grazie and writes 'Nature and Our Ideals' for her. He attends her salon, where he meets many priests, theologians, and philosophers, who will become his friends. Meanwhile, the director of the Goethe Archive in Weimar requests his collaboration with the *Sophien* edition of Goethe's works, particularly the writings on colour.

1887:   At the beginning of the year, Rudolf Steiner is very sick. As the year progresses and his health improves, he becomes increasingly 'a man of letters,' lecturing, writing essays, and taking part in Austrian cultural life. In August–September, the second volume of Goethe's *Scientific Writings* appears.

1888: January–July: Rudolf Steiner assumes editorship of the 'German Weekly' (*Deutsche Wochenschrift*). He begins lecturing more intensively, giving, for example, a lecture titled 'Goethe as Father of a New Aesthetics.' He meets and becomes soul friends with Friedrich Eckstein (1861–1939), a vegetarian, philosopher of symbolism, alchemist, and musician, who will introduce him to various spiritual currents (including Theosophy) and with whom he will meditate and interpret esoteric and alchemical texts.

1889: Rudolf Steiner first reads Nietzsche (*Beyond Good and Evil*). He encounters Theosophy again and learns of Madame Blavatsky in the Theosophical circle around Marie Lang (1858–1934). Here he also meets well-known figures of Austrian life, as well as esoteric figures like the occultist Franz Hartman and Karl Leinigen-Billigen (translator of C.G. Harrison's *The Transcendental Universe*). During this period, Steiner first reads A.P. Sinnett's *Esoteric Buddhism* and Mabel Collins's *Light on the Path*. He also begins travelling, visiting Budapest, Weimar, and Berlin (where he meets philosopher Edouard von Hartmann).

1890: Rudolf Steiner finishes volume 3 of Goethe's scientific writings. He begins his doctoral dissertation, which will become *Truth and Science* (CW 3). He also meets the poet and feminist Rosa Mayreder (1858–1938), with whom he can exchange his most intimate thoughts. In September, Rudolf Steiner moves to Weimar to work in the Goethe-Schiller Archive.

1891: Volume 3 of the Kurschner edition of Goethe appears. Meanwhile, Rudolf Steiner edits Goethe's studies in mineralogy and scientific writings for the *Sophien* edition. He meets Ludwig Laistner of the Cotta Publishing Company, who asks for a book on the basic question of metaphysics. From this will result, ultimately, *The Philosophy of Freedom* (CW 4), which will be published not by Cotta but by Emil Felber. In October, Rudolf Steiner takes the oral exam for a doctorate in philosophy, mathematics, and mechanics at Rostock University, receiving his doctorate on the twenty-sixth. In November, he gives his first lecture on Goethe's 'Fairy Tale' in Vienna.

1892: Rudolf Steiner continues work at the Goethe-Schiller Archive and on his *Philosophy of Freedom*. *Truth and Science*, his doctoral dissertation, is published. Steiner undertakes to write introductions to books on Schopenhauer and Jean Paul for Cotta. At year's end, he finds lodging with Anna Eunike, née Schulz (1853–1911), a widow with four daughters and a son. He also develops a friendship with Otto Erich Hartleben (1864–1905) with whom he shares literary interests.

1893: Rudolf Steiner begins his habit of producing many reviews and articles. In March, he gives a lecture titled 'Hypnotism, with Reference to Spiritism.' In September, volume 4 of the Kurschner edition is completed. In November, *The Philosophy of Freedom* appears. This year, too, he meets John Henry Mackay (1864–1933), the anarchist, and Max Stirner, a scholar and biographer.

1894: Rudolf Steiner meets Elisabeth Förster Nietzsche, the philosopher's sister, and begins to read Nietzsche in earnest, beginning with the as yet unpublished *Antichrist*. He also meets Ernst Haeckel (1834–1919). In the fall, he begins to write *Nietzsche, A Fighter against His Time* (CW 5).

1895: May, *Nietzsche, A Fighter against His Time* appears.

1896: January 22: Rudolf Steiner sees Friedrich Nietzsche for the first and only time. Moves between the Nietzsche and the Goethe-Schiller Archives, where he completes his work before year's end. He falls out with Elisabeth Förster Nietzsche, thus ending his association with the Nietzsche Archive.

1897: Rudolf Steiner finishes the manuscript of *Goethe's Worldview* (CW 6). He moves to Berlin with Anna Eunike and begins editorship of the *Magazin für Literatur*. From now on, Steiner will write countless reviews, literary and philosophical articles, and so on. He begins lecturing at the 'Free Literary Society.' In September, he attends the Zionist Congress in Basel. He sides with Dreyfus in the Dreyfus affair.

1898: Rudolf Steiner is very active as an editor in the political, artistic, and theatrical life of Berlin. He becomes friendly with John Henry Mackay and poet Ludwig Jacobowski (1868–1900). He joins Jacobowski's circle of writers, artists, and scientists—'The Coming Ones' (*Die Kommenden*)— and contributes lectures to the group until 1903. He also lectures at the 'League for College Pedagogy.' He writes an article for Goethe's sesquicentennial, 'Goethe's Secret Revelation,' on the 'Fairy Tale of the Green Snake and the Beautiful Lily.'

1898–99: 'This was a trying time for my soul as I looked at Christianity. . . . I was able to progress only by contemplating, by means of spiritual perception, the evolution of Christianity. . . . Conscious knowledge of real Christianity began to dawn in me around the turn of the century. This seed continued to develop. My soul trial occurred shortly before the beginning of the twentieth century. It was decisive for my soul's development that I stood spiritually before the Mystery of Golgotha in a deep and solemn celebration of knowledge.'

1899: Rudolf Steiner begins teaching and giving lectures and lecture cycles at the Workers' College, founded by Wilhelm Liebknecht (1826–1900). He will continue to do so until 1904. Writes: *Literature and Spiritual Life in the Nineteenth Century; Individualism in Philosophy; Haeckel and His Opponents; Poetry in the Present;* and begins what will become (fifteen years later) *The Riddles of Philosophy* (CW 18). He also meets many artists and writers, including Käthe Kollwitz, Stefan Zweig, and Rainer Maria Rilke. On October 31, he marries Anna Eunike.

1900: 'I thought that the turn of the century must bring humanity a new light. It seemed to me that the separation of human thinking and willing from the spirit had peaked. A turn or reversal of direction in human evolution seemed to me a necessity.' Rudolf Steiner finishes *World and Life Views in the Nineteenth Century* (the second part of what will become *The Riddles of Philosophy*) and dedicates it to Ernst Haeckel. It is published in March. He continues lecturing at *Die Kommenden*, whose leadership he assumes after the death of Jacobowski. Also, he gives the Gutenberg Jubilee lecture before 7,000 typesetters and printers. In September, Rudolf Steiner is invited by Count and Countess Brockdorff to lecture in the Theosophical Library. His first lecture is on Nietzsche. His second lecture is titled 'Goethe's Secret Revelation.' October 6, he begins a lecture cycle on the mystics that will become *Mystics after Modernism* (CW 7). November–December: 'Marie von Sivers appears in the audience....' Also in November, Steiner gives his first lecture at the Giordano Bruno Bund (where he will continue to lecture until May, 1905). He speaks on Bruno and modern Rome, focusing on the importance of the philosophy of Thomas Aquinas as monism.

1901:   In continual financial straits, Rudolf Steiner's early friends Moritz Zitter and Rosa Mayreder help support him. In October, he begins the lecture cycle *Christianity as Mystical Fact* (CW 8) at the Theosophical Library. In November, he gives his first 'Theosophical lecture' on Goethe's 'Fairy Tale' in Hamburg at the invitation of Wilhelm Hubbe-Schleiden. He also attends a gathering to celebrate the founding of the Theosophical Society at Count and Countess Brockdorff's. He gives a lecture cycle, 'From Buddha to Christ,' for the circle of the *Kommenden*. November 17, Marie von Sivers asks Rudolf Steiner if Theosophy needs a Western-Christian spiritual movement (to complement Theosophy's Eastern emphasis). 'The question was posed. Now, following spiritual laws, I could begin to give an answer....' In December, Rudolf Steiner writes his first article for a Theosophical publication. At year's end, the Brockdorffs and possibly Wilhelm Hubbe-Schleiden ask Rudolf Steiner to join the Theosophical Society and undertake the leadership of the German section. Rudolf Steiner agrees, on the condition that Marie von Sivers (then in Italy) work with him.

1902:   Beginning in January, Rudolf Steiner attends the opening of the Workers' School in Spandau with Rosa Luxemburg (1870–1919). January 17, Rudolf Steiner joins the Theosophical Society. In April, he is asked to become general secretary of the German Section of the Theosophical Society, and works on preparations for its founding. In July, he visits London for a Theosophical congress. He meets Bertram Keightly, G.R.S. Mead, A.P. Sinnett, and Annie Besant, among others. In September, *Christianity as Mystical Fact* appears. In October, Rudolf Steiner gives his first public lecture on Theosophy ('Monism and Theosophy') to about three hundred people at the Giordano Bruno Bund. On October 19–21, the German Section of the Theosophical Society has its first meeting; Rudolf Steiner is the general secretary, and Annie Besant attends. Steiner lectures on practical karma studies. On October 23, Annie Besant inducts Rudolf Steiner into the Esoteric School of the Theosophical Society. On October 25, Steiner begins a weekly series of lectures: 'The Field of Theosophy.' During this year, Rudolf Steiner also first meets Ita Wegman (1876–1943), who will become his close collaborator in his final years.

1903:   Rudolf Steiner holds about 300 lectures and seminars. In May, the first issue of the periodical *Luzifer* appears. In June, Rudolf Steiner visits

London for the first meeting of the Federation of the European Sections of the Theosophical Society, where he meets Colonel Olcott. He begins to write *Theosophy* (CW 9).

1904: Rudolf Steiner continues lecturing at the Workers' College and elsewhere (about 90 lectures), while lecturing intensively all over Germany among Theosophists (about 140 lectures). In February, he meets Carl Unger (1878–1929), who will become a member of the board of the Anthroposophical Society (1913). In March, he meets Michael Bauer (1871–1929), a Christian mystic, who will also be on the board. In May, *Theosophy* appears, with the dedication: 'To the spirit of Giordano Bruno.' Rudolf Steiner and Marie von Sivers visit London for meetings with Annie Besant. June: Rudolf Steiner and Marie von Sivers attend the meeting of the Federation of European Sections of the Theosophical Society in Amsterdam. In July, Steiner begins the articles in *Luzifer-Gnosis* that will become *How to Know Higher Worlds* (CW 10) and *Cosmic Memory* (CW 11). In September, Annie Besant visits Germany. In December, Steiner lectures on Freemasonry. He mentions the High Grade Masonry derived from John Yarker and represented by Theodore Reuss and Karl Kellner as a blank slate 'into which a good image could be placed.'

1905: This year, Steiner ends his non-Theosophical lecturing activity. Supported by Marie von Sivers, his Theosophical lecturing—both in public and in the Theosophical Society—increases significantly: 'The German Theosophical Movement is of exceptional importance.' Steiner recommends reading, among others, Fichte, Jacob Boehme, and Angelus Silesius. He begins to introduce Christian themes into Theosophy. He also begins to work with doctors (Felix Peipers and Ludwig Noll). In July, he is in London for the Federation of European Sections, where he attends a lecture by Annie Besant: 'I have seldom seen Mrs. Besant speak in so inward and heartfelt a manner....' 'Through Mrs. Besant I have found the way to H.P. Blavatsky.' September to October, he gives a course of thirty-one lectures for a small group of esoteric students. In October, the annual meeting of the German Section of the Theosophical Society, which still remains very small, takes place. Rudolf Steiner reports membership has risen from 121 to 377 members. In November, seeking to establish esoteric 'continuity,' Rudolf Steiner and Marie von Sivers participate in a 'Memphis-Misraim' Masonic ceremony. They pay forty-five marks for membership. 'Yesterday, you saw how little remains of former esoteric institutions.' 'We are dealing only with a "framework"... for the present, nothing lies behind it. The occult powers have completely withdrawn.'

1906: Expansion of Theosophical work. Rudolf Steiner gives about 245 lectures, only 44 of which take place in Berlin. Cycles are given in Paris, Leipzig, Stuttgart, and Munich. Esoteric work also intensifies. Rudolf Steiner begins writing *An Outline of Esoteric Science* (CW 13). In January, Rudolf Steiner receives permission (a patent) from the Great Orient of the Scottish A & A Thirty-Three Degree Rite of the Order of the Ancient

Freemasons of the Memphis-Misraim Rite to direct a chapter under the name 'Mystica Aeterna.' This will become the 'Cognitive-Ritual Section' (also called 'Misraim Service') of the Esoteric School. (See: *Freemasonry and Ritual Work: The Misraim Service*, CW 265). During this time, Steiner also meets Albert Schweitzer. In May, he is in Paris, where he visits Edouard Schuré. Many Russians attend his lectures (including Konstantin Balmont, Dimitri Mereszkovski, Zinaida Hippius, and Maximilian Woloshin). He attends the General Meeting of the European Federation of the Theosophical Society, at which Col. Olcott is present for the last time. He spends the year's end in Venice and Rome, where he writes and works on his translation of H.P. Blavatsky's *Key to Theosophy*.

1907: Further expansion of the German Theosophical Movement according to the Rosicrucian directive to 'introduce spirit into the world'—in education, in social questions, in art, and in science. In February, Col. Olcott dies in Adyar. Before he dies, Olcott indicates that 'the Masters' wish Annie Besant to succeed him: much politicking ensues. Rudolf Steiner supports Besant's candidacy. April-May: preparations for the Congress of the Federation of European Sections of the Theosophical Society—the great, watershed Whitsun 'Munich Congress,' attended by Annie Besant and others. Steiner decides to separate Eastern and Western (Christian-Rosicrucian) esoteric schools. He takes his esoteric school out of the Theosophical Society (Besant and Rudolf Steiner are 'in harmony' on this). Steiner makes his first lecture tours to Austria and Hungary. That summer, he is in Italy. In September, he visits Edouard Schuré, who will write the introduction to the French edition of *Christianity as Mystical Fact* in Barr, Alsace. Rudolf Steiner writes the autobiographical statement known as the 'Barr Document.' In *Luzifer-Gnosis*, 'The Education of the Child' appears.

1908: The movement grows (membership: 1,150). Lecturing expands. Steiner makes his first extended lecture tour to Holland and Scandinavia, as well as visits to Naples and Sicily. Themes: St. John's Gospel, the Apocalypse, Egypt, science, philosophy, and logic. *Luzifer-Gnosis* ceases publication. In Berlin, Marie von Sivers (with Johanna Mücke (1864–1949) forms the *Philosophisch-Theosophisch* (after 1915 *Philosophisch-Anthroposophisch*) *Verlag* to publish Steiner's work. Steiner gives lecture cycles titled *The Gospel of St. John* (CW 103) and *The Apocalypse* (104).

1909: *An Outline of Esoteric Science* appears. Lecturing and travel continues. Rudolf Steiner's spiritual research expands to include the polarity of Lucifer and Ahriman; the work of great individualities in history; the Maitreya Buddha and the Bodhisattvas; spiritual economy (CW 109); the work of the spiritual hierarchies in heaven and on earth (CW 110). He also deepens and intensifies his research into the Gospels, giving lectures on the Gospel of St. Luke (CW 114) with the first mention of two Jesus children. Meets and becomes friends with Christian Morgenstern (1871–1914). In April, he lays the foundation stone for the Malsch model—the building that will lead to the first Goetheanum. In May, the International Congress of the Federation of European Sections of the

Theosophical Society takes place in Budapest. Rudolf Steiner receives the Subba Row medal for *How to Know Higher Worlds*. During this time, Charles W. Leadbeater discovers Jiddu Krishnamurti (1895–1986) and proclaims him the future 'world teacher,' the bearer of the Maitreya Buddha and the 'reappearing Christ.' In October, Steiner delivers seminal lectures on 'anthroposophy,' which he will try, unsuccessfully, to rework over the next years into the unfinished work, *Anthroposophy (A Fragment)* (CW 45).

1910:   New themes: *The Reappearance of Christ in the Etheric* (CW 118); *The Fifth Gospel; The Mission of Folk Souls* (CW 121); *Occult History* (CW 126); the evolving development of etheric cognitive capacities. Rudolf Steiner continues his Gospel research with *The Gospel of St. Matthew* (CW 123). In January, his father dies. In April, he takes a month-long trip to Italy, including Rome, Monte Cassino, and Sicily. He also visits Scandinavia again. July–August, he writes the first mystery drama, *The Portal of Initiation* (CW 14). In November, he gives 'psychosophy' lectures. In December, he submits 'On the Psychological Foundations and Epistemological Framework of Theosophy' to the International Philosophical Congress in Bologna.

1911:   The crisis in the Theosophical Society deepens. In January, 'The Order of the Rising Sun,' which will soon become 'The Order of the Star in the East,' is founded for the coming world teacher, Krishnamurti. At the same time, Marie von Sivers, Rudolf Steiner's co-worker, falls ill. Fewer lectures are given, but important new ground is broken. In Prague, in March, Steiner meets Franz Kafka (1883–1924) and Hugo Bergmann (1883-1975). In April, he delivers his paper to the Philosophical Congress. He writes the second mystery drama, *The Soul's Probation* (CW 14). Also, while Marie von Sivers is convalescing, Rudolf Steiner begins work on *Calendar 1912/1913*, which will contain the 'Calendar of the Soul' meditations. On March 19, Anna (Eunike) Steiner dies. In September, Rudolf Steiner visits Einsiedeln, birthplace of Paracelsus. In December, Friedrich Rittelmeyer, future founder of the Christian Community, meets Rudolf Steiner. The *Johannes-Bauverein*, the 'building committee,' which would lead to the first Goetheanum (first planned for Munich), is also founded, and a preliminary committee for the founding of an independent association is created that, in the following year, will become the Anthroposophical Society. Important lecture cycles include *Occult Physiology* (CW 128); *Wonders of the World* (CW 129); *From Jesus to Christ* (CW 131). Other themes: esoteric Christianity; Christian Rosenkreutz; the spiritual guidance of humanity; the sense world and the world of the spirit.

1912:   Despite the ongoing, now increasing crisis in the Theosophical Society, much is accomplished: *Calendar 1912/1913* is published; eurythmy is created; both the third mystery drama, *The Guardian of the Threshold* (CW 14) and *A Way of Self-Knowledge* (CW 16) are written. New (or renewed) themes included life between death and rebirth and karma and reincarnation. Other lecture cycles: *Spiritual Beings in the Heavenly Bodies and in the Kingdoms of Nature* (CW 136); *The Human Being in the Light of Occultism, Theosophy, and Philosophy* (CW 137); *The Gospel of St. Mark* (CW 139); and *The Bhagavad Gita and the Epistles of Paul* (CW 142). On May 8, Rudolf Steiner celebrates White Lotus Day, H.P. Blavatsky's death day, which he had faithfully observed for the past decade, for the last time. In August, Rudolf Steiner suggests the 'independent association' be called the 'Anthroposophical Society.' In September, the first eurythmy course takes place. In October, Rudolf Steiner declines recognition of a Theosophical Society lodge dedicated to the Star of the East and decides to expel all Theosophical Society members belonging to the order. Also, with Marie von Sivers, he first visits Dornach, near Basel, Switzerland, and they stand on the hill where the Goetheanum will be built. In November, a Theosophical Society lodge is opened by direct mandate from Adyar (Annie Besant). In December, a meeting of the German section occurs at which it is decided that belonging to the Order of the Star of the East is incompatible with membership in the Theosophical Society. December 28: informal founding of the Anthroposophical Society in Berlin.

1913:   Expulsion of the German section from the Theosophical Society. February 2–3: Foundation meeting of the Anthroposophical Society. Board members include: Marie von Sivers, Michael Bauer, and Carl Unger. September 20: Laying of the foundation stone for the *Johannes Bau* (Goetheanum) in Dornach. Building begins immediately. The third mystery drama, *The Soul's Awakening* (CW 14), is completed. Also: *The Threshold of the Spiritual World* (CW 147). Lecture cycles include: *The Bhagavad Gita and the Epistles of Paul* and *The Esoteric Meaning of the Bhagavad Gita* (CW 146), which the Russian philosopher Nikolai Berdyaev attends; *The Mysteries of the East and of Christianity* (CW 144); *The Effects of Esoteric Development* (CW 145); and *The Fifth Gospel* (CW 148). In May, Rudolf Steiner is in London and Paris, where anthroposophical work continues.

1914:   Building continues on the *Johannes Bau* (Goetheanum) in Dornach, with artists and coworkers from seventeen nations. The general assembly of the Anthroposophical Society takes place. In May, Rudolf Steiner visits Paris, as well as Chartres Cathedral. June 28: assassination in Sarajevo ('Now the catastrophe has happened!'). August 1: War is declared. Rudolf Steiner returns to Germany from Dornach—he will travel back and forth. He writes the last chapter of *The Riddles of Philosophy*. Lecture cycles include: *Human and Cosmic Thought* (CW 151); *Inner Being of Humanity between Death and a New Birth* (CW 153); *Occult Reading and Occult Hearing* (CW 156). December 24: marriage of Rudolf Steiner and Marie von Sivers.

1915:   Building continues. Life after death becomes a major theme, also art. Writes: *Thoughts during a Time of War* (CW 24). Lectures include: *The Secret of Death* (CW 159); *The Uniting of Humanity through the Christ Impulse* (CW 165).

1916:   Rudolf Steiner begins work with Edith Maryon (1872–1924) on the sculpture 'The Representative of Humanity' ('The Group'—Christ, Lucifer, and Ahriman). He also works with the alchemist Alexander von Bernus on the quarterly *Das Reich*. He writes *The Riddle of Humanity* (CW 20). Lectures include: *Necessity and Freedom in World History and Human Action* (CW 166); *Past and Present in the Human Spirit* (CW 167); *The Karma of Vocation* (CW 172); *The Karma of Untruthfulness* (CW 173).

1917: Russian Revolution. The U.S. enters the war. Building continues. Rudolf Steiner delineates the idea of the 'threefold nature of the human being' (in a public lecture March 15) and the 'threefold nature of the social organism' (hammered out in May–June with the help of Otto von Lerchenfeld and Ludwig Polzer-Hoditz in the form of two documents titled *Memoranda*, which were distributed in high places). August– September: Rudolf Steiner writes *The Riddles of the Soul* (CW 20). Also: commentary on 'The Chemical Wedding of Christian Rosenkreutz' for Alexander Bernus (*Das Reich*). Lectures include: *The Karma of Materialism* (CW 176); *The Spiritual Background of the Outer World: The Fall of the Spirits of Darkness* (CW 177).

1918: March 18: peace treaty of Brest-Litovsk—'Now everything will truly enter chaos! What is needed is cultural renewal.' June: Rudolf Steiner visits Karlstein (Grail) Castle outside Prague. Lecture cycle: *From Symptom to Reality in Modern History* (CW 185). In mid-November, Emil Molt, of the Waldorf-Astoria Cigarette Company, has the idea of founding a school for his workers' children.

1919: Focus on the threefold social organism: tireless travel, countless lectures, meetings, and publications. At the same time, a new public stage of Anthroposophy emerges as cultural renewal begins. The coming years will see initiatives in pedagogy, medicine, pharmacology, and agriculture. January 27: threefold meeting: ' We must first of all, with the money we have, found free schools that can bring people what they need.' February: first public eurythmy performance in Zurich. Also: 'Appeal to the German People' (CW 24), circulated March 6 as a newspaper insert. In April, *Towards Social Renewal* (CW 23) appears— 'perhaps the most widely read of all books on politics appearing since the war.' Rudolf Steiner is asked to undertake the 'direction and leadership' of the school founded by the Waldorf-Astoria Company. Rudolf Steiner begins to talk about the 'renewal' of education. May 30: a building is selected and purchased for the future Waldorf School. August– September, Rudolf Steiner gives a lecture course for Waldorf teachers, *The Foundations of Human Experience (Study of Man)* (CW 293). September 7: Opening of the first Waldorf School. December (into January): first science course, the *Light Course* (CW 320).

1920: The Waldorf School flourishes. New threefold initiatives. Founding of limited companies *Der Kommende Tag* and *Futurum A.G.* to infuse spiritual values into the economic realm. Rudolf Steiner also focuses on the sciences. Lectures: *Introducing Anthroposophical Medicine* (CW 312); *The Warmth Course* (CW 321); *The Boundaries of Natural Science* (CW 322); *The Redemption of Thinking* (CW 74). February: Johannes Werner

Klein—later a cofounder of the Christian Community—asks Rudolf Steiner about the possibility of a 'religious renewal,' a 'Johannine church.' In March, Rudolf Steiner gives the first course for doctors and medical students. In April, a divinity student asks Rudolf Steiner a second time about the possibility of religious renewal. September 27–October 16: anthroposophical 'university course.' December: lectures titled *The Search for the New Isis* (CW 202).

1921: Rudolf Steiner continues his intensive work on cultural renewal, including the uphill battle for the threefold social order. 'University' arts, scientific, theological, and medical courses include: *The Astronomy Course* (CW 323); *Observation, Mathematics, and Scientific Experiment* (CW 324); the *Second Medical Course* (CW 313); *Color*. In June and September-October, Rudolf Steiner also gives the first two 'priests' courses' (CW 342 and 343). The 'youth movement' gains momentum. Magazines are founded: *Die Drei* (January), and—under the editorship of Albert Steffen (1884–1963)—the weekly, *Das Goetheanum* (August). In February–March, Rudolf Steiner takes his first trip outside Germany since the war (Holland). On April 7, Steiner receives a letter regarding 'religious renewal,' and May 22–23, he agrees to address the question in a practical way. In June, the Klinical-Therapeutic Institute opens in Arlesheim under the direction of Dr. Ita Wegman. In August, the Chemical-Pharmaceutical Laboratory opens in Arlesheim (Oskar Schmiedel and Ita Wegman are directors). The Clinical Therapeutic Institute is inaugurated in Stuttgart (Dr. Ludwig Noll is director); also the Research Laboratory in Dornach (Ehrenfried Pfeiffer and Gunther Wachsmuth are directors). In November–December, Rudolf Steiner visits Norway.

1922: The first half of the year involves very active public lecturing (thousands attend); in the second half, Rudolf Steiner begins to withdraw and turn toward the Society—'The Society is asleep.' It is 'too weak' to do what is asked of it. The businesses—*Der Kommende Tag* and *Futurum A.G.*—fail. In January, with the help of an agent, Steiner undertakes a twelve-city German lecture tour, accompanied by eurythmy performances. In two weeks he speaks to more than 2,000 people. In April, he gives a 'university course' in The Hague. He also visits England. In June, he is in Vienna for the East–West Congress. In August–September, he is back in England for the Oxford Conference on Education. Returning to Dornach, he gives the lectures *Philosophy, Cosmology, and Religion* (CW 215), and gives the third priests' course (CW 344). On September 16, The Christian Community is founded. In October–November, Steiner is in Holland and England. He also speaks to the youth: *The Youth Course* (CW 217). In December, Steiner gives lectures titled *The Origins of Natural Science* (CW 326), and *Humanity and the World of Stars: The Spiritual Communion of Humanity* (CW 219). December 31: Fire at the Goetheanum, which is destroyed.

1923: Despite the fire, Rudolf Steiner continues his work unabated. A very hard year. Internal dispersion, dissension, and apathy abound. There is conflict—between old and new visions—within the Society. A wake-up call is needed, and Rudolf Steiner responds with renewed lecturing vitality. His focus: the spiritual context of human life; initiation science; the course of the year; and community building. As a foundation for an artistic school, he creates a series of pastel sketches. Lecture cycles: *The Anthroposophical Movement; Initiation Science* (CW 227) (in England at the Penmaenmawr Summer School); *The Four Seasons and the Archangels* (CW 229); *Harmony of the Creative Word* (CW 230); *The Supersensible Human* (CW 231), given in Holland for the founding of the Dutch society. On November 10, in response to the failed Hitler-Ludendorf putsch in Munich, Steiner closes his Berlin residence and moves the *Philosophisch-Anthroposophisch Verlag* (Press) to Dornach. On December 9, Steiner begins the serialization of his *Autobiography: The Course of My Life* (CW 28) in *Das Goetheanum*. It will continue to appear weekly, without a break, until his death. Late December–early January: Rudolf Steiner re-founds the Anthroposophical Society (about 12,000 members internationally) and takes over its leadership. The new board members are: Marie Steiner, Ita Wegman, Albert Steffen, Elizabeth Vreede, and Guenther Wachsmuth. (See *The Christmas Meeting for the Founding of the General Anthroposophical Society*, CW 260). Accompanying lectures: *Mystery Knowledge and Mystery Centres* (CW 232); *World History in the Light of Anthroposophy* (CW 233). December 25: the Foundation Stone is laid (in the hearts of members) in the form of the 'Foundation Stone Meditation.'

1924:   January 1: having founded the Anthroposophical Society and taken over its leadership, Rudolf Steiner has the task of 'reforming' it. The process begins with a weekly newssheet ('What's Happening in the Anthroposophical Society') in which Rudolf Steiner's 'Letters to Members' and 'Anthroposophical Leading Thoughts' appear (CW 26). The next step is the creation of a new esoteric class, the 'first class' of the 'University of Spiritual Science' (which was to have been followed, had Rudolf Steiner lived longer, by two more advanced classes). Then comes a new language for Anthroposophy—practical, phenomenological, and direct; and Rudolf Steiner creates the model for the second Goetheanum. He begins the series of extensive 'karma' lectures (CW 235–40); and finally, responding to needs, he creates two new initiatives: biodynamic agriculture and curative education. After the middle of the year, rumors begin to circulate regarding Steiner's health. Lectures: January–February, *Anthroposophy* (CW 234); February: *Tone Eurythmy* (CW 278); June: *The Agriculture Course* (CW 327); June–July: *Speech Eurythmy* (CW 279); *Curative Education* (CW 317); August: (England, 'Second International Summer School'), *Initiation Consciousness: True and False Paths in Spiritual Investigation* (CW 243); September: *Pastoral Medicine* (CW 318). On September 26, for the first time, Rudolf Steiner cancels a lecture. On September 28, he gives his last lecture. On September 29, he withdraws to his studio in the carpenter's shop; now he is definitively ill. Cared for by Ita Wegman, he continues working, however, and writing the weekly installments of his *Autobiography* and *Letters to the Members/Leading Thoughts* (CW 26).

1925: Rudolf Steiner, while continuing to work, continues to weaken. He finishes *Extending Practical Medicine* (CW 27) with Ita Wegman.

On March 30, around ten in the morning, Rudolf Steiner dies.

INDEX

Abraham, 4
abstraction, 169
Adam, 15, 29, 42–43, 45, 59–60, 68
Adam and Eve, 3–4, 43
admonition, 45
adversary powers, xii, 151
Aegisthus, 118–119
Aerope, 118
Aeschylus, 121
Agamemnon, 118–119
Ahriman, xii, 23, 102, 104, 136,
    144–147, 149–155
  as spawn of evil, 104
Ahriman-Lucifer, 38
ahrimanic, 61, 93, 103–104, 146, 150,
    152
ambition, 114
Ambrose, St, 34
angels/angelic, 28, 31, 51–54
  as messenger, 52
animal world, 130, 146–147, 161
anthroposophical/anthroposophy. *See*
  spiritual science
antinomics, 151, 178
antipathy, 41, 190
Aphrodite, goddess, 127
Apollo, 118
  Apollo figure, 147
  Apollo-type, 150
  Apollo-way (form), 145
apostles, 37–39
Apostle's (Apostolic) Creed, 184,
    186–187, 189
Aquinas, Thomas, 160, 164–165
  Thomism, 164–165
archetypal, 16, 36
architecture, 135
archon, 38–39
Aristotle, 50, 160, 169

art/artistic, 124, 132–135, 146,
    154–155, 187
  black art, 109
  white art, 109
ascend/ascending, 122, 138, 144, 185
association, 182
Åsteson, Olaf, 81
astral body, 8, 76, 79, 99–102, 142, 148,
    173, 182
  affects male/female form, 142
  consciousness of, 79–80
Athena, goddess, 127
  Athena-type, 150
  Athena-way (form), 145
Atlantean/Atlantis, 143
  fifth through seventh epochs,
    143–145, 150
  the flood, 144
Atreus, 117–119
Atridae, 118, 120
Augustine, St, 34
aura, 107, 123, 190
  earth's, 5, 17–18, 149, 153
awe, 10

balance, xii, 149
  balance of power, 91
Bartholomew, 38
Basilides, 173, 175
Bauer, Mr, 178–179
beauty, 120, 150, 168
belief in authority, 85
Bethlehem, 12, 56
Bible (Holy), 3, 10, 42, 55
birth (and conception), 7, 17, 20, 43,
    129, 132, 143
blessedness, 28
blood/blood system, 76, 132
Books of Jeu, 35, 37, 47–48